italian

Lydia Vellaccio

and

Maurice Elston

D1173290

TEACH YOURSELF BOOKS

For UK order queries: please contact Bookpoint Ltd, 130 Milton Park, Abingdon, Oxon OX14 4SB. Telephone: (44) 01235 827720, Fax: (44) 01235 400454. Lines are open from 09.00–18.00, Monday to Saturday, with a 24 hour message answering service. Email address: *orders@bookpoint.co.uk*

For U.S.A. order enquiries: please contact McGraw-Hill Customer Services, P.O. Box 545, Blacklick, OH 43004-0545, U.S.A. Telephone: 1-800-722-4726. Fax: 1-614-755-5645.

For Canada order enquiries: please contact McGraw-Hill Ryerson Ltd., 300 Water St, Whitby, Ontario L1N 9B6, Canada. Telephone: 905 430 5000. Fax: 905 430 5020.

Long renowned as the authoritative source for self-guided learning – with more than 30 million copies sold worldwide – the *Teach Yourself* series includes over 300 titles in the fields of languages, crafts, hobbies, business and education.

British Library Cataloguing in Publication Data
A catalogue record for this title is available from The British Library

Library of Congress Catalog Card Number: On file

First published in UK 1998 by Hodder Headline Plc, 338 Euston Road, London NW1 3BH.

First published in US in 1998 by Contemporary Books, A Division of The McGraw-Hill Companies, 4255 West Touhy Avenue, Lincolnwood (Chicago), Illinois 60712-1975 U.S.A.

The 'Teach Yourself' name and logo are registered trade marks of Hodder & Stoughton Ltd.

Copyright © 1998 Lydia Vellaccio and Maurice Elston

Typeset by Transet Limited, Coventry, Warwickshire.
Printed in Great Britain for Hodder & Stoughton Educational, a division of Hodder Headline Plc, 338 Euston Road, London NW1 3BH by Cox & Wyman Ltd, Reading, Berkshire.

Impression number   10
Year   2002 2001

CONTENTS

INTRODUCTION

Welcome to *Teach Yourself Italian*

Is this the right course for you?

If you are an adult learner with no previous knowledge of Italian and studying on your own, then this is the course for you. Perhaps you are taking up Italian again after a break from it, or you are intending to learn with the support of a class? Again, you will find this course very well suited to your purposes.

Developing your skills

The language introduced in this course is centred around realistic everyday situations. The emphasis is first and foremost on *using* Italian, but we also aim to give you an idea of how the language works, so that you can create sentences of your own.

The course covers all four of the basic skills – listening and speaking, reading and writing. If you are working on your own, the audio recordings will be all the more important, as they will provide you with the essential opportunity to listen to Italian and to speak it within a controlled framework. You should therefore try to obtain a copy of the audio recordings if you haven't already done so.

Use it or lose it!

Language learning is a bit like jogging – you need to do it regularly for it to do any good! Ideally, you should find a 'study buddy' to work through the course with you. This way you will have someone to try out your Italian on. And when the going gets tough, you will have someone to chivvy you on until you reach your target.

Where can I find real Italian?

Don't expect to be able to understand everything you hear or read straight away. If you watch Italian-speaking programmes on TV or buy Italian magazines, you should not get discouraged when you realise how quickly native-speakers talk and how much vocabulary there is still to be learned. Just concentrate on a *small* extract – either a video/audio clip or a short article – and work through it till you have mastered it. In this way, you'll find that your command of Italian increases steadily.

Sources of real Italian

Newspapers (e.g. *La Stampa, La Repubblica, Il Corriere della Sera*).
Magazines (e.g. *Oggi, Panorama, L'Espresso, Grazia*).
Radio stations, Spectrum International, MW 558. Vatican MW 526.
Satellite: there are many Italian channels on satellite.

The Italian Cultural Institute runs regular courses in Italian Language and Literature. It is also the venue for many talks and lectures. Address: 39 Belgrave Square, London SW1 (0171 235 1461).

The structure of this course

The course book contains **25 course units** plus a **reference section** at the back of the book. There is also a **90-minute audio cassette** which you really do need to have if you are going to get maximum benefit from the course.

The course units

The course units can be divided roughly into the following categories, although of course there is a certain amount of overlap from one category to another.

Statement of aims

You will be told what you can expect to learn, mostly in terms of what you will be able to *do* in Italian by the end of the unit.

Presentation of new language

Usually in the form of dialogues 💬 which are recorded on the audio 📼 and also printed in the book. Some assistance with vocabulary is also given 🔑. The language is presented in manageable chunks, building carefully on what you have learned in earlier units.

Practice of the new language

Practice ✅ is graded, so that activities which require mainly *recognition* come first. As you grow in confidence in manipulating the language forms, you will be encouraged to *produce* both in writing and in speech.

Description of language forms

In these section 🔧 you learn about the *forms* of the language, thus enabling you to construct your own sentences correctly. For those who are daunted by grammar, assistance is given in various ways.

Pronunciation and intonation

The best way to acquire good pronunciation and intonation is to listen to native speakers and try to imitate them. But most people do not actually notice that certain sounds in Italian are pronounced differently from their English counterparts, until this is pointed out to them. For this reason we include specific advice within the course units.

Information on Italian

Here ✳️ you will find information on Italy and various aspects of Italian life – from the level of formality that is appropriate when you talk to strangers, to how the health service works if you should fall ill.

The reference section contains

- ■ a glossary of grammar terms
- ■ a key to the activities
- ■ transcripts of the audio recordings
- ■ an Italian–English vocabulary

How to use this course

At the beginning of each course unit make sure that you are clear about what you can expect to learn.

Read any background information that is provided. Then listen to the dialogues on the audio recording. Try to get the gist of what is being said before you look at the printed text in the book. Refer to the printed text and the Key Words and Phrases in order to study the dialogues in more detail.

Don't fall into the trap of thinking you have 'done that' when you have listened to the audio a couple of times and worked through the dialogues in the book. You may *recognise* what you hear and read, but you almost certainly still have some way to go before you can *produce* the language of the dialogues correctly and fluently. This is why we recommend that you keep listening to the audio at every opportunity – sitting on the tube or bus, waiting at the dentist's or stuck in a traffic jam in the car, using what would otherwise be 'dead' time. Of course, you must also be internalising what you hear and making sense of it – just playing it in the background without really paying attention is not enough!

Some of the recordings are listen-only exercises. The temptation may be to go straight to the transcriptions in the back of the book, but try not to do this. The whole point of the listening exercises is to improve your listening skills. You will not do this by reading first. The transcriptions are there to help you if you get stuck.

As you work your way through the exercises, check your answers carefully in the back of the book. It is easy to overlook your own mistakes. If you have a study buddy, it's a good idea to check each other's answers. Most of the exercises have fixed answers, but some are a bit more open-ended, especially when we are asking you to talk about yourself. We then, in most cases, give you a model answer which you can adapt for your own purposes.

We have tried to make the grammar explanations as user-friendly as possible, because we recognise that many people find grammar daunting. But in the end, it is up to you just how much time you spend on studying and sorting out the grammar points. Some people find that they can do better by getting an ear for what sounds right, others need to know in detail how the language is put together.

Before you move on to a new unit always use the checklist to make sure that you know all the new words and phrases in the current unit. Try covering up the English side of the page and producing the English equivalents of the Italian. If you find that relatively easy, go on to cover up the Italian side of the page and produce the Italian equivalents of the English. You will probably find this more difficult. Trying to recall the context in which words and phrases were used may help you learn them better.

Italian in the Modern World

Italian is spoken by about 60 million people in Italy (including Sicily and Sardinia), the Ticino Canton in Switzerland, Corsica, and parts of Istria and Dalmatia in the former Yugoslavia. Massive emigration over the past 100 years has led to the establishment of Italian-speaking communities worldwide, especially in the United States, Brazil, Argentina, and, more recently, Australia. Early pre-eminence in European architecture, banking, painting and music has enriched the English language with many words of Italian origin: dome, cupola, bank, fresco and concerto are a few of the more obvious examples. The great appeal of Italy has long been its land-scape and artistic heritage, but it is important to remember too that, like Great Britain, it is a great manufactuirng and trading nation.

* * *

We hope you enjoy working your way through *Teach Yourself Italian*. Don't get discouraged. Mastering a new language takes time and perseverance, and sometimes things can seem just too difficult. But then you'll come back to it another day and things will begin to make more sense again.

1 | SCUSI!
Excuse me!

In this Unit you will learn how to:

■ attract someone's attention
■ exchange information about the languages you speak
■ make and respond to simple enquiries or requests
■ say you don't know
■ greet someone formally
■ accept or refuse what is offered to you

Dialogo 1 Parla inglese? *Do you speak English?*

Il portiere (*the porter*) of a small hotel in Rome is having difficulties communicating with his foreign guests. He is looking for an Italian who speaks English and German to help out. He addresses **la signorina Anna Muti** (*Miss Anna Muti*) because he has heard she speaks several languages.

Listen to the following dialogue carefully, and without looking at the text answer the following questions orally:

(a) How does the porter ask her: 'Do you speak English?'

Portiere	Scusi, signorina!
Sig.na M.	Sì..? Prego?
Portiere	Parla inglese?
Sig.na M.	Sì. Parlo inglese e francese. *anche*
Portiere	Ah, benissimo! Parla anche tedesco, vero?
Sig.na M.	No. Mi dispiace. Non parlo tedesco.

Sì..? Prego?	*Yes..? Can I help you?*	**No. Mi dispiace.**	*No. I'm sorry*
Benissimo!	*Splendid! Great!*		*(I don't).*
Parla anche tedesco, vero?		e	*and*
You speak German too, don't you?			

(b)   How does Anna say: 'I speak English and French'?

(c)   How does she say: 'I don't speak German'?

Listen to the following list of languages. Tick the ones that have appeared in the dialogue. Can you guess the others? If in doubt, check them in the vocabulary at the back of the book.

italiano ☐	**russo** ☐	**tedesco** ☐	**cinese** ☐	**giapponese** ☐
spagnolo ☐	**greco** ☐	**francese** ☐	**inglese** ☐	**portoghese** ☐

(d)   How would you say you speak the following languages?
       _____ inglese. _____ francese. _____ tedesco.

(e)   How would you say you don't speak the following?
       _____ cinese. _____ giapponese. _____ russo.

(f)   Now ask someone: 'Do you speak Italian?' _____

Parla also means *he is speaking* or *she is speaking*.

  Pablo Serra parla spagnolo.   *Pablo Serra is speaking Spanish.*
  Anna Muti parla italiano.   *Anna Muti is speaking Italian.*

(g)   Match each picture with the correct caption (the first one is done for you), and complete the captions for **Gérard Dupont** and **Helga Weil**.

(i)   (ii)   (iii)   (iv)

  Pablo Serra
  parla spagnolo.

Anna Muti parla italiano.
Gérard Dupont _____ .
Betty Warren parla inglese.
Helga Weil _____ .

Dialogo 2 Sì, è lì   *Yes, it's (over) there*

Two guests ask the porter for information.

The first one, **una signora** (*a woman*) asks him where the lift and telephone are.

(a) How does she attract the porter's attention and ask where the lift is?

Signora   Scusi, l'ascensore, per favore?
Portiere   L'ascensore? Sì, è lì.
Signora   E il telefono?
Portiere   È qui, a sinistra.
Signora   Grazie.
Portiere   Prego.

l'ascensore *the lift*	**prego** *don't mention it, you're*
per favore *please*	*welcome*
è qui, a sinistra *it's here,*	
on the left	

(b) How does she say: 'Thank you'?
(c) How would *you* attract someone's attention and ask where the telephone is?

Dialogo 3 Non lo so *I don't know*

The second guest, **un signore** (*a man*) asks him where the station and the bank are. Being new to Rome, **il portiere** doesn't know all the answers.

(a) There is another way of saying *please* in this dialogue: what is it?

Signore   Scusi, la stazione, per piacere?
Portiere   Sempre dritto, poi a destra. Dopo il semaforo.
Signore   E la banca?
Portiere   Mi dispiace. Non lo so.

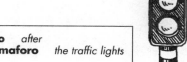

sempre dritto *straight on*	**dopo** *after*
poi *then*	**il semaforo** *the traffic lights*
a destra *on the right*	

(b) How does the porter say: 'I'm sorry'?
(c) How would *you* attract someone's attention and ask where the bank is?
(d) If you were asked the same question how would you reply: 'I don't know'?
(e) Listen to the above dialogues and mark where the stress falls in the following words:
    Esempio: scusi
    sinistra, stazione, ascensore, grazie, telefono

Vero o falso? *True or false?*

Look at the following town signs. Are the statements underneath each one true or false? Correct the false statements.

(i)   (ii)   (iii)   (iv)

| STAZIONE → | ← POSTA | MUSEO → | POLIZIA → |

La stazione è   **La posta è**   **Il museo è**   **La polizia è**
a sinistra   **a destra**   **a destra**   **a sinistra**

Someone asks you: **Scusi! Il Duomo?** (*the Cathedral*)

(f)   **duomo ↑**   Look at the sign. What do you answer?

La posta is *the post-office.* Can you guess what **il museo** and **la polizia** are?

Dialogo 4 Buongiorno. Come sta?   *Good morning. How are you?*

Un professore (*a teacher*) meets **Giulia**, one of his students. They exchange greetings. How does the teacher greet **Giulia**? What does **Giulia** say when she leaves?

Professore	Buongiorno, signorina Giulia.
Giulia	Buongiorno, professore. Come sta?
Professore	Bene, grazie. E lei? *Lay*
Giulia	Molto bene, grazie.
Professore	Ci vediamo domani! Arrivederci!
Giulia	Arrivederci, professore.

E lei?	*And you?*	**Ci vediamo domani.**	*See you tomorrow!*
(molto) bene	*(very) well*		

Dialogo 5 Un gelato?   *An ice cream?*

Il professore goes into a café where **un dottore** (*a doctor*) and other friends of his are waiting for him. He offers them something to drink.

(a)   What does the teacher say to offer an ice cream to the young woman?

Professore	Un tè, signora?
Signora	No, grazie.
Professore	Un gelato, signorina?

Signorina	Sì, grazie.
Professore	E per lei, dottore? Un caffè o una birra?
Dottore	Un espresso e una pasta, grazie.

per *for* **una pasta** *a cake*
o *or*

BAR
ITALIA

acqua
minerale

tè

caffè

birra

espresso

limonata

cioccolato *choco*

(b) What expressions are used for *no thank you* and *yes please*?

(c) Guess what the drinks in the dialogue are. Check your answers in the vocabulary at the back of the book.

(d) Listen to/read the above dialogue and concentrate on the list of drinks that follows it. See which ones you can recognise: tick them off on the **Bar Italia** board (above right). Look up those you don't understand. If you are listening to the tape, there should be one left over: which is it? Respond to the pictures as in the example. ✓ = you accept. ✗ = you refuse.

Esempio: Un espresso? No grazie.

(i)   (ii)   (iii)

✗   ✓   ✗   ✓

Pronuncia   *Pronunciation*

Vocali   *Vowels*

Italian has five vowels: **a, e, i, o, u**. The vowels **a, i** and **u** each represent one sound only. When the vowel is stressed it is slightly longer.

a is pronounced as in *bat*: listen to the following words: pasta, limonata, parla, banana. Notice particularly how, in the Italian word **banana**, the vowel **a** has exactly the same sound throughout, even though the second **a** is longer because of the stress: **ba-na-na**.

i is pronounced as in English *machine:* sì, sinistra, scusi, birra.

u is pronounced as in English *rule:* un, una, museo, scusi, cappuccino

ATTENZIONE! *Beware!* Pronounce *u* as in *rule* NOT as in *tune*.

e has two sounds:

as in English *get*: è, prego, telefono, destra, caffè.
as in English *they*: e, francese, piacere, sera, arrivederci

o has two sounds:

  as in English *got*: n**o**, p**o'**, p**o**sta.

  as in English *ought*: R**o**ma, c**o**me, parl**o**

Stress

1 Stress usually falls on the last syllable but one: pr**e**go, stazi**o**ne, limon**a**ta.
2 An accent on the final vowel of a word must be stressed: caff**è**.
3 Occasionally, the stress falls on the last syllable but two: tel**e**fono, gr**a**zie, **u**tile, sem**a**foro.

Accents

There is only one accent in Italian (`` ` ``).

Apart from showing final stress (**caffè**) an accent can distinguish between the meaning of two words: **e** *and*, but **è** *is*.

▣ Spiegazioni *Explanations*

1 Grazie, prego, per favore/per piacere

grazie	*thank you*
prego	*not at all, don't mention it*
per favore ⎱	
per piacere ⎰	*please*

Although **grazie** normally means *thank you* and **per piacere** or **per favore** *please*, care must be taken to use only **sì, grazie/no, grazie** when someone is offering you something:

Un caffè, dottore?	*A coffee (Doctor)?*
Sì, grazie.	*Yes please.*
Un cioccolato, signora?	*A chocolate (Madam)?*
No, grazie.	*No thank you.*

In response to thanks Italians instinctively reply **prego**:

Grazie.	*Thank you.*
Prego.	*Not at all, you're welcome, don't mention it.*

When **Prego?** is used as a question it means *Can I help you?* or *Pardon?*

2   Parlo, parla

(Io) parlo	*I speak, I am speaking.*
(Lei) parla	*You speak, you are speaking.*

Parla can also mean *he/she speaks* or *he/she is speaking.*

*The pronouns (**io** *I*, **lei** *you*, etc.) are only used for emphasis, contrast, or to avoid ambiguity. The context will usually make it clear whether **parla** refers to *you*, *he* or *she*. Notice also that the auxiliary verb 'to be' is **not** used. Therefore in Italian *I am speaking* is the same as *I speak*: **parlo**.

3   **Domande e risposte**   *Questions and answers*

To ask a question, Italians simply change the intonation of their voice. Listen to all the questions on the audio very carefully and compare the intonation with that of statements.

Parla italiano?	*Do you speak Italian?*
Sì. Parlo italiano e inglese.	*Yes. I speak Italian and English.*
Parla inglese?	*Does he/she speak English?*

Vero (literally *true*) added to the end of a question is the equivalent of the English *don't you? isn't it? aren't they?* etc.

Maria parla tedesco, vero?	*Maria speaks German, doesn't she?*
No. Parla spagnolo.	*No. She speaks Spanish.*
È lì, vero?	*It's (over) there, isn't it?*
Sì. È lì.	*Yes. It's (over) there.*

In answer to questions such as *Do you speak Italian?* we would normally answer in English: *Yes, I do* or *No, I don't.* Italians simply answer: **Sì** or **No**, or they repeat the whole sentence: **Sì. Parlo italiano** or **No. Non parlo italiano**. They do **not** express *do* or *don't*.

4   **Negativo**   *The negative*

In negative sentences use **non** before the verb:

parlo	*I speak*	**non parlo** *I don't speak*
Anna parla inglese, ma		*Anna speaks English, but*
non parla tedesco.		*she doesn't speak German.*
Non è qui Roberto?		*Isn't Robert here?*

*If you are not sure what verbs, nouns, pronouns, etc. are, see Grammar glossary p 323.

5   *Greetings and titles*

Buongiorno (lit. *good day*) *hello, good morning, goodbye*

Buonasera (lit. *good evening*) is used for the late afternoon and evening.

Buonanotte *goodnight*

Arrivederci *goodbye* (at any time of day)

Note the various meanings of the following words and their abbreviated forms from the dialogues:

signore (sig.)	*(gentle)man, Mr, sir*
signora (sig.ra)	*lady, Mrs, madam*
signorina (sig.na)	*young lady/woman, Miss*
professore (prof.)	any professor or teacher
dottore (dott.)	any university graduate; not restricted to the medical profession

Italians normally use titles when addressing each other formally:

Buongiorno, signora.	*Good morning (madam).*
Buonasera, signorina.	*Good evening (miss).*
Grazie, dottore. Arrivederci!	*Thank you (doctor). Goodbye.*

6   *Articles*: (*singular*) il, la, l' *(the)*; un, una *(a, an, one)* + noun

In Italian most words end in a vowel.

Names for men usually end in **-o** – Carl**o** *Charles*, Franc**o** *Frank*, amic**o** *friend (male)*.

Names for women usually end in **-a** – Ann**a** *Anne*, Mari**a** *Mary*, amic**a** *friend* (female).

Names for things usually end in **-o** or **-a** – gelat**o**, post**a**.

If they end in **-o** they are called masculine nouns.

If they end in **-a** they are called feminine nouns.

Some nouns end in **-e**, and these can be either masculine or feminine. Learn them as you meet them. However, nouns ending in **-ore** are normally masculine and those ending in **-zione** are normally feminine: **il** dott**ore**, **il** profess**ore**, **la** sta**zione**, **la** le**zione** (*the lesson*).

Il, **un** are used with masculine nouns.

la, **una** are used with feminine nouns.

l' is used with masculine or feminine nouns beginning with a vowel.

Masculine		Feminine	
il cioccolato	*the chocolate*	la birra	*the beer*
il museo	*the museum*	la polizia	*the police*
il dottore	*the doctor*	la lezione	*the lesson*
l'amico	*the friend (male)*	l'amica	*the friend (female)*
un cappuccino	*a cappuccino*	una pasta	*a cake*
un gelato	*an ice cream*	una parola	*a word*
un tè	*a tea*	una stazione	*a station*

Come si dice in italiano? *How do you say it in Italian?*

How to:

1 attract someone's attention — **Scusi!**
  reply to someone attracting your attention — **Prego?**

2 ask someone whether they speak English — **Parla inglese?**
  say that you speak English and Italian — **Parlo inglese e italiano.**

3 say that you don't speak Spanish — **Non parlo spagnolo.**

4 make a simple enquiry — **Il museo, per favore?**
  say whether something is: here/(over) there /on the right/on the left/straight ahead — **È: qui/lì/a destra/a sinistra/ sempre dritto.**
  make a simple request — **Una birra, per piacere.** **Un tè, per favore.**

5 greet someone:
  (morning/early afternoon) — **Buongiorno!**
  (later afternoon/evening) — **Buonasera!**
  (before going to bed) — **Buonanotte!**
  (on departure) — **Arrivederci!**

6 offer someone a coffee — **Un caffè?**
  accept/refuse what you are offered — **Sì, grazie./No, grazie.**

7 say you don't know — **Non lo so.**

8 say thank you — **Grazie.**
  respond to thanks — **Prego.**

Now cover up the right-hand side and try to give the Italian.

✅ Attività   *Activities*

1

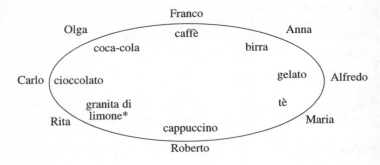

crushed ice flavoured with lemon

Look at this group of friends sitting round a café table; go round clockwise and write down what drink each person is asking for. Choose carefully between **un** and **una**.

Esempio: (a) Franco: **'Un caffè, per favore.'**   (e) Roberto: _____

          (b) Anna: _____   (f) Rita: _____

          (c) Alfredo: _____   (g) Carlo: _____

          (d) Maria: _____   (h) Olga: _____

2   Now help the waiter when he returns by telling him which drink is for which person. Choose carefully between **il** and **la**. **Esempio: Il caffè è per Franco**.

3   Look at the following table which tells you what language(s) Olga and her friends speak. If you were talking about **Olga** you would write: **Olga parla inglese, francese e spagnolo**.

What would you write about (a) **Franco**, (b) **Rita**, (c) **Carlo**? (d) How would you write that **Carlo** speaks German but (**ma**) doesn't speak French?

	inglese	francese	tedesco	spagnolo
Olga	✓	✓		✓
Franco	✓			
Rita		✓		✓
Carlo			✓	✓

Ora tocca a te! *Now it's your turn.*

(e) How would you say: 'I don't speak Spanish'?

(f) How would you ask someone: 'Do you speak French?'

(g) Pretend you are **Olga** and say which languages you speak; which languages you don't speak.

Note that capital letters are not used for languages in Italian.

4 Dialogo A tourist stops you in the street and asks you the way. Complete your side of the following conversation:

(If you are using the audio, use 'pause' to give you time to answer.)

Turista	Scusi!
You	*(Respond to him).*
Turista	La posta, per favore?
You	*(It's over there on the left).*
Turista	E la stazione?
You	*(Straight ahead).*
Turista	Grazie.
You	*(Don't mention it).*

5 Check your answers on page 277, then reverse the roles.

Informazioni *Information*

1 Espresso, cappuccino

The general word for coffee in Italian is **caffè**. **Espresso** (*black*) coffee is served in very small cups as it is quite strong. A **cappuccino** is a frothy white coffee given a distinctive flavour by a sprinkling of chocolate.

2 Il bar

Il bar is the normal name for an Italian café. Both alcoholic and non-alcoholic drinks are served there. In most, you have to pay at the cashier's desk first, obtain a ticket/receipt (**scontrino**) and present it at the counter to get your drink. If you sit at a table, you pay more. Don't throw away any receipts you are given (in any cafes, restaurants or shops) while you are in the vicinity. The police may want to see them: not to check on you, but on the vendors for tax purposes!

2 IN GIRO PER LA CITTÀ
Out and about in town

In this Unit you will learn how to:

■ identify things and places
■ ask and say where people and places are
■ order a snack or drink and ask for the bill

Dialogo 1 Cos'è? *What is it?*

Franco is showing **Roberta** round the town.

(a) What are the words he uses to point out the Cathedral?

Franco	Ecco il Duomo!
Roberta	E cos'è questo?
Franco	Questo è il Museo Nazionale.
Roberta	Bello! E questo palazzo? Cos'è? È una banca?
Franco	Sì. Questa è la Banca Commerciale.

questo/questa	*this*	**palazzo**	*building*
bello/bella	*beautiful, nice*		

(b) How does he say: 'The National Museum' and 'the Commercial Bank'?
(c) How would *you* say: 'This is the museum'?

Dialogo 2 Dov'è? *Where is it?*

Roberta now wants to know where the Europa Hotel is and where the shops are.

(a) How does **Franco** say: 'After the American Consulate'?
(b) There are two words for *street* in this dialogue. What are they? What is the word for *main*?

Roberta	Dov'è l'Albergo Europa? Non è qui?
Franco	No. È più avanti. Dopo il Consolato Americano.
Roberta	Ma dove sono i negozi?
Franco	I grandi magazzini sono in Via Roma: la strada principale.
Roberta	Ah, sì! Vicino a Villa Millefiori.
Franco	No, no. Sono vicino a Piazza Municipio.

più avanti *further on*	**Piazza Municipio** *the Town Hall*
i negozi *the shops*	*Square*
i grandi magazzini *the*	**è** *(it) is, it's*
department stores	**sono** *(they) are*
vicino a *next to, near*	

(c) How would *you* ask: 'Where is the Town Hall Square, please?'

(d) How would *you* say: 'It's near Via Roma?'

(e) How would *you* ask: 'Where are the shops, please?'

Dialogo 3 Cosa prende?   *What are you having?*

Franco and **Roberta** are now at the **Bar-Ristorante Roma**. They say in turn what they are having. Then **Franco** calls the waiter (**cameriere**).

(a) How does **Franco** say: 'I'm having a pizza and a glass of wine'?

Franco	Io prendo una pizza e un bicchiere di vino. Lei, Roberta, cosa prende?
Roberta	Un panino con formaggio.
Franco	Cameriere! Un panino con formaggio e una pizza.
Cameriere	Va bene. E da bere?
Roberta	Un'acqua minerale con limone e senza gas.
Franco	E per me, vino, vino rosso. E poi, due caffè.

un bicchier(e) di vino *a glass of*	**e da bere?** *and to drink?*
wine	**un'acqua minerale** *a mineral*
Cosa prende? *What are you*	*water*
having?	**con/senza** *with/without*
un panino con formaggio	**poi, due ...** *then, two ...*
a cheese roll	
va bene *alright*	

(b) How does he ask **Roberta**: 'What are you having?'
(c) What is *red wine* in Italian?
(d) How would *you* ask for a sparkling mineral water?
(e) How would *you* ask for a glass of red wine?

Dialogo 4 Il conto, per favore! *The bill, please!*

(a) How does the waiter ask whether they want anything else?

Cameriere	Ecco: Il panino e l'acqua minerale per la signorina, e il vino e la pizza per lei. Altro?
Franco	No, grazie. Il conto, per favore.
Roberta	E lo zucchero...!
Cameriere	Subito, signorina.

lo zucchero	*the sugar*	**subito**	*straight away*

(b) How does Roberta ask for the sugar?
(c) How would you say: 'The sugar please'?

Listen to the numbers in Italian from 0–10:

0	1	2	3	4	5	6	7	8	9	10
zero	**uno, una**	**due**	**tre**	**quattro**	**cinque**	**sei**	**sette**	**otto**	**nove**	**dieci**

Dialogo 5 Un tavolo per dieci persone *A table for ten*

Una guida (*a guide*) enters the **bar-ristorante** with a group of tourists and orders for all of them.

(a) How many beers, how many sandwiches and how many ice creams are ordered?

Guida	Un tavolo per dieci persone.
Cameriere	Va bene qui?
Guida	Sì. Va bene. Sette birre e cinque tramezzini con prosciutto crudo.
Cameriere	E per i bambini? I gelati sono molto buoni.
Guida	Allora: un gelato misto e un'aranciata fresca.
Cameriere	Ecco: le birre, i tramezzini, il gelato e l'aranciata.

Va bene qui?	*Is it alright here?*	**i gelati sono molto buoni**	*the*
tramezzini	*sandwiches*	*ice creams are very good*	
prosciutto crudo	*Parma ham*	**misto/a**	*mixed*
i bambini	*the children*	**fresco/a**	*cool, fresh*
allora	*then*		

Pronuncia

Consonanti *Consonants*

Most consonants in Italian correspond roughly to their English equivalents, but double consonants (**mm**, **gg**, **cc**, etc.) must be heard: they are more deliberately pronounced than in English.

c and **g** need particular care before **e** and **i**:

c followed by **e** or **i** is pronounced
  as in English *child*: vi**ci**no, **ci**nque, die**ci**, di**ce**, **ce**nto, uffi**ci**o, farma**ci**a.

c followed by **a**, **o**, **u** or a consonant is pronounced
  as in *cat*:   ban**ca**, **co**n, **ca**meriere, **co**sa, **co**me.

ch is as in *architect*: **ch**e, bic**ch**iere, zuc**ch**ero, ma**cch**ina

g followed by **e** or **i**
  as in *general*:   **ge**lati, forma**ggi**o, An**ge**la, **gi**ro.

g followed by **a**, **o**, **u** or a consonant
  as in *gun*:   **gr**anita, ne**go**zio, **gui**da, alber**go**.

g followed by **h**
  as in *gherkin*:   alber**ghi**.

gn as *ni* in *onion*: si**gn**ore, si**gn**ora, si**gn**orina.

Spiegazioni

1 Cosa, dove

Cosa, **che cosa** and **che** can all be used to mean *what* in English.
Cos'è stands for **cosa** + **è**; the final **-a** is dropped for ease of pronunciation.

Che cos'è?
Cos'è? } *What is it?*

Cosa
Che cosa } **prende?**   *What are you having?*
Che

Dov'è stands for **dove** (*where*) + **è**. The final **-e** of **dove** is dropped for the same reason.

Dov'è?	*Where is it/he/she? Where are you?*
Dov'è la stazione?	*Where's the station?*
Dov'è Roberto?	*Where's Robert?*
Dove sono i negozi?	*Where are the shops?*

2 Verbs

Parlo and **parla** (Unit 1) are parts of the verb **parlare** (infinitive) *to speak*. Here are the corresponding parts for **prendere** *to have, to take*:

prend -o *I have, I take*; **prend -e** *you have/take, he/she has/takes*.

È *you are, he/she/it is/it's*, and **sono** *they are*, are parts of the verb **essere** *to be* (Unit 3, p 33).

3 Plural of nouns

Nouns ending in **-o** (masc.) change the final **-o** to **-i**:

   muse**o**   muse**i** *(museums)*

Nouns ending in **-a** (fem.) change the final **-a** to **-e**:

   birr**a**   birr**e** *(beers)*

Nouns ending in **-e** (masc. or fem.) change the final **-e** to **-i**:

   masc: ristorant**e**   ristorant**i** *(restaurants)*

   fem: stazion**e**   stazion**i** *(stations)*

Nouns ending in a consonant or in an accented vowel do not change:

   caff**è**   due caff**è** *(two coffees)*

   ba**r**   tre ba**r** *(three cafes)*

4 Articles: un', uno a, an   lo, i, le the

un' is used only before feminine words beginning with a vowel: **un'a**cqua minerale.

But **un** *(masc.)* is used before consonants or vowels: **un a**lbergo *(a hotel, inn)*, **un a**scensore *(a lift)*, **un g**elato.

Notice: **un** ami**co** (without an apostrophe) but **un'**ami**ca** (with an apostrophe).

Lo and **uno** are used before masculine singular nouns beginning with **z** or **s + consonant**:

*uno s*contrino *a ticket/receipt*   *uno s*tudente *a student*
*lo z*ucchero *the sugar*
*lo s*contrino *the ticket/receipt*   *lo s*tudente *the student*

I, **le** *the* (plural)

il becomes **i** before masculine plural nouns: *il* **muse***o*, *i* **muse***i*; *il* **duom***o*, *i* **duom***i*.

la becomes **le** before feminine plural nouns: *la* **birra**, *le* **birre**; *la* **stazione**, *le* **stazion***i*.

5 Piazza, Via

La piazza *the square*, **la via** *the road*; but when the square or the road is named, omit the article: **Piazza Municipio, Via Roma.**

6 *Adjectives*

Adjectives agree in number and gender with the nouns they qualify:

il vin*o* **ross***o*   *the red wine*   **la mel***a* **ross***a*   *the red apple*
un panin*o* **fresc***o*   *a fresh roll*   **un'aranciat***a* **fresc***a*
                                               a cool orangeade

Quest**o**/quest**a** must also agree:

Quest*o* **palazz***o* **è bell***o*.   *This building is beautiful.*
Quest*a* **piazz***a* **è bell***a*.   *This square is beautiful.*

Unlike English, adjectives in Italian often follow the noun they refer to:
vino *rosso*, **acqua** *minerale*, **aranciata** *fresca*, **prosciutto** *crudo*.

However, one or two very common ones such as **bello/bella** *beautiful, nice* often come before: **una bella città**   *a beautiful town*

7 *Numbers* (for 0–10 see p 20)

un, **una**, besides meaning *a* or *an*, also mean *one*. It is the only number which agrees with the noun following it. The others do not change. When there is no noun following, use **uno, una**: **un museo** but **(numero) uno** (*number*) *one*.

Quanti caffè...? Uno!   *How many coffees...? One!*
Quante pizze...? Una!   *How many pizzas...? One!*

8 con *with;* **senza** *without*

Un panino con formaggio	*a cheese roll* (literally means 'a roll with cheese')
un'acqua minerale con gas	*sparkling mineral water*
un'acqua minerale senza gas	*still* or *natural mineral water*
con/senza: limone, zucchero, latte, burro	*with/without lemon, sugar, milk, butter*

9 prosciutto crudo

Literally *raw ham,* i.e. Parma ham. **Prosciutto cotto** is cooked ham.

Come si dice in italiano?

How to:

1	ask what something is	**Cos'è?/Cos'è questo/questa?**
	say what it is	**È un museo. È una banca.**
2	ask what things are	**Cosa sono?/Cosa sono Standa e Upim?**
	say what they are	**Sono grandi magazzini.**
3	ask where a thing or person is	**Dov'è?/Dov'è la posta? Dov'è Franco?**
	say where he, she or it is	**È qui, è lì, ecc.**
4	ask where things or people are	**Dove sono i negozi? Dove sono Anna e Roberta?**
5	ask what someone is having	**Cosa prende?**
	say what you are having	**(Io) prendo un tè ...**
6	say that you are having ... with ...	**Prendo un tè con latte.**
7	say that you are having ... without ...	**Prendo un caffè senza zucchero.**
8	ask for the bill	**Il conto, per favore!**

Attività

1 Listen to this list of towns, then to the list of famous places that follows: **Milano, Firenze, Londra, Parigi, Pisa, Napoli, Roma, Venezia.**

Il Colosseo, Piazza San Marco, il Vesuvio, il Ponte Vecchio, la Torre Eiffel, il Palazzo del Parlamento, la Torre Pendente, La Scala.

Try repeating them.

2 Look at the illustrations below, match the name of the place with the name of the town as in the example.

La Scala: Milano

Check that they are correctly paired.

3 To say *in Rome, in Venice, etc.* use **a: a Roma, a Venezia**.

Dov'è La Scala? A Milano. *Where is La Scala? In Milan.*

Form similar questions and answers for **il Colosseo**, **il Vesuvio**, and **la Torre Eiffel**.

Now make statements about where the rest are. Start with: **La Scala è ...**

4 Use the diagram to form questions and answers on these places as in the example:

(a) **il Consolato Americano**
(b) **Piazza Garibaldi**
(c) **il Duomo**
(d) **l'Albergo Miramare**

Esempio: Scusi, dov'è il Consolato Spagnolo?
È a sinistra, dopo il Consolato Americano.

Lei è qui
You are here

(e) Now answer the following question: **Dove sono i consolati?**

5 Cosa sono? *What are they?*

Sort this list of words into three columns: Drinks, Food, Places, and precede each by **il**, **la** or **l'**:

> • **banca** • **Duomo** • **limonata** • **piazza** • **pizza** • **pasta** • **museo**
> • **birra** • **formaggio** • **albergo** • **acqua minerale** • **panino**
> **aranciata** • **tè** • **prosciutto**

6 Con o senza? *With or without?*

How do they take their tea? With or without sugar, etc? Look at the table and make two statements, one about **Marta** and one about **Filippo**. Start with: **Marta prende il tè ...**

	limone	latte	zucchero
Marta		✓	✓
Filippo	✓		✕

Ora tocca a te! How do you take yours?

7 Cos'è questo/questa?

Look at the illustrations immediately after Dialogue 5 (p. 10) in Unit 1 and form a question and answer for each using **Cos'è questo?** or **Cos'è questa?** depending on whether the nouns are masculine or feminine.

✳ Informazioni

1 Il Palazzo

Strictly speaking, **palazzo** means *palace*, but it is generally used to describe any large building or block of flats.

2 Strada, via

Although **strada** means *road* or *street* it is never used in naming any particular one. **Via** is used for this. **Via** may also mean *way* or *route*.

3 La piazza

In Italian towns **la piazza** is the centre of social life where everyone meets for a date, a coffee or a chat. One of the most famous is **Piazza San Marco** (*St Mark's Square*) in Venice.

4 I grandi magazzini

The most popular department stores are **Upim, Standa, La Rinascente** and **Coin**.

They can be found in most Italian towns. **Upim** and **Standa** especially are reasonably priced and there are large food departments in some of them. Shop opening hours vary between regions. Most of them are open from 8.30/9.00 am to 12.30/1.00 pm and from 3.30/4.00 pm until 7.00/8.00 pm. Many of them observe half-day closing during the week, usually Monday morning, others one whole day. The latter, such as tobacconists, chemists, hairdressers and some restaurants, may close on a rota system.

5 La pizza

The **pizza** is a speciality of Naples and the **Campania** region. It can be bought in a variety of sizes either in a **pizzeria**, which is like a restaurant but cheaper, or in a **rosticceria**, a take-away which often has limited seating space for customers. You may also have a **pizza** cut from a large slab in which case it is called **pizza al metro** or **al taglio**. You may ask for your **taglio** (*cut*) by weight, size or value.

6 Here are some more Italian town signs: how many can you guess? Look up those you don't know:

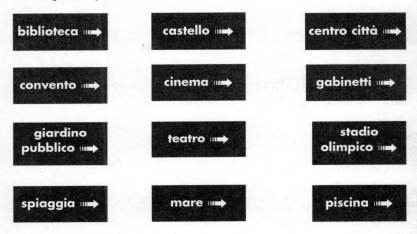

3 | COME SI CHIAMA?
What's your name?

In this Unit you will learn how to:

■ exchange personal details formally and informally
■ introduce yourself and others; respond to introductions

Listen to the following ordinal numbers:

1st	2nd	3rd	4th
primo, prima	**secondo, seconda**	**terzo, terza**	**quarto, quarta**

Dialogo 1 A che piano...? *On what floor...?*

Il signor Russo asks **il Portiere** on what floor **i signori Nuzzo** (*Mr & Mrs Nuzzo*) live: he has been invited to a party at their home.

(a) How does he ask on what floor they live?

Sig. Russo	A che piano abitano i signori Nuzzo, per favore?
Portiere	Terzo piano, numero 20. Quarta porta a destra.
Sig. Russo	Grazie mille.
Portiere	Prego.

porta *door*	**grazie mille** *many thanks*

Dialogo 2 Come si chiama? (formal) *What's your name?*

Il sig. Russo meets **la sig.na Finzi** for the first time.

(a) How does he ask: 'What's your name?' How does he give his own name?

Sig. Russo	Come si chiama?
Sig.na Finzi	Sandra Finzi. E lei?
Sig. Russo	Mi chiamo Marco Russo.

Sig. na Finzi Di dov'è?
Sig. Russo   Sono di Napoli.
Sig.na Finzi Io sono di Torino.

(b) How does she ask: 'Where are you from?' How does he answer?

🎧 Dialogo 3 Di dove sei? (informal)   *Where are you from?*

In another part of the room **Elena** and **Massimo** (*Max*), two younger people, meet on a more informal basis. Compare this dialogue (which is informal) with the second dialogue (which is formal).

(a) How does **Elena** ask: 'What's your name?' Compare it with the same question that **il Sig. Russo** asked in the second dialogue.

Elena	Come ti chiami?
Massimo	Massimo. E tu?
Elena	Elena. Sei di Milano?
Massimo	No. Sono di Firenze. E tu, di dove sei?
Elena	Io sono di Milano.
Massimo	Che cosa fai?
Elena	Sono segretaria.
Massimo	Io sono ragioniere. Lavoro in banca.

Che cosa fai?	*What do you do?*	**Lavoro in banca.**	*I work in a*
ragioniere (m)	*accountant*		*bank.*

(b) How does she say: 'I'm from Milan'?
(c) How does he ask what she does and how does she answer: 'I'm a secretary'?

🎧 Dialogo 4 Di che nazionalità è? (formal)   *What's your nationality?*

Il sig. Russo is now talking to **la sig.na Galli**.

(a) How does he ask her nationality and how does she answer: 'I'm Italian'?

Sig. Russo   Di che nazionalità è, signorina?
Sig.na Galli Sono italiana. Sono di Palermo.
Sig. Russo   Anch'io sono italiano. Chi è questa bella ragazza?

Sig.na Galli	Maria Toffalis. È greca. Non parla italiano.
Sig. Russo	Ho capito. È qui in vacanza?
Sig.na Galli	Chi, io? Sono a Roma per studiare l'informatica.

Chi è ...? *Who is ...?*	**per studiare** *to study*
ragazza *girl*	**l'informatica** *information*
Ho capito *I understand (Lit. I have*	*technology*
understood)	

(b) How does he say: 'I'm Italian too'?

(c) How does la **sig.na Galli** say: 'She's Greek'?

Dialogo 5 Quanti anni hai? (informal) *How old are you?*

Elena and **Massimo** are interrupted in mid-conversation by **Ugo** (*Hugh*). **Massimo** introduces first himself, then **Elena** to him.

(a) How does **Massimo** introduce himself to **Ugo**?

(b) How does he introduce **Elena** to **Ugo**? How does she respond?

Massimo	Io sono Massimo, e questa è Elena.
Elena	Piacere.
Ugo	Piacere, Ugo.
Massimo	Dunque… Elena, quanti anni hai?
Elena	Ho diciotto anni.
Massimo	Beata te! Io ho ventisei anni.

At this point **Sandra**, in a hurry to be off, spots **Massimo**, who is a friend of hers, and greets him.

Sandra	Ciao, Massimo!
Massimo	Ciao! Come stai?
Sandra	Non c'è male, grazie. E tu?
Massimo	Abbastanza bene, grazie. Ci vediamo più tardi. Ciao!
Sandra	Ciao!

piacere *how do you do?*	**non c'è male** *not too bad*
dunque ... *well, where was I ...*	**abbastanza bene** *quite well*
Beata te! *Lucky you!*	**più tardi** *later*
Ciao! Come stai? *Hi! How are you?*	

(c) How does **Massimo** ask how old **Elena** is and how does she answer?

Dialogo 6 Quanti figli ha? (formal)   *How many children have you (got)?*

Finally, in another group, **Ugo** talks to la **sig.ra Dini**.

(a) How does **la sig.ra Dini** say she's married?

Nino

Ugo	È sposata?
Sig.ra Dini	Sì. Sono sposata.
Ugo	Quanti figli ha, signora?
Sig.ra Dini	Due: Luisa e Paolo.
Ugo	Quanti anni hanno?
Sig.ra Dini	Il ragazzo ha undici anni e va a scuola. La bambina ha solo quattro anni.
Ugo	Ah, sono piccoli! Io non sono sposato. Mio fratello invece è sposato. Ma è separato.
Sig.ra Dini	Quanti fratelli e quante sorelle ha?
Ugo	Ho un fratello e una sorella. Io sono il secondo.

(b) **Quanti fratelli e quante sorelle ha Nino?**

figli	*children*	**piccolo/a**	*young, small*
ragazzo	*boy*	**invece**	*but, on the other hand*
va a scuola	*goes to school*	**fratello, sorella**	*brother, sister*

(c) How does **Ugo** ask how many children she has?
(d) How does he ask their age?
(e) How does **la sig.ra Dini** say the little girl is only four?

Pronuncia

Consonanti (continued)

s has two sounds:

  s as in English *song*: secondo, solo, Massimo, sono, suo, inglese
  s as in *toes* (usually between vowels): musica, scusi, sposato

sc followed by **e** or **i** is pronounced as in English *she*: ascensore

z has two sounds:

  ts as in ca*ts*: stazione, grazie, ragazza
  ds as in o*dds*: zero, zucchero, gorgonzola

▓ Spiegazioni

1 Subject pronouns

singular		plural	
io	I	**noi**	we
tu	you (informal)	**voi**	you (plural)
lei	you (formal)		
lui, lei	he, she	**loro**	they

The familiar form **tu** (2nd person singular) is used with relatives, friends and children. Use **Ciao!** to say *hello* or *goodbye* when you are on **tu** terms with someone (as in Dialogue 5, p 31). The **tu** form of the verb normally ends in **-i**. **Lei** means both *you* and *she* and is used whether you are talking directly to a man or a woman formally, or talking about a girl or woman. The context should make it clear.

2 Verbs

Present tense (irregular) of **essere** and **avere**:

	essere *to be*		**avere** *to have*	
(io)	**sono**	I am	**ho**	I have
(tu)	**sei**	you are (informal)	**hai**	you have (informal)
(lei)	**è**	you are (formal)	**ha**	you have (formal)
(lui, lei)	**è**	he, she, (it) is	**ha**	he, she, (it) has
(noi)	**siamo**	we are	**abbiamo**	we have
(voi)	**siete**	you (plural) are	**avete**	you (plural) have
(loro)	**sono**	they are	**hanno**	they have

The plural of both **tu** and **lei** is **voi**.

Attenzione! The letter 'h' is never pronounced in Italian.

Present tense (regular) of -are verbs

The infinitives of regular verbs end in **-are**, **-ere** or **-ire**. For the present tense of **-are** verbs add the endings written below in bold characters to the stem (**parl-**).

Notice that *the first person singular* of the present tense of a verb always ends in **-o**.

Present tense		**parlare** to speak
(io)	**parl -o**	I speak, I am speaking
(tu)	**parl -i**	you (informal) speak, you are speaking
(lei)	**parl -a**	you (formal) speak, you are speaking
(lui, lei)	**parl -a**	he, she, (it) speaks, he, she, (it) is speaking
(noi)	**parl -iamo**	we speak, we are speaking
(voi)	**parl -ate**	you (plural) speak, you are speaking
(loro)	**parl -ano**	they speak, they are speaking

In this unit you have met **abitano** (from **abitare**), **lavoro** (from **lavorare**)
and **studiare** which are all conjugated like **parlare**. But verbs ending in
-iare do not double the final **-i** in the second person singular **tu** form: tu
stud**i**.

Notice how for all verbs the stress falls on the same vowel in the first
person singular and the third person plural: **parlo parlano**; **abito abitano**;
studio studiano; **telefono telefonano** (from **telefonare** to phone)

3 Titles

Signore (Mr), **Signora** (Mrs), **Signorina** (Miss), **Signori** (Mr & Mrs)

Titles ending in **-ore**, such as **signore**, **dottore** and **professore**, drop the
final **-e** when followed by a proper name: **Buongiorno**, dott**ore**! becomes
Buongiorno, dott**or Nuzzo**! **Buongiorno**, profess**ore**! becomes
Buongiorno, profess**or Salviati**!

When you are not addressing people directly, but talking about them, you
must use the definite article before the title: **il signore**, **la signora**, etc.

Dov'è **il dottore**?   *Where is the doctor?*
Dov'è **il dottor** Nuzzo?   *Where is Doctor Nuzzo?*

Although **signori** is masculine plural it can refer to both men and women:

I signori Spada   *Mr and Mrs Spada*

Similarly, **ragazzi** can mean *boys* or *boys and girls*; **figli**, *sons*, or *sons
and daughters*, etc.

4 Numbers (continued)

First, second, third, etc., are adjectives in Italian:

il prim**o** pian**o** *the 1st floor*   la terz**a** porta *the 3rd door*
il second**o** dialog**o** *the 2nd dialogue*   la quart**a** strada a destra
                                                the 4th road on the right

5 Come si chiama? *What's your name?*

(lei) Come si chiama? literally *How do you call yourself?* is the normal way of asking someone's name. (**Come** means *how*.)

(io) Mi chiamo Antonia.	*My name is Antonia.*
(lei) Come si chiama?	*What's your name?* (formal)
(tu) Come ti chiami?	*What's your name?* (informal)

6 *Adjectives (continued)*

Like nouns there are two types of adjectives:

those ending in **-o/-a**: piccol**o/a** *small*; ricc**o/a** *rich*;
those ending in **-e** (m. & f.): intelligent**e** *intelligent*;
interessant**e** *interesting*.

As we have seen in Unit 2, p 23, adjectives agree with the nouns they qualify. In the following examples notice the endings in bold:

Masculine singular	Feminine singular
un giardin**o** piccol**o** *a small garden*	un**a** cas**a** piccol**a** *a small house*
un uom**o** ricc**o** *a rich man*	un**a** donn**a** ricc**a** *a rich woman*
un ragazz**o** intelligent**e**	un**a** ragazz**a** intelligent**e**
an intelligent boy	an intelligent girl
un dottor**e** ingles**e**	un**a** ragionier**a** ingles**e**
an English doctor	an English accountant

The plural of adjectives corresponds to the plural of nouns (see unit 2, p 22). For mixed genders use masculine adjectives.

Masculine plural	Feminine plural
i gelat**i** italian**i**	**le** pizz**e** italian**e**
i dottor**i** ingles**i**	**le** ragionier**e** ingles**i**
i ristorant**i** frances**i**	**le** lezion**i** interessant**i**

Quanti, quante are also adjectives and must agree with the noun they qualify:

Quant**i** fratell**i** e quant**e** sorell**e** ha?	*How many brothers and sisters have you?*

7 Anch'io   *I am also/me too*

Notice how subject pronouns (**io**, **tu**, **lu**i, **ecc**.) are used after **anche** for emphasis:

> **Mangia anche lei? Sì. Mangio**   *Are you eating too?*
> **anch'io!**   *Yes, I'm eating too.*
>
> **Aspettate anche voi?**   *Are you waiting too?*
> **Sì. Aspettiamo anche noi.**   *Yes, we are (waiting) too.*

8 Chi?   *who/whom?*

Chi? is used to refer to people:

> **Chi è questa ragazza?**   *Who is this girl?*
> **(È) Maria**.   *(It's) Maria.*

Notice how Italians answer this question when a pronoun is involved:

> Chi è? Sono **io**.   *Who is it? It's me.*
> È **lui**, è **lei**.   *It's him, it's her/you.*

9 Età   *age*

To express age in Italian, use the verb **avere** (*to have*):

> Quanti anni **ha** Bruno?   *How old is Bruno?*
> **Ha** trentaquattro anni.   *He's thirty-four (years old).*

10 Mio fratello   *my brother* (possessives with family relations)

Mio/mia *m*y, **tuo/tua** *your*, **suo/sua** *your* are adjectives and must therefore agree with the nouns they qualify. Say **tuo/tua** when using the informal **tu**, and **suo/sua** when using **lei**. Take special care with **suo/sua**, which apart from *your* can each mean *his* or *her*, depending on the context.

> **sua sorella**   *his sister, her sister, your sister*
> **suo padre**   *his father, her father, your father*

Come si dice in italiano?

How to:

1   ask someone's name   **Come si chiama?** (form.)/
   (a) formally (b) informally   **Come ti chiami** (inform.)**?**
   give your name   **Mi chiamo …/Sono …**

2   ask where someone is from   **Di dov'è?** (form.)/**Di dove sei?** (inf.)
    (a) formally (b) informally;
    say where you are from   **Sono di Londra, sono di**
    (referring to town)   **Parigi, ecc.**

3   ask what someone's job is   **Che cosa fa?** (form.)/
    (a) formally (b) informally   **Che cosa fai?** (inf.)

4   ask someone's nationality   **Di che nazionalità è?** (form.)/
    (a) formally (b) informally   **Di che nazionalità sei?** (inf.)
    give your nationality   **Sono inglese, sono americano/a,**
                           ecc.

5   ask someone's age   **Quanti anni ha?** (form.)/
    (a) formally (b) informally   **Quanti anni hai?** (inf.)
    give your age   **Ho venticinque anni,**
                           ho ventotto anni, ecc.

6   ask and say who someone is   **Chi è questa ragazza? È Maria.**
    introduce yourself/others   **Io sono …/ Questo/questa è …**
    respond to introduction   **Piacere.**

Attività

1   Repeat the numbers from 11–50 as you hear them. Listen carefully to
    21, 28, 31, 38, 41 and 48. What difference do you notice between
    these six numbers and the other numbers from 20 to 50?

11	12	13	14	15	16
undici	**dodici**	**tredici**	**quattordici**	**quindici**	**sedici**
17	18	19	20	21	22
diciassette	**diciotto**	**diciannove**	**venti**	**ventuno**	**ventidue**
23	24	25	26	27	
ventitrè	**ventiquattro**	**venticinque**	**ventisei**	**ventisette**	
28	29	30	31	32	33
ventotto	**ventinove**	**trenta**	**trentuno**	**trentadue**	**trentatrè**
34	35	36	37	38	
trentaquattro	**trentacinque**	**trentasei**	**trentasette**	**trentotto**	
39	40	41	42		
trentanove	**quaranta**	**quarantuno**	**quarantadue**		

43	44	45	46
quarantatrè	quarantaquattro	quarantacinque	quarantasei
47	48	49	50
quarantasette	quarantotto	quarantanove	cinquanta

2 You will hear the names of five people on the audio with the number of the floor they live on and their door number. Fill them in as in the example. (The Roman numeral denotes the floor.)

(a)   (b)

Dott. Colombo **PROFESSORE** **II 21**	**Prof. P. Russo** **ARCHITETTO**	**Carlo Pini** **RAGIONIERE**

secondo piano   **Primo piano,**   **Quarto piano,**
numero ventuno   **numero dodici.**   **numero quarantasette.**

(c)   (d)

Olga Fulvi **DENTISTA**	**Anna Biondi** **GIORNALISTA**

Primo piano,   **Terzo piano,**
numero tredici.   **numero trentotto.**

3 Using the information from the nameplates above, write down what each person's occupation is. **Esempio: Il dottor Colombo è professore**.

4 Languages are masculine and don't change: **greco**, **russo**, ecc. (see p. 8). The same words are used for nationalities except that in this case they are adjectives and must agree with the nouns they qualify: Ug**o** è italian**o**; Pipp**a** è italian**a**. Here is a list of countries and people. Can you tell from the countries what nationality these people are?

Esempio: Inghilterra: Rita e Olga. Rita e Olga sono inglesi.

(a) **Germania**: Helga. (b) **Francia**: Gérard e Philippe. (c) **Spagna**: Juanita. (d) **Russia**: Ivan e Natasha. (e) **Italia**: Anna e Pina.

5 Now say what town they are from. **Esempio: Londra. Rita e Olga sono di Londra.**

(a) **Bonn** (b) **Nizza** (c) **Barcellona** (d) **Omsk** (e) **Trento**.

6 Finally, say what town they live in. **Esempio: Rita e Olga abitano a Londra.**

7 Here is the beginning of a letter from **Luisa**, who is writing to her new pen-pal **Anna**.

```
                                      Roma,
                               3 novembre
Cara Anna,
mi chiamo Luisa. Ho quindici anni. Sono di
Trento, ma abito a Roma. Ho una sorella. Si
chiama Vittoria e ha tredici anni. Mio
padre è francese e mia madre è italiana...
```

Write the beginning of **Anna's** letter to **Luisa** in which she gives the following information. Start your letter: **Cara Luisa,**

Age 17	Father: Italian
Town she comes from: **Siena**	Mother: German
Town she lives in: **Lucca**	Brother: Luigi 18 years old

3 Informazioni

Chi è questa bella ragazza? (Dialogue 4, p 30)

Making and receiving compliments is an essential feature of Italian daily life. They are not meant to be offensive or patronising. They are linked to another aspect of Italian culture: **fare bella figura** – that is, 'keeping up appearances'; it is important to make the right impression, in dress, bearing and general attitude. Perhaps equally, if not more important, is not 'to create a bad impression': **fare brutta figura**.

4 | QUANT'È?
How much is it?

In this Unit you will learn:

- ■ how to ask about opening and closing times
- ■ about the days of the week
- ■ how to ask the price and pay for purchases
- ■ how to talk about the colour and size (of shoes and clothing)

 Listen to the main divisions of the clock:

Alle due, alle tre, alle due e un quarto, alle tre e un quarto,
at 2.00   *at* 3.00   *at* 2.15   *at* 3.15

alle quattro e mezza
at 4.30

alle cinque e mezza, alle sei meno un quarto, alle sette meno un quarto,
at 5.30   *at* 5.45   *at* 6.45

all'una, all'una e un quarto, all'una e mezza
at 1.00   *at* 1.15   *at* 1.30

 Dialogo 1 A che ora apre il tabaccaio?   *At what time does the tobacconist's open?*

 (a) How does **B** say: 'At eight o'clock'?

A   Scusi, signore, a che ora apre il tabaccaio?
B   Alle otto.
A   E a che ora chiude? ~~quede~~ ~~costa~~ q-de
B   Alle dodici.

I giorni della settimana   *The days of the week*

Listen to the days of the week and notice particularly where the stress falls. In Italy the week starts on Monday and the days are written without capitals.

lunedì, martedì, mercoledì, giovedì, venerdì, sabato, domenica.

Dialogo 2 Che giorno parte? *What day are you leaving?*

Il tabaccaio (*the tobacconist*) asks **il dottore**, a regular customer of his, on what day he is leaving for Paris.

(a) What are the words for 'morning' and 'evening' in this conversation?

Tabaccaio Che giorno parte per Parigi? Giovedì o venerdì?
Dottore Giovedì.
Tobaccaio Quando ritorna?
Dottore Parto giovedì mattina e ritorno domenica sera.

Now listen to these numbers and repeat them.

1000   2000   20,000   120,000   220,000
mille duemila ventimila centoventimila duecentoventimila

Cento 100, **mille** 1000 and **mila** 1000s are indispensable for expressing the price of everyday purchases.

Dialogo 3 Vorrei tre francobolli *I'd like three stamps*

(a) How much did the stamp on the right cost?
(b) How does **il tabaccaio** ask: 'Do you want these?'

Dottore Vorrei tre francobolli.
Tabaccaio Per l'estero?
Dottore Sì. Per l'Inghilterra. E tre cartoline.
Tabaccaio Queste sono belle. Vuole queste?
Dottore Sì. E questi due giornali.
Tabaccaio E poi…?
Dottore Nient'altro, grazie. Quant'è?

Fontana di Trevi

(c) È una cartolina di Londra o di Roma?

Tabaccaio	I giornali, 3.000 lire; le cartoline, 1.500 lire; i francobolli, 2.550 lire.
Dottore	Mi dispiace, non ho spiccioli. Ho solo un biglietto da cinquantamila.
Tabaccaio	Non importa. Ecco il resto.
Dottore	Grazie. Buonasera.

(d) Look at the bank notes. Which one did **il dottore** pay with: (i), (ii), (iii) or (iv)?

per l'estero	*for abroad*	**non ho spiccioli**	*I haven't any change*
la cartolina	*postcard*	**solo**	*only*
il giornale	*the newspaper*	**un biglietto**	*a (bank) note*
nient'altro	*nothing else*	**non importa**	*it doesn't matter*

i)

ii)

iii)

iv)

(e) How many postcards and how many newspapers does **il dottore** want to buy?

Dialogo 4 A che ora aprono i negozi? *At what time do the shops open?*

(a) How does **A** say: 'Very kind of you'?

A Scusi, a che ora aprono i negozi la mattina?
B Alle nove.
A E a che ora chiudono? *y de no*
B All'una.
A E di pomeriggio?
B Aprono alle quattro e chiudono alle otto.
A Grazie. Molto gentile.
B Prego. Si figuri!

---

di pomeriggio *in the afternoon* **molto gentile** *very kind of you*
si figuri! *not at all!*

(b) Write down in figures at what time the shops open in the morning and at what time they close at night.

Dialogo 5 Vorrei un vestito *I would like a dress*

(a) How does **la commessa** (*shop assistant*) ask: 'Can I help you?'

Commessa Buongiorno, signora. Desidera?
Cliente Vorrei un vestito e una camicetta.
Commessa Di che colore, signora?
Cliente Il vestito? Bianco o nero.
Commessa Che taglia?
Cliente La quaranta.
Commessa Ecco: questo nero è semplice, ma elegante.
Cliente Infatti. È molto carino. Lo posso provare?
Commessa Certo, signora. Di qua, prego.
Cliente Sì. Questo va bene. Quanto costa?
Commessa Centoquarantamila. Non costa molto.
Cliente No. Non è caro.
Commessa E la camicetta, signora? Non vuole la camicetta?
Cliente No. La camicetta è troppo cara.

vestito dress	**Lo posso provare?** Can I try it on?
camicetta blouse	**Di qua, prego** This way, please
bianco/a, nero/a white, black	**Questo va bene** This one is (fits)
che taglia? what size?	alright
carino/a pretty, nice	

(b) How does **la cliente** ask: 'How much does it cost?'

(c) How does she say: 'The blouse is too dear'?

Dialogo 6   Quanto costano queste scarpe?
How much do these shoes cost?

(a) How does **il cliente** say: 'I'll take a pair of brown sandals'?

Cliente	Scusi, quanto costano queste scarpe?
Commesso	Trecentoventimila.
Cliente	Sono bellissime! Ma sono troppo care. Prendo un paio di sandali marroni e un paio di calzini beige.
Commesso	D'accordo. Che numero?
Cliente	Il quarantuno.
Commesso	Ecco…
Cliente	Sì. Sono proprio comodi.
Commesso	Desidera altro, signore?
Cliente	No, grazie. Quant'è?
Commesso	Non paga qui. Paga alla cassa.

d'accordo fine	**Paga alla cassa** You pay at the
proprio comodo/a really comfortable	desk

(b) How does the **Commesso** ask: 'What size?' (for the sandals)

Pronuncia

Consonanti (continued)

gu before a vowel is like *gu*
   in *linguist*:   **lingu**a, **gu**ida, **gu**anto

qu before a vowel is like *qu*
   in *quite*:   **qu**i, ac**qu**a, **qu**arto, **qu**aranta

Mark the stress in these words: **lunedì, sabato, domenica, aprono, chiudono**.

Spiegazioni

1 *Present tense (regular of -ere and -ire verbs)*

As with **-are** verbs, the endings in bold are added to the stem which is obtained by taking off **-ere** and **-ire**, respectively. Compare the **lei**, **voi** and **loro** endings with those of **-are** verbs (p. 34).

Present tense	**chiud-ere** *to close*	
(io)	chiud-**o**	*I close, I am closing*
(tu)	chiud-**i**	*you (informal) close, you are closing*
(lei)	chiud-**e**	*you (formal) close, you are closing*
(lui, lei)	chiud-**e**	*he, she, (it) closes, is closing*
(noi)	chiud-**iamo**	*we close, we are closing*
(voi)	chiud-**ete**	*you close, you are closing*
(loro)	chiud-**ono**	*they close, they are closing*
Present tense	**apr-ire** *to open*	
(io)	apr-**o**	*I open, I am opening*
(tu)	apr-**i**	*you open (inf.), you are opening*
(lei)	apr-**e**	*you (form.) open, you are opening*
(lui, lei)	apr-**e**	*he, she (it) opens, is opening*
(noi)	apr-**iamo**	*we open, we are opening*
(voi)	apr-**ite**	*you open, you are opening*
(loro)	apr-**ono**	*they open, they are opening*

Prendere *to take, to have* is conjugated like **chiudere**. **Sentire** *to hear* or *to feel* and **partire** *to leave* behave like **aprire**.

2 A che ora ...? *At what time ...?*

To say at *2 o'clock, 3 o'clock, 4 o'clock,* etc. up to 12 o'clock, use **alle** for *at*: **alle due, alle tre, alle quattro, alle dodici.**

For *at* one o'clock use **all'una**.

3 Di che colore?　*What colour?*

Colours are adjectives and therefore agree with the noun they qualify.
Like most adjectives they follow the noun.

azzurro *blue*　　**bianco** *white*　　**giallo** *yellow*　　**grigio** *grey*
nero *black*　　**rosso** *red*

il vestito giallo	*the yellow dress*
i vestiti gialli	*the yellow dresses*
la gonna rossa	*the red skirt*
le gonne rosse	*the red skirts*

To ask what colour a thing is/things are: **Di che colore è?/Di che colore
sono?**

Di che colore è la giacca?	*What colour is the jacket?*
Di che colore sono i guanti?	*What colour are the gloves?*
La giacca è grigia e i guanti sono neri.	*The jacket is grey and the gloves are black.*

Colours that end in **-e** in the singular (m. & f.), such as **verde** *green* and
marrone *brown*, end in **-i** in the plural (m. & f.):

singular		plural	
il vestito　　*dress, suit*	verd**e**/marrone	**i** vestiti	verd**i**/marron**i**
la magliett**a** *T shirt*		**le** magliett**e**	

The following colours never change their endings: **beige** *beige* **blu** *navy
blue* and **rosa** *pink*.

4 Quant'è?　*How much is it?*

Quant'è stands for **quanto è**. **Quant'è** is especially used when you are
buying more than one thing and want to know what the total comes to:

　　Quant'è (in tutto)?　　　　*How much is it (altogether)?*

5 Un paio di guanti　*A pair of gloves*

The plural of **paio** (m.) *pair* is **paia** (f.): **un paio** but **due paia**.

　　due paia di scarpe　　　　*two pairs of shoes*

6 Quanto costa? Quanto costano?   *How much does it cost?*
How much do they cost?

Make sure to use the plural **costano** when asking the price of more than one article:

> **Quanto costa il vestito?**   *How much does the dress/suit cost?*
> **Quanto costano queste scarpe?**   *How much do these shoes cost?*

7 -issimo   *very*

To give the idea of very, subtract the final vowel from an adjective and add **-issimo/a** for the singular or **issimi/e** for the plural:

> **bello/a** → **bell-** → **bellissimo/a**   *very beautiful*
> **caro/a** → **car-** → **carissimo/a**   *very dear*
>
> **una camicia bellissima**   *a very beautiful shirt*
> **due quadri carissimi**   *two very expensive pictures*

8 Non ho spiccioli   *I haven't any change*

In negative sentences in the plural, such as *I haven't any change, I haven't any brothers*, *any* remains unexpressed in Italian:

> **Non ho soldi.**   *I haven't any money.*

Similarly, *any* is omitted when negative questions are in the plural:

> **Non ha amici italiani?**   *Haven't you got any Italian friends?*

9 L'Inghilterra   *England*

Countries are normally preceded by the definite article in Italian:

> **L'Italia ha circa 60 milioni**   *Italy has about 60 million*
> **di abitanti.**   *inhabitants.*
> **Vorrei due francobolli per**   *I'd like two stamps for*
> **la Svizzera.**   *Switzerland.*

10 Centoquarantamila

Notice how numbers are all written in one word, however long. When giving the price you don't need to add the word **lire**:

> **Quant'è? Centomila.**   *How much is it? 100,000 lire.*

Notice that with **cento**   *a/one hundred* and **mille** *a/one thousand*, the indefinite article *a* or the number *one* is not expressed:

| cento sterline; mille dollari | *a hundred pounds, a thousand dollars* |
| centomila persone | *one hundred thousand people* |

but *1 million* is **un** milione **di**

| **un** milione **di** franchi | *a million francs* |
| **due** milioni **di** lire | *2 million lire* |

11 Ci vediamo!   *I'll see you!*

Use **ci vediamo** by itself, with days, dates or parts of the day:

Ci vediamo	{ **stamattina** **dopo** **oggi** **stasera**	*I'll see you*	{ *this morning* *later* *today* *this evening/tonight*

Other ways of using **ci vediamo**:

Ci vediamo	**domani** **dopodomani** **lunedì** **martedì**	**mattina** **pomeriggio** **sera**	*I'll see you*	*tomorrow* *the day after tomorrow* *on Monday* *on Tuesday*	*morning* *afternoon* *evening/ night*

12 Prepositions

Here is a list of some Italian prepositions. Their English equivalents are very approximate but they can be a useful guide to understanding:

di	*of*	**a**	*at, to*	**da**	*from, by*
in	in	**con**	*with*	**su**	*on*
per	*for*	**tra/fra**	*between* or *among*	**senza**	*without*

It must be emphasised, however, that their meanings vary enormously according to the context.

Come si dice in italiano?

How to:

1 ask at what time a place opens/closes	**A che ora apre/chiude?**
say at what time it opens/closes	**Apre/chiude alle …/all'…**
2 ask on what day someone is leaving	**Che giorno parti** (informal)/ **parte** (formal)?
say on what day you are leaving	**Parto lunedì/giovedì, ecc.**
3 say what you would like (to buy)	**Vorrei una cartolina, un francobollo, ecc.**
4 ask about the colour	**Di che colore?**
the size: (a) clothes in general	**Che taglia?**
(b) footwear.	**Che numero?**
5 ask how much a thing/things cost	**Quanto costa?/Quanto costano?**
ask what the price comes to	**Quant'è?**

Attività

(a)

(b)
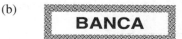

(c)

(d)

(e)
I GRANDI MAGAZZINI

1 Listen to the audio and write down in figures the opening and closing times of the above places.

(a) La mattina il consolato apre alle nove e mezza e chiude all'una.

(b) Il pomeriggio la banca apre alle tre e chiude alle quattro.

(c) Il museo apre alle nove e chiude alle due.
(d) L'Istituto Europeo apre alle nove e chiude all'una e mezza.
(e) I grandi magazzini aprono alle nove e chiudono alle sette e
     mezza.

2   Match the words below with the correct pictures. Look up those you
    don't know.

i jeans	la camicia
i pantaloni	le scarpe
la gonna	i sandali
la camicetta	la cravatta
la giacca	la maglietta
i guanti	il vestito

3 Form questions to ask (a) how much the T shirt costs; (b) how much the trousers cost; (c) how much the shoes cost. Write down in words the price of each.

4 (a) Write down what **Carlo** buys, using the information in the table below. On the left-hand side you see the clothes he buys. The figures refer to the number he buys of each, and at the top of the table you will see what colours he chooses (**comprare** *to buy*).

	rosso	giallo	nero	verde
maglietta	1	3		
cravatta		1		1
paio di scarpe			2	
paio di pantaloni		1		1

Start: **Carlo compra una ...**

(b) Assuming **Carlo** pays the prices given in **2** above, how much does he pay in total?

5 **Ora tocca a te!** Add your side to the dialogue.

Tabaccaio	Desidera?
You	*Two stamps.*
Tabaccaio	Per l'estero?
You	*Yes. For France.*
Tabaccaio	Altro?
You	*A postcard of Rome and this newspaper.*
Tabaccaio	Poi...
You	*Nothing else. How much does it come to?*
Tabaccaio	3.700 lire.
You	*Here you are.*

Informazioni

1 Prezzo   *Price*

In markets and small shops you can often bargain for the price of an article or ask for a discount (**uno sconto**) unless, that is, the sign **prezzi fissi** *fixed prices* is displayed.

2 Tabaccaio

In Italy tobacco and salt are state monopolies. They are both sold in tobacconists' shops, **Sali e Tabacchi**, which also sell stamps. **Carta**

bollata and **marche da bollo** are also obtainable there. The first is government stamped paper: it is used for a variety of official purposes such as drawing up contracts and making statements to the police. The second are revenue stamps used for, among other things, official receipts.

3

What do you think **CHIUSO**, **APERTO** and **SALDI** mean in the signs above? Check the meanings in the vocabulary.

Look up the words you don't know in this advert. What are they offering a discount for? When?

5 IL COLLOQUIO
The interview

In this Unit you will learn how to:

■ exchange information about where you are going (country, town)
■ ask why … and say because …
■ ask and say how something is spelt
■ ask and tell the time
■ ask for someone's address and phone number

Dialogo 1 Dove vai? *Where are you going?*

Barbara tells her friend **Beatrice** that she is going to Bologna for her job interview (**il colloquio**).

(a) How does Barbara say 'I'm going to Bologna'?

Beatrice Dove vai?
Barbara Vado a Bologna per il colloquio.
Beatrice Come vai? In macchina?
Barbara In treno. Ma anche tu parti, no?
Beatrice Sì. Vado in Inghilterra con la mia amica francese. Andiamo a Londra.
Barbara Per quanto tempo?
Beatrice Oh! Solo per dieci giorni.
Barbara Andate in albergo o a casa di amici?
Beatrice Andiamo in una piccola pensione. Gli alberghi sono cari.

in macchina *by car*		**per quanto tempo?** *how long for?*	
in treno *by train*		**a casa di amici** *to a friend's house*	
andiamo *we are going*		**una pensione** *a guest house*	

(b) How does **Barbara** say: 'By train'?
(c) How does **Beatrice** say: 'Only for ten days'?

Dialogo 2   Quanto tempo ci vuole?   *How long does it take?*

Barbara is asking **un passante** *a passer-by* if he knows where the shoe factory is.

(a) Barbara asks where the shoe factory is in a slightly different way from the one you have already learnt: can you spot the difference and repeat the question?

Barbara Scusi, sa dov'è la fabbrica di scarpe?
Passante Certo, signora. Sempre dritto dopo la chiesa.
Barbara È lontano da qui?
Passante No. Non è lontano. È vicino.
Barbara Quanto tempo ci vuole?
Passante A piedi, mezz'ora.
Barbara E in autobus?
Passante Solo cinque minuti.
Barbara Ho capito. Che ore sono adesso, per piacere?
Passante Sono le dieci.
Barbara Già le dieci? Allora prendo l'autobus.

(b) What is **una fermata**?

FERMATA
7 PIAZZA CAVOUR
19 DUOMO

chiesa *church*	**che ore sono?** *What time is it?*
lontano *far*	**adesso** *now*
a piedi *on foot*	**già** *already*
mezz'ora *half an hour*	

(c) How does the **passante** say: 'It's not far.'?

Dialogo 3   Il suo nome?   *Your name?*

Barbara is being interviewed by **il dottor Verga**, **Direttore del Personale** *the Personnel Manager*.

(a) What expression does he use to ask her to spell her name?

Dottor Verga Il suo nome, signora?
Barbara Barbara Setzler.
Dottor Verga Setzler?... Come si scrive?
Barbara Dunque: S come Salerno, E come Empoli, T come Torino,

Z come Zara, L come Livorno, E come Empoli, R come Roma.

Dottor Verga Non è italiana?
Barbara Sì. Sono italiana. Mio marito è svizzero.
Dottor Verga Capisce l'inglese?
Barbara Capisco tutto, ma non parlo bene.

---

come si scrive?	*how do you spell*	**marito**	*husband*
	it/how is it spelt?	**tutto**	*everything*

(b) How does **Barbara** say: 'My husband is Swiss'?

(c) How does she say 'I understand everything'?

Dialogo 4 Qual è il suo indirizzo? *What's your address?*

The interview continues. **Barbara** says where she was born.

(a) How does she say: 'I was born in Lucca, but I live in Sienna.'?

Dottor Verga Dove abita?
Barbara Sono nata a Lucca, ma abito a Siena.
Dottor Verga Dove lavora?
Barbara A Firenze: in uno studio legale.
Dottor Verga Perchè vuole cambiare il suo lavoro attuale?
Barbara Perchè vorrei usare le lingue che conosco.
Dottor Verga Quante lingue parla?
Barbara Quattro. Tre abbastanza bene.
Dottor Verga Qual è il suo indirizzo?
Barbara Via Lazio 68.
Dottor Verga E il numero di telefono?
Barbara Il mio numero di telefono è 3355541.

---

studio legale *lawyer's office*	**attuale** *present/current*	
perchè vuole cambiare ...?	**le lingue che conosco** *the*	
Why do you want to change ...?	*languages that I know*	
cambiare *to change*	**abbastanza bene** *quite well*	

(b) How does **il dott. Verga** ask: 'How many languages do you speak?'

Pronuncia

The Italian alphabet has 21 letters: **a, b, c, d, e, f, g, h, i , l, m, n, o, p, q, r, s, t, u, v, z.** For spelling names, the town alphabet is normally used:

a **A come Ancona**	h **Acca come Hotel**	q **Cu come Quebec**
b **Bi come Bari**	i **I come Imola**	r **Erre come Roma**
c **Ci come Capri**	l **Elle come Livorno**	s **Esse come Salerno**
d **Di come Domodossola**	m **Emme come Modena**	t **Ti come Torino**
e **E come Empoli**	n **Enne come Napoli**	u **U come Urbino**
f **Effe come Firenze**	o **O come Ostia**	v **Vi come Verona**
g **Gi come Genova**	p **Pi come Palermo**	z **Zeta come Zara**

The following are not part of the Italian alphabet but may be required for spelling foreign names:

j **I lunga come Jazz**	w **Doppia vu come Washington**
k **Kappa come Kaiser**	x **Ix come raggi X**
y **Ipsilon come York**	

Spiegazioni

1 *Verbs*

In Dialogue 1 **vai** *you* (informal) *are going* is part of the irregular verb **andare** *to go*.

Present tense	**andare**	*to go*		
(io) vado	*I go, am going*	**(noi) andiamo**	*we go, are going*
(tu) vai	*you (inf.) go, are going*	**(voi) andate**	*you (pl.) go,*
(lei) va	*you (form.) go, are going*		*are going*
(lui, lei) va	*he/she/it goes, is going*	**(loro) vanno**	*they go, are going*

Capisce is part of **capire** *to understand*, another type of **-ire** verb. The endings in bold are added to the stem **cap-**.

Present tense	**capire**	*to understand*	
(io) cap-**isco**	*I understand*	**(noi)** cap-**iamo**	*we understand*
(tu) cap-**isci**	*you* (inf.) *understand*	**(voi)** cap-**ite**	*you* (pl.) *understand*
(lei) cap-**isce**	*you* (form.) *understand*		
(lui, lei) cap-**isce**	*he/she/it understands*	**(loro)** cap-**iscono**	*they understand*

The most common verbs like **capire** are: **finire** *to finish*, **preferire** *to prefer* and **pulire** *to clean*. e.g. fin-**isco**, fin-**isci**, fin-**isce**, fin-**iamo**, fin-**ite**, fin-**iscono**; prefer-**isco**, prefer-**isci**, **ecc.**; pul-**isco**, pul-**isci**, **ecc.**

Ho capito (Lit: *I have understood*) is what Italians usually say to show that they understand what has been said to them:

Ripeto?	*Shall I repeat?*
No, no. Va bene. Ho capito.	*No, no. That's alright. I understand.*

Notice that when **capire** is used, the language is preceded by the article:
   Capisce l'inglese? Sì. Capisco l'inglese e il tedesco.

2 Andare a/in ...   *to go to ...*

With towns, use **andare a ...**; with countries, use **andare in ...**

Vado a Nizza, a Pisa...	*I'm going to Nice, to Pisa...*
Andiamo in Italia, in Francia...	*We're going to Italy, to France...*

3 *Articles*: Gli   *the*

Gli (plural of **lo** and **l'**) is used before masculine plural words beginning with a vowel, s + consonant, or z:

4 Amici, alberghi

Singular		Plural	
l' + vowel		**amici**	*the friends*
		alberghi	*the hotels*
		uffici	*the offices*
	gli		
		studenti	*the students*
lo + s + consonant		**stranieri**	*the foreigners*
lo + z		**zii**	*the uncles*

amico (*male*) *friend* takes the plural form **amici**.
but **amica** (*female*) *friend* takes the plural form **amiche**.

Take care with words ending in **-co, -ca, -go, -ga**. They often insert an **h** in the plural to preserve the same **c** or **g** sound (see **Pronuncia**, Unit 2 p 21): **la banca**, **le banche** (*the banks*); **il lago**, **i laghi** (*the lakes*).

5 Perchè ...? Perchè ... *Why ...? Because ...*

Perchè means both *why* and *because*:

> **Perchè non va in albergo?** *Why don't you go to a hotel?*
> **Perchè gli alberghi sono cari.** *Because hotels are expensive.*

6 Scusi, sa dov'è ...? *Excuse me, do you know where ... is?*

As in English, this expression is frequently used as another way of asking **Dov'è ...?**

7 Quanto tempo ci vuole? *How long does it take?*

Use this expression to ask or say how long something takes:

> **Quanto tempo ci vuole per** *How long does it take to go*
> **andare a casa di Maria?** *to Mary's house?*
> **Ci vuole un'ora.** *It takes an hour.*

For plural nouns: **ore** *hours*, **minuti** *minutes*, **giorni** *days*, etc., **ci vuole** becomes **ci vogliono**.

> **Quanto tempo ci vuole per** *How long does it take to return/*
> **ritornare?** *get back?*
> **Ci vogliono cinque minuti.** *It takes five minutes.*

8 Che ora è? Che ore sono? *What time is it?*

To ask the time, either of the above may be used, but the answer will depend on whether the time is singular or plural. Always use **sono le ...** in your answer unless talking about *one o'clock*, *midday* or *midnight*. **Sono le due, sono le cinque, sono le sei,** but **è l'una, è l'una e mezza, è mezzogiorno, è mezzanotte**.

The clocks (**gli orologi**) opposite show how **e** is used on the right-hand side of the clock to say '*past*', and **meno** (*less*) on the left to say '*to*'.

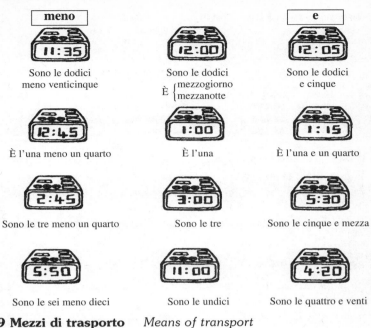

meno		**e**
11:35	12:00	12:05
Sono le dodici meno venticinque	È {mezzogiorno / mezzanotte}	Sono le dodici e cinque
12:45	1:00	1:15
È l'una meno un quarto	È l'una	È l'una e un quarto
2:45	3:00	5:30
Sono le tre meno un quarto	Sono le tre	Sono le cinque e mezza
5:50	11:00	4:20
Sono le sei meno dieci	Sono le undici	Sono le quattro e venti

9 Mezzi di trasporto   *Means of transport*

andare + in ...   *to go by ...*

	aereo		air
	autobus		bus
	bicicletta		bike
Vado in	macchina	*I'm going by*	car
	metropolitana		underground
	treno		train
	vaporetto		boat

but **Vado a piedi** *I'm going on foot/I'm walking*

10 Possessive adjectives

When referring to *one member* of the family *only* (**mio fratello, sua sorella ecc.** see Unit 3, p 36) the article is not used before **mio, tuo, ecc**. In other cases, however, the definite article is required and must precede the possessive:

Le mie sorelle e i tuoi fratelli   *My brothers and your sisters*
vanno a casa.   *are going home.*

Here are the possessive adjectives for *my, your, his, her.*

Singular	Masc.	Fem.	Plural	Masc.	Fem.	
(io)	**il mio**	**la mia**		**i miei**	**le mie**	*my*
(tu)	**il tuo**	**la tua**		**i tuoi**	**le tue**	*your* (informal)
(lui/lei)	**il suo**	**la sua**		**i suoi**	**le sue**	*his, her; your* (formal)

il mio orologio; il suo orologio   *my watch; his/her/your watch*
la mia città; la sua città   *my town; his/her/your town*
i miei amici; i suoi amici   *my friends; your/his/her friends*
                                          (m.)
le mie amiche; le sue amiche   *my friends; your/his/her friends*
                                          (f.)

11 Sono nato/a a ...   *I was born in ...*

It is important to use the *present* tense of **essere**, not the past, when saying
when or where you were born:

Dov'è nato/a?   *Where were you born?*
Sono nato/a a Roma.   *I was born in Rome.*

12 Come si scrive?   *How do you spell (write) it?/How is it spelt?*

To ask *'How do you spell...?'* Italians say *'How do you write..?'*

Si means *one, you, people in general* and is used frequently in Italian. It
is always used with the third person of the verb, and precedes it.

Come si dice in italiano?   *How do you say it in Italian?*
Qui si parla italiano.   *Italian is spoken here.* (Lit: *here*
                                          one speaks Italian)
In questo ristorante si mangia   *You can eat well in this*
bene.   *restaurant.*

Come si dice in italiano?

How to:

1   ask where someone is going   **Dove va?** (formal)/**Dove vai?**
                                          (informal)

say where you are going (country, town)	**Vado in Italia, a Genova**.
2 ask why ... and say because...	**Perchè ...? Perchè ...**
3 ask how something is spelt	**Come si scrive?**
4 ask and tell the time	**Che ora è?/Che ore sono?**
	È l'una.../Sono le due ...
5 ask for someone's address/ phone number	**Qual è il suo** (formal)/**il tuo** (informal) **indirizzo?**
	Qual è il suo (formal)/**il tuo** (informal) **numero di telefono?**

After this Unit only the **lei** form (formal *you*) will be used in the **Come si dice in italiano** section unless **tu** is more appropriate.

◤ Attività

1 I numeri *numbers (continued)*

First repeat the round numbers from **60–100** as you hear them.

60	70	80	90	100
sessanta	**settanta**	**ottanta**	**novanta**	**cento**

Now use your pause button so that you can say the following numbers before you hear them:

61	68	82	88	91	97
sessantuno	**sessantotto**	**ottantadue**	**ottantotto**	**novantuno**	**novantasette**

98	99	100
novantotto	**novantanove**	**cento**

Finally, listen to the ordinal numbers 5th–10th and repeat them:

5th	6th	7th	8th	9th	10th
quinto/a	**sesto/a**	**settimo/a**	**ottavo/a**	**nono/a**	**decimo/a**

2   In the eight addresses below, the house numbers are written out in full. See if you can recognise what they are by listening to the audio. Write them down in figures.

(a)   Via Nazionale settantasei
(b)   Via Quattro Novembre ottantacinque
(c)   Via Cavour sessantotto
(d)   Via Martelli settantanove
(e)   Via Romolo centosettanta

(f)   Via Mercuri centonovantotto

(g) Via Vittorio Emanuele centosettantasette

(h) Via Terni centodue

3   Say where **Carlo**, **Roberto**, etc. are going to, and how they get there.

(a) **Carlo** _____ in ufficio   _____.

(b) **Roberto** _____ Parigi   _____.

(c) **Franco** _____ Roma   _____.

(d) **Anna** _____ a casa   _____.

(e) **I bambini** —— a scuola   _____.

(f) **Francesca** _____ Milano   _____.

4   Now imagine a conversation with Carlo: the information given in **Attività 3** could be rendered in question and answer form:

    – Dove vai, Carlo?   **– Come vai?**

    – Vado in ufficio.   **– In bicicletta.**

    Write similar conversations with **Franco, Anna** and **Francesca.**

5   Write these times out in letters starting with **È ...** or **Sono ...** (see p. 58 § 8)

    (a) 10.05   (b) 12.45   (c) 2.50   (d) 3.20   (e) 5.45   (f) 6.30

    (g) 12.00 (noon)   (h) 12.00 (midnight)

6   **Ora tocca a te!** You have a short interview with **il Dirigente** *the Manager*. You are Pat Brown, 33 years old and American. You work **in un'agenzia di viaggi** *a travel agency*. Use the pause button to complete your side of the interview.

Dirigente	Il suo nome?
You	*Pat Brown.*
Dirigente	Brown? Come si scrive?
You	*(Spell it for him.)*
Dirigente	È inglese, vero?
You	*No. I'm American but I live in London.*
Dirigente	Quanti anni ha?
You	*I am 33.*
Dirigente	Che lavoro fa?
You	*I work in a travel agency.*
Dirigente	Parla francese e tedesco?
You	*I understand everything but I don't speak well.*

✳ Informazioni

1   Buses are the most usual form of public transport in Italian towns, though trams and trolley buses still exist. You must buy your ticket before boarding the bus, otherwise you are liable to a fine (**la multa**). You normally buy **un blocchetto** of 10 before the journey, at the tobacconist's, newsagent's or in bars.

2

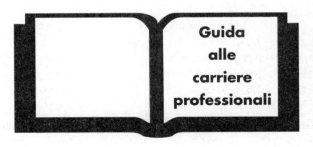

Guida
alle
carriere
professionali

What is this handbook for?

6 | ALLA STAZIONE
At the station

In this Unit you will learn how to:

■ buy a rail ticket and book a seat
■ ask the time of the next train, etc.
■ ask from what platform it leaves
■ ask whether you have to change and where

Dialogo 1 A che ora parte il prossimo treno?
At what time does the next train leave?

At the railway station **un viaggiatore** *a traveller* is buying a ticket to Turin.

(a) How does **l'impiegato** *the (booking) clerk* say 'at 3.25 p.m.'?

Viaggiatore	Vorrei un biglietto per Torino.
Impiegato	Prima o seconda classe?
Viaggiatore	Prima classe. A che ora parte il prossimo treno?
Impiegato	Alle quindici e venticinque. Fra dieci minuti.
Viaggiatore	Da che binario?
Impiegato	Dal binario diciotto.
Viaggiatore	A che ora arriva a Torino?
Impiegato	Alle venti e cinquanta.
Viaggiatore	Devo cambiare?
Impiegato	No. È diretto. Guardi, signore, l'orario dei treni è là in fondo.

prossimo/a *next*	**Devo cambiare?** *Do I have to change?*
fra dieci minuti *in ten minutes*	**l'orario dei treni** *the train*
Da che/quale binario? *From*	*timetable*
what platform?	**là in fondo** *down there*

(b) How does **il viaggiatore** ask: 'From what platform?'

🔊 Dialogo 2 **Vorrei prenotare ...**   *I'd like to book ...*

At the railway station a man is trying to book three seats for tomorrow morning, but there will be a strike (**sciopero**) on.

(a) How does **A** say: 'Three seats for tomorrow morning'?

A Vorrei prenotare tre posti per domani mattina.
B Domani? Impossibile!
A Perchè impossibile?
B Perchè domani c'è lo sciopero.
A Un altro sciopero? Ci sono sempre scioperi. Tre posti per dopodomani, allora.
B C'è l'Eurostar alle otto e trenta e un espresso alle dieci e quaranta.
A Meglio l'Eurostar. Tre biglietti, andata e ritorno.

| **ci sono sempre ...** | *there are always ...* | **dopodomani** | *the day after tomorrow* |
| **meglio** | *better* | **andata e ritorno** | *return ticket* |

(b) You have now learnt two meanings for **espresso** and two for **biglietto**: what are they?

🔊 Dialogo 3 **C'è un treno diretto...?**   *Is there a through train...?*

A traveller wants to go to Florence and asks for the times of the trains (**l'orario dei treni**) at the enquiry desk (**Ufficio Informazioni**).

(a) How does **l'impiegato** say: 'It's two minutes late'?

Viaggiatore C'è un treno diretto per Firenze o devo cambiare?
Impiegato Se vuole prendere l'espresso, deve aspettare tre ore, fino alle diciotto e quarantacinque.
Viaggiatore Non c'è un treno prima della sette meno un quarto?
Impiegato L'Eurostar. Ma deve cambiare a Bologna.
Viaggiatore È in orario l'Eurostar?
Impiegato No. È in ritardo di due minuti.
Viaggiatore Meno male! Da quale binario parte?
Impiegato È in partenza dal binario nove. Se ha già il biglietto, può pagare il supplemento in treno.

Se vuole prendere... *If you want to take...*	**prima di** *before*
aspettare *to wait for*	**in orario/in ritardo** *on time/late*
fino a *until*	**meno male!** *thank goodness!*
	può pagare *you can pay*

(b) 'The train is now leaving from platform 9.' What is the Italian equivalent?

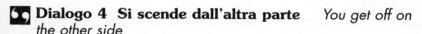

Dialogo 4 Si scende dall'altra parte   *You get off on the other side*

Il signor Neri asks a passenger whether the bus (**l'autobus**) on which they are travelling goes to the main line station.

(a) How does **il sig. Neri** ask: 'Where's the 68 bus stop?'

Sig. Neri	Va alla stazione centrale quest'autobus, per favore?
Passeggiero	No, signore. Deve prendere il 68.
Sig. Neri	E dov'è la fermata del 68, per cortesia?
Passeggiero	Davanti all'università. Dopo il municipio.
Sig. Neri	Grazie. Può dirmi quando devo scendere?
Passeggiero	Certamente. Alla prossima fermata.
Sig. Neri	Ho capito. Scendo e vado davanti all'università.
Passeggiero	Guardi, alla prossima fermata scendo anch'io.
Sig. Neri	Allora scendiamo insieme. Si scende da qui?
Passeggiero	No. Si scende dall'altra parte. Da qui si sale solamente.

per cortesia *please*	**insieme** *together*
davanti a *in front of*	**da qui** *over here*
Può dirmi...? *Can you tell me...?*	**si sale (salire** irr.**)** *you get on*
Guardi... *Look...*	**solamente** *only*

(b) How does **il passeggiero** say: 'I'm getting off at the next stop too'?
(c) What are the three expressions you have met for 'please' up to now?

Pronuncia

a + i   vai, stai, ai binari
e + u   l'Albergo Europa, l'Istituto Europeo, la Comunità Europea
i + e   le mie amiche, i miei amici, l'impiegato
u + o   può, vuoi andare, i suoi fratelli.

Spiegazioni

1 L'orario dei treni   *The train timetable*

The 24-hour clock is normally used for all official purposes: **dodici e quindici** *12.15*; **quindici e quarantacinque** *15.45*; **diciotto e trenta** *18.30*; **venti e cinquanta** *20.50*.

2 Prossimo/a   *next*

To ask when the first, second, next, or last train leaves:

A che ora parte	**il primo treno?** **il secondo treno?** **il prossimo treno?** **l'ultimo treno?**	*At what time does*	*the first train* *the second train* *the next train* *the last train*	*leave?*

3 A, da + *definite article* (contracted prepositions)

When the above prepositions combine with the article they are called contracted prepositions. We have already seen **alle (a + le)** used with times (Unit 4, p 45). Always place the definite article before the noun first, as in column 1 below. Then remember that **a + il** *at the* contracts to **al**. In all other cases you put **a** before the article and double the '**l**' if there is one. Note that **il cinema** is masculine.

il cinema	**a + il = al**		**al** cinema		*the cinema*
lo sportello	**a + lo = allo**		**allo** sportello	*at*	*the counter*
l'entrata	**a + l' = all'**		**all'**entrata		*the entrance*
la biglietteria	**a + la = alla**	**(davanti)**	**alla** biglietteria	*(in front of)*	*the ticket office*
i bambini	**a + i = ai**		**ai** bambini		*the children*
gli studenti	**a + gli = agli**		**agli** studenti	*to*	*the students*
le ragazze	**a + le = alle**		**alle** ragazze		*the girls*

Like **davanti a**: **vicino a** *near*:

    Ci vediamo vicino alla fontana!   *See you near the fountain!*
    Il cinema è vicino all'albergo.   *The cinema is near the hotel.*

Da + definite article behaves in exactly the same way. Don't forget that **da + il** becomes **dal**:

Il ristorante è lontano dal centro. *The restaurant is far from the centre.*
L'albergo è lontano dall'aeroporto. *The hotel is far from the airport.*

4 Di + *definite article*   *of the*

When **di** combines with the definite article it becomes **de**. Once this change is made, and you remember that **di + il** becomes **del**, you will see that the same pattern as **a + definite article** holds good.

In the following examples notice where the English differs from the Italian rendering: whereas we say 'the station clock', Italians say 'the clock of the station'.

il mare	**di + il = del**	l'acqua **del** mare	*seawater*
lo sport	**di + lo = dello**	La Gazzetta **dello** Sport	*The Sports Gazzette*
l'autobus	**di + l' = dell'**	la fermata **dell'**autobus	*the bus stop*
la stazione	**di + la = della**	l'orologio **della** stazione	*the station clock*
i negozi	**di + i = dei**	le vetrine **dei** negozi	*the shop windows*
gli affari	**di + gli = degli**	il mondo **degli** affari	*the business world*
le vacanze	**di + le = delle**	la fine **delle** vacanze	*the end of the holidays*

5 Devo cambiare?   *Do I have to change?*

Devo comes from **dovere** *to have to*. It means *I have to* or *I must*. **Vuol(e)** and **vorrei** come from **volere** *to wish* or *to want*. Both **dovere** and **volere** are irregular.

Present tense		**dovere** *to have to*		
(io)	**devo**	*I have to, I must*	**(noi) dobbiamo**	*we have to, we must*
(tu)	**devi**	*you (inf.) have to, you must*	**(voi) dovete**	*you (pl) have to, you must*
(lei)	**deve**	*you (formal) have to, must*		
(lui, lei) deve		*he, she has to, must*	**(loro) devono**	*they have to, they must*

Present tense		**volere** *to want, to wish*		
(io)	**voglio**	*I want*	**(noi) vogliamo**	*we want*
(tu)	**vuoi**	*you (informal) want*	**(voi) volete**	*you (pl) want*
(lei)	**vuole**	*you (formal) want*		
(lui, lei) vuole		*he/she wants*	**(loro) vogliono**	*they want*

From now on the second person singular **lei** form will be omitted as it is always the same as the third person singular.

Attenzione! Verbs immediately after **volere** and **dovere** must be in the infinitive:

Voglio	**partire**	*I want*	*leave*
Vorrei }	**telefonare**	*I would like* } *to*	*phone*
Devo	**mangiare**	*I have*	*eat*
	andare in banca		*go to the bank*

> **Perchè non vuoi andare alla discoteca con i tuoi amici?** — *Why don't you want to go to the discotheque with your friends?*
> **Perchè devo studiare.** — *Because I have to study.*

6 C'è, Ci sono   *There is, there are*

C'è = ci + è.

Use **c'è** to say *there is, is there?* Use **ci sono** to say *there are, are there?* For the negative, use **non c'è** *there isn't,* **non ci sono** *there aren't.*

> **(Non) c'è un espresso per Firenze?** — *Is(n't) there an express to Florence?*
> **No, perchè c'è lo sciopero.** — *No, because there's a strike.*
> **(Non) ci sono treni la domenica?** — *Are(n't) there any trains on Sundays?*

7 Aspettare *to wait for,* ascoltare *to listen to,* guardare *to look at*

Aspettare is followed by a direct object in Italian. The preposition *for* is not expressed:

> **Aspetta l'autobus?** — *Are you waiting for the bus?*
> **Aspetto un mio amico.** — *I'm waiting for a friend of mine.*

Guardare *to look at* and **ascoltare** *to listen to* behave similarly: *at (look at)* and *to (listen to)* are not expressed:

> **Guardo spesso la televisione.** — *I often look at (watch) television.*
> **Ascoltiamo la radio.** — *We listen to the radio.*

8 Prima di   *before*

Note how **prima di** is used with times. **Di** combines with **l'** and **le** to become **dell'** and **delle**:

prima dell'una, prima delle due, prima delle sei, ecc.	*before 1 o'clock, before 2 o'clock, before 6 o'clock, etc.*

but **prima di mezzogiorno, prima di mezzanotte** *before midday, before midnight*

9 Fare, comprare   *to buy*

Although **comprare** means *to buy*, the normal way of saying *to buy a ticket* is **fare il biglietto** (Lit. *to make the ticket*).

10 Fra dieci minuti   *In 10 minutes*

Fra always refers to the future:

Fra mezz'ora.	*In half an hour's time.*
Fra un paio di settimane.	*In a couple of weeks' time.*

11 In ritardo, in orario   *late, on time*

Il treno è	in { anticipo / arrivo / partenza	The train is	early / arriving / leaving

Come si dice in italiano?

How to:

1. buy a second class ticket

   single/return

2. ask the time of departure of the next train, etc.

3. ask from what platform it leaves

4. ask whether you have to change and where

   ask if there's a through train

5. ask to book a seat

Vorrei un biglietto di seconda classe andata/andata e ritorno.

A che ora parte il prossimo treno, ecc?

Da che binario parte?

Devo cambiare?
Dove?
C'è un treno diretto?

Vorrei prenotare un posto.

Attività

1   Listen to the four dialogues below which all take place at a booking-
    office. For each conversation in turn fill in the details on the grid below.

(a) **A**   Un biglietto per Siena.

    B   Andata?

    A   Sì. Andata. Seconda classe.

    B   Trentamila.

    A   A che ora parte il treno?

    B   Alle sedici e venti dal binario tre.

(b) **A**   Buongiorno. Vorrei due biglietti per Roma.

    B   Seconda classe?

    A   Prima classe. Quando parte il treno?

    B   Parte alle dieci e quaranta e arriva a Roma alle quindici e venti.

    A   Da che binario parte?

    B   Dal binario quindici.

(c) **A**   A che ora parte l'ultimo treno per Genova?

    B   Alle ventitrè e cinquantacinque.

    A   Dal binario dodici?

    B   No. L'ultimo treno parte dal binario sette.

    A   Un biglietto, allora. Seconda classe.

(d) **A**   Uno per Novara. Prima classe.

    B   Solo andata?

    A   Andata e ritorno. Quant'è?

    B   Sessantamilasettecento.

    A   A che ora parte il treno?

    B   Alle diciotto e trenta. Primo binario. Buon viaggio!

	Destinazione	Numero di Biglietti	Classe	Ora di Partenza	Binario
(a)					
(b)					
(c)					
(d)					

2   Using each contracted preposition from the box only once fill in the gaps.

    (a)   Non so il prezzo _____ orologio.

    (b)   Il professore parla _____ studenti.

    (c)   L'appartamento _____ ragazze italiane è molto bello.

    (d)   Vuoi comprare la macchina _____ zio di Giulia?

    (e)   Vuole accompagnare Mario _____ stadio domenica prossima?

    (f)   L'orario _____ autobus è lì.

    (g)   A che ora va _____ istituto?

    (h)   Il treno parte _____ diciotto e quindici.

    (i)   Il dirigente _____ fabbrica è occupato.

    (j)   Aspettiamo Massimo davanti _____ bar.

dell'	**dello**	**della**	**degli**	**delle**
al	**allo**	**all'**	**agli**	**alle**

3   Which line from the right-hand column fits with (i)? You can see that (e) makes most sense. Fit the others together in the same way.

(i)	Voglio comprare le scarpe	(a)	Perchè non ho il suo numero di telefono.
(ii)	Lucia deve andare alla biglietteria	(b)	perchè è disoccupato *(unemployed).*
(iii)	Devo prendere l'autobus	(c)	perchè voglio andare a lavorare in Italia.
(iv)	Perchè non telefoni a Mario?	(d)	perchè ho un messaggio importante per lei *(for her).*
(v)	Giorgio non ha soldi	(e)	perchè ci sono i saldi.
(vi)	Studio l'italiano	(f)	perchè è troppo caro.
(vii)	Devo vedere Francesca	(g)	perchè c'è lo sciopero dei treni.
(viii)	Non compro il vestito	(h)	Perchè non ho il suo indirizzo.
(ix)	Perchè non scrivi a Fabrizio?	(i)	perchè vuole fare il biglietto per Livorno.

4 C'è/Ci sono

Here is a list of buildings (**edifici**) and monuments (**monumenti**) in various places. Using **c'è** or **ci sono** as appropriate, make a statement about each, modelling it on the first example which is done for you:

Esempio: In Via Rossini ci sono due banche.

Via Rossini: La Banca Commerciale, La Banca Nazionale del Lavoro.
Via Terni: L'Albergo Alba, l'Albergo Luxor, l'Albergo Rialto.
Piazza Dante: Il Palazzo Visconti.
Piazza Cavour: Il Bar Parini, il Bar Stella, il Bar Verdi, il Bar Marotta.
Roma: (L'Aeroporto) Ciampino, (l'Aeroporto) Fiumicino.

5   From the two sentences provided, make a statement using **fra** as in the example:

Esempio: Sono le nove meno un quarto. Adriano va a scuola alle nove.

Adriano va a scuola *fra* un quarto d'ora.

(a)   Sono le dieci. Pina va in banca alle undici.
(b)   È mezzogiorno. Giorgio va al colloquio alle tre.
(c)   Sono le sei e mezza. Enrico ritorna a casa alle sette meno un quarto.
(d)   Sono le undici e venti. Carlo va alla discoteca alle undici e mezza.
(e)   Sono le sette e mezza. Il treno arriva alle sette e trentacinque.

6   **Ora tocca a te!** You would like to book three seats to Livorno, *Leghorn*. Complete your side of the conversation.

Impiegato	Sì… Prego?
You	*I would like to book three seats for the day after tomorrow, Thursday.*
Impiegato	Destinazione?
You	*Leghorn.*
Impiegato	Vuole partire la mattina o la sera?
You	*Isn't there a through train at 11.00 o'clock?*
Impiegato	No, ma c'à un espresso che parte a mezzogiorno.
You	*All right. Three seats for Thursday then. Second class.*

3 Informazioni

1 I biglietti   *tickets*

Before boarding your train you must validate your ticket (**convalidare il biglietto**) in a machine which stamps the time and date on it.

2 Ferrovie dello Stato

(a)   What are the two advantages claimed for the **Amicotreno** railcard?
(b)   **Ferrovie dello Stato**: are they state-owned or privately run?
(c)   What number would you phone for information regarding **Amicotreno**?

(d) What two numbers would you phone for rail travel information?

Viaggi meglio e spendi meno, con la Carta Amicotreno.

Nuova Carta Amicotreno.
Il viaggiare intelligente che diventa conveniente.

Per informazioni: 📞 167-431784

FERROVIE DELLO STATO

*Si applica la tariffa "ragazzi". Lo sconto non è cumulabile con altre riduzioni e non è valido per viaggi interamente compresi nella provincia di Trento.

Ferrovie dello Stato S.p.A.
Informazioni viaggiatori
Civitavecchia	**24975**
Tivoli	**20268**

7 AL RISTORANTE
At the restaurant

In this Unit you will learn how to:

- ask/say whether a place is open/closed
- order a meal
- ask for more bread/wine, etc; say that it's enough
- ask the waiter what he recommends
- say that it doesn't matter

Dialogo 1

Listen to these snippets of conversation and circle the appropriate letter for the correct situation. Try making a guess before looking anything up!

A

> **Buon appetito!**
> **Grazie altrettanto!**

This is taking place:
- (a) just before a meal.
- (b) immediately after a meal.
- (c) at the cash desk.
- (d) just before the end of the meal.

B

> **Un altro po'**
> **di vino?**
> **No. Basta così.**

The second speaker:
- (a) wants some more wine.
- (b) doesn't like the wine.
- (c) is refusing more wine.
- (d) wants a glass of red wine.

C

> **Scusi, è**
> **occupato questo posto?**
> **No. È libero. Prego,**
> **si accomodi!**

The second speaker says that:
- (a) the seat is clean.
- (b) the seat is taken.
- (c) the seat is dangerous.
- (d) the seat is free.

D

> **Il menù a prezzo fisso?**
> **No. Alla carta.**

The second speaker wants:

(a) to pick and choose from the menu.
(b) the set meal.
(c) the wine list.
(d) the meal of the day.

 Dialogo 2 Che facciamo? *What shall we do?*

A couple are deciding whether to eat in the hotel or to have a meal out.

(a) How does **il marito** say: 'Excellent idea'?

Marito Dunque. Che facciamo oggi? Mangiamo qui in albergo?

Moglie No. Usciamo! Andiamo a pranzo fuori! Magari, stasera torniamo qui per la cena.

Marito Ottima idea!

Usciamo! *Let's go out!*
pranzo *lunch*
magari *perhaps*

tornare = ritornare *to return*
cena *dinner*

 Dialogo 3 'Da Peppino' è aperto *'Da Peppino' is open*

Having decided to go out they make enquiries.

(a) How does **il signore** say: 'But it's closed today'?

Marito Scusi, signore, c'è un buon ristorante qui vicino?

Signore Sì. Il ristorante 'Da Peppino'. È buono e non è caro. Ma oggi è chiuso.

Signora No. La trattoria è chiusa. 'Da Peppino' è aperto.

Marito Allora, andiamo lì, no ...?

Moglie Come vuoi!

---

trattoria *modest restaurant*   **Come vuoi!** *As you wish!*

(b) How does **il marito** ask: 'Is there a good restaurant nearby?'

 Dialogo 4 Conosco un ristorante vicino al mare
I know a restaurant by the sea

Listen to another person giving information about a restaurant.

A Conosco un ristorante vicino al mare dove si mangia molto bene.
B Quando è aperto?
A Tutti i giorni, eccetto il lunedì.

(a) How does the first speaker say: 'Every day except Monday'?

Dialogo 5 Vogliono ordinare? *Do you wish to order?*

Before reading this dialogue look at the **Informazioni** section
(p 85–6) where you will find out about meals in restaurants and see some
of the vocabulary for food. The waiter tells **Anna** and **Silvia** that if they
prefer to lunch outside, **all'aperto**, they'll have to wait. They decide to
remain where they are.

(a) How does the waiter say: 'There are a lot of people today'?

Cameriere	Ecco il menù. Vogliono ordinare subito? Se preferiscono pranzare all'aperto, devono aspettare un po'. C'è molta gente oggi.
Anna	No. Non fa niente. Pranziamo qui. Per antipasto io prendo melone con prosciutto.
Silvia	Io, coppa di gamberetti. E per primo, risotto alla milanese.
Anna	Risotto anche per me.
Cameriere	Mi dispiace, ma il risotto non c'è. È finito.
Silvia	Allora, spaghetti alle vongole.
Anna	E per me, lasagne al forno.
Cameriere	Benissimo. E per secondo piatto: carne o pesce?
Anna	Carne: bistecca ai ferri. E per contorno patatine fritte e fagiolini.
Cameriere	Bene. Bistecca anche per lei, signorina?
Silvia	No, no. Non mangio carne. Che cosa mi consiglia?
Cameriere	Il fritto misto di pesce. È una specialità della casa. E il pesce è freschissimo.
Silvia	Beh… no. Preferisco sogliola alla griglia con insalata verde.
Cameriere	D'accordo. E da bere? Vino rosso o vino bianco?
Anna	Rosso. Una bottiglia di Barolo. E ci porti un po' di ghiaccio per l'acqua, per piacere.
Silvia	E un po' di vino bianco… locale.

Non fa niente	*It doesn't matter*	**E da bere?**	*Anything to drink?*
Che cosa mi consiglia?	*What*	**ci porti**	*bring us*
do you recommend (me)?		**un po' di ghiaccio**	*some ice*

(b) How does **il cameriere** say: 'It's a speciality of the house'?

Dialogo 6 Tutto bene?   *Is everything all right?*

Il Cameriere asks whether they want dessert.

(a) How does **il Cameriere** ask: 'A little more wine?'

Cameriere	Tutto bene…? Un altro po' di vino?
Silvia	No. Va bene. Basta così. Grazie.
Cameriere	Dolce o frutta?
Anna	Formaggio, e una macedonia.
Silvia	Per me niente. Solo un caffè e un amaro.

Va bene.	*That's OK.*	**un amaro**	*a bitter after-dinner*
Basta così.	*That's enough.*		*liqueur*
Per me niente.	*Nothing for me.*		

(b) How does **Silvia** say: 'Nothing for me'?

Pronuncia

Doppie consonanti   *double consonants*

Primo pia**tt**o, patatine fri**tt**e, spaghe**tt**i, un po' di ghia**cc**io, una bo**tt**iglia di la**tt**e, una bi**rr**a, fru**tt**a, forma**gg**io, biste**cc**a, e**cc**e**tt**o.

Spiegazioni

1 *Verbs*

Here is the present tense of the irregular verbs **fare** *to do, make* and **uscire** *to go out*.

Present tense	**fare** *to do, make*		
(io) faccio	*I do, am doing, make, etc.*	**(noi) facciamo**	*we do, are doing, make, etc.*
(tu) fai	*you do, are doing, make, etc.*	**(voi) fate**	*you (pl.) do, are doing, make, etc.*
(lui, lei)* fa	*he/she does is doing, makes, etc.*	**(loro) fanno**	*they do, are doing, make, etc.*

*As explained in Unit 6, p 69, the **lei** form 2nd person singular (formal 'you') is omitted from now on because it is exactly the same as the 3rd person singular: (**lei fa** = *you do, make*, etc.)

Present tense		**uscire** *to go out*	
(io) esco	*I go out, am going out*	**(noi) usciamo**	*we go out, are going out*
(tu) esci	*you go out, are going out*	**(voi) uscite**	*you (pl.) go out, are going out*
(lui, lei) esce	*he/she goes out, is going out*	**(loro) escono**	*they go out, are going out*

Attenzione! Note the difference between **uscire** *to go out* and **andare** *to go.*

Esci...?	*Are you going out?*
Dove vai?	*Where are you going?*

Uscire used with **da** means *to leave, to come out of, to go out of:*

Escono dall'ufficio alle due.	*They leave the office at two.*
Usciamo dalla banca a mezzogiorno.	*We leave the bank at midday.*

But

La mattina esco *di casa* alle otto.	*In the morning I leave home at eight.*

2 Present tense as immediate future

The present tense is also used in Italian to express an intention or a suggestion where we would use the future in English:

Mangiamo qui stasera?	*Shall we eat here this evening/tonight?*
Oggi prendo l'autobus.	*Today I'll take the bus.*

The first person plural present ending **-iamo** also denotes the imperative: *let us ...*

Andiamo! *Let's go!*	**Usciamo!** *Let's go out!*

The context and the tone of voice will make the meaning clear.

3 Un buon ristorante   *a good restaurant*

Buono/a is nearly always shortened to **buon** before a masculine singular noun. It follows the pattern of the indefinite article **un/uno/una**. It is often heard in expressions where Italians wish each other something:

Buon divertimento! *Have a good time!* **Buon Natale!** *Merry Christmas!*
Buona giornata! *Have a good day!* **Buon Anno!** *Happy New Year!*
Buon appetito! *Have a good meal!* **Buon viaggio!** *Have a good journey!*

4 Tutto, tutti

In the singular **tutto/a** means *whole, all, everything*:

Tutta la famiglia è in vacanza.	*The whole family is on holiday.*
Mangia tutto.	*He eats everything.*
È tutto per me.	*It's all for me.*

In the plural **tutti/e** means *all, every*:

Tutti i negozi sono aperti.	*All the shops are open.*
Usciamo tutti i giorni.	*We go out every day.*

5 Il lunedì   On Mondays

When the definite article precedes the day it gives the idea of every:

È chiuso il lunedì.	*It's closed on Mondays/ every Monday.*
È aperto la domenica.	*It's open on Sundays/ every Sunday.*

6 La gente   people

La gente is singular in Italian:

La gente parla.	*People talk.*
In piazza c'è poca gente.	*There are few people in the square.*

7 molto/a, molti/e, molto

Molto may be used either as an adverb (*very*) or as an adjective (*a lot of, many*). When used as an adverb it is invariable.

È *molto* brava. (adverb)	*She's very good/clever.*
Questi musei sono *molto* interessanti. (adverb)	*These museums are very interesting.*
Il negozio all'angolo ha *molta* roba. (adj.)	*The corner shop has a lot of stuff.*
In Italia ci sono *molti* mercati.	*There are many markets in Italy.*

Troppo behaves in the same way:

La camicetta è *troppo* cara. (adverb)	*The blouse is too dear.*
In classe ci sono *troppi* studenti. (adj.)	*There are too many students in class.*

8 Vogliono ordinare? *Do you wish to order?*

The plural of **tu** and **lei** is **voi**. But in **Dialogo 5** the waiter asks: 'Vogliono ordinare?' This third person plural **loro** form, is very much used instead of **voi** by waiters, hotel staff and shop assistants when addressing more than one person.

9 Non fa niente *It doesn't matter*

When Italian uses a negative word such as **niente** *nothing*, unlike English, **non** must still be used: **Non voglio niente** literally means *I don't want nothing*. The main negative expressions are: **non ... niente** *nothing*; **non ... mai** *never*; **non ... nessuno** *no-one*.

Lino non mangia niente.	*Lino is not eating anything.*
Non bevo mai a quest'ora.	*I never drink at this time.*
Non c'è nessuno a casa.	*There isn't anyone at home.*
Non capisce niente!	*He doesn't understand anything!*

10 Risotto alla milanese

a + definite article is used to show that food or drink is cooked, served or prepared in a particular style. **Risotto alla milanese** is therefore a rice dish cooked in the Milanese style (see **Informazioni**, p 85–6). **Un tè al limone** is tea served with lemon, i.e. *lemon tea*. **Un tè al latte** is *tea with milk*.

11 Da bere

There are many expressions where **da** followed by an infintive means *to*:

C'è molto da bere.	*There's lots to drink.*
Ho molto da fare.	*I've a lot to do.*
Non c'è niente da mangiare.	*There's nothing to eat.*

You should note examples as you come across them throughout the book.

12 Un po' di ghiaccio *a bit of (some) ice*

The easiest way to express 'some' when it means 'a little of something' is to use **un po'di** (Lit. *a bit of*):

Vorrei: un po' di formaggio,	*I'd like: some cheese,*
un po' di pane, un po' di vino,	*some bread, some wine,*
un po' d'acqua.	*some water.*

13 Basta così   *that's enough*

As with **costa, costano** (Unit 4, p 47) it is important to distinguish between singular and plural:

Mezza bottiglia basta.   *Half a bottle is enough.*
Due sterline bastano.   *Two pounds is enough.*

 # Come si dice in italiano?

How to:

1 ask/say whether a place is   **È aperto/a(?) / È chiuso/a(?)**
   open/closed

2 order a meal   **Per antipasto, per primo,
                                        per secondo, per contorno,
                                        prendo ...**

3 ask for some (more) bread/wine,   **Un (altro) po' di pane / di vino,
   etc.   ecc.**
   say that it's enough   **Basta così.**

4 ask the waiter what he recommends   **Che cosa mi consiglia?**

5 say that it doesn't matter   **Non fa niente / Non importa**

Attività

1 Opposite there are some examples of Italian food and drink, many of
   which are explained in **Informazioni**. Fit them into the menu below
   in the appropriate place.

```
┌────────────────────────────────────────┐
│                 𝔐 𝔈 ℜ 𝔘                │
│                                         │
│     Antipasti                           │
│     Primi Piatti                        │
│     Secondi Piatti                      │
│     Contorni                            │
│     Frutta - Dolci                      │
│     Da Bere                             │
└────────────────────────────────────────┘
```

> **acqua minerale** ● **antipasto misto** ● **coppa di gamberetti**
> ● **bistecca alla griglia** ● **fagiolini** ● **fritto misto di pesce** ● **frutta
> fresca** ● **gelati misti** ● **insalata mista** ● **lasagne al forno**
> ● **macedonia di frutta** ● **melone con prosciutto** ● **patatine fritte**
> ● **pollo arrosto** ● **risotto alla milanese** ● **sogliola alla griglia**
> ● **spaghetti alle vongole** ● **vino bianco** ● **vino rosso**

2   To denote flavours in ice creams, Italian uses **al, alla, ecc. Un gelato
     alla fragola** is *a strawberry ice cream.*

     I signori Lambrini are treating each of their four children to an ice
     cream. Say what kind of an ice cream each is having. Start: **Aldo
     prende ...**

     (a)   Aldo – fragola
     (b)   Giulia – limone
     (c)   Bruno – caffè
     (d)   Silvia – cioccolato.
     (e)   Finally, how would you say that Mr and Mrs Lambrini are having
            a lemon tea?

3   Which of the phrases on the right complete the sentences on the left?
     To do this exercise you need to look at the verb endings carefully.

     (i)   E tu Mario,   (a)   non mangia carne.
     (ii)   Anche noi   (b)   restare a casa stasera.
     (iii) Anche voi   (c)   vanno sempre al ristorante
                                                la domenica.
     (iv)   Maria è vegetariana: (d)   cosa vuoi?
     (v)   Anch'io   (e)   mangiate fuori stasera?
     (vi)   Tutta la famiglia Ferni   (f)   vado 'Da Peppino' oggi.
     (vii) Giovanni e Antonella   (g)   va in pizzeria.
     (viii) I miei amici vogliono   (h)   preferiamo la cucina italiana.

4 Here are four restaurant advertisements. Make sure you understand them, then answer the questions below.

(a)

> LA TORINESE
> *Ristorante*
> *Caratteristico*
> *Vasto Parcheggio*
> *Giochi per bambini*
>
> *(Chiuso il mercoledì)*

(b)

> **La Bella Napoli**
> Ristorante
> e
> Pizzeria
>
> *Aperto solo la sera*

(c)

> **TEMPIO di DIANA**
>
> **Hotel Ristorante con cucina francese**
> **Vasto parco nel bosco**
> **MARTEDÌ CHIUSO**

(d)

> VILLA TOTÒ
> *Ristorante*
> *specialità marinare*
> *Si mangia bene e si*
> *mantiene la linea*
>
> DOMENICA SERA E
> LUNEDÌ RIPOSO

(i) It's Monday lunch time: are there any of the above that you couldn't go to?

(ii) Where would you go if you liked seafood?

(iii) Which one of these restaurants is unlikely to be in the town centre? Why?

(iv) Which one would you consider if you were on a diet?

(v) Which two would probably offer better parking facilities?

 5 **Ora tocca a te!** You are ordering a meal in a restaurant.

Cam. Cosa prende?
You *I'd like a selection of appetisers.*
Cam. E per primo?
You *Vegetable soup.*
Cam. Vuole ordinare il secondo adesso?
You *Why not? What do you recommend (me)?*
Cam. Oggi il pesce è buonissimo.
You *I don't eat fish. Grilled steak.*

Cam.	Certo. E per contorno, cosa desidera?
You	*I'll have a mixed salad and chips.*
Cam.	E da bere?
You	*Half a bottle of local wine.*
Cam.	Bianco o rosso?
You	*Better the red wine with the steak.*
Cam.	Subito!
	... .
Cam.	Tutto bene?
You	*Yes. Fine. A bit more bread, please.*
Cam.	Ecco. Desidera altro?
You	*No thank you. That's enough.*

● aceto	● bicchiere	● coltello	● cucchiaio	● forchetta
● olio	● pepe	● piatto	● sale	● tovagliolo

Can you label each of these using the words from the box? Look up the words you don't know in the vocabulary at the back.

Informazioni

1 Pasti italiani   *Italian meals*

Before starting your meal it is customary to say: **Buon appetito!** The response is **Grazie, altrettanto!** *(Thank you) the same to you!*

La cucina italiana   *Italian cooking* is regional: names of dishes vary from one part of the country to another.

Antipasti *starters* or *hors d'oeuvres*. Among other things, these appetisers consist of a variety of cooked or cured meats such as **prosciutto crudo** (this is often served with melon), **mortadella, salame**; seafood such as **coppa di gamberetti** *prawn cocktail*, and various vegetables, raw or preserved in oil such as **carciofi** *artichokes* and **funghi** *mushrooms*. **Antipasto misto** is a selection of appetisers: ham, salame, mortadella, olives (**olive**), etc.

I primi (**il primo piatto** *the first course*) would offer **minestra** *soup*, **minestrone** *vegetable soup* or a choice of **pasta** dishes e.g: **spaghetti alle vongole** *spaghetti with clams*, **lasagne al formo** *layers of pasta slices with meat sauce and mozzarella cheese baked in the oven*, **tagliatelle al pomodoro** *pasta strips in tomato sauce*, etc. **Risotto alla milanese** is *rice cooked in broth with onions*.

I secondi (**il secondo piatto** *the second course*) consist of (**la**) **carne** *meat* or (**il**) **pesce** *fish*. **Alla griglia** or **ai ferri** both mean *grilled*. **Bistecca** is *steak*, **pollo arrosto** is *roast chicken*, **sogliola** is *sole*, **fritto misto di pesce** *mixed fry* of smaller Mediterranean fish.

I contorni *side dishes* could be **insalata** (**mista**) *(mixed) salad* or a selection of vegetables such as **fagiolini** *green beans*, **patatine fritte** *chips*, **zucchini** *courgettes*.

Frutta *fruit*: this is often eaten at mealtimes instead of **dolci** *dessert*; **macedonia di frutta** *fruit salad*; **gelati** *ice cream*.

Barolo is a famous red wine from the Piedmont region in Northern Italy. Most regions produce their own local wine, **vino locale**, which is usually excellent value.

Your restaurant bill will probably include a cover charge: **pane e coperto**. Where the service charge is included in the price, you will see **servizio compreso** *service included*. You yourself may ask: '**È compreso il servizio?**' *'Is service included?'* However, even when it is, it is customary to leave a tip (**la mancia**) on top of this.

2 La trattoria

La trattoria is normally cheaper than a restaurant. But in some places it may have a sort of snob value and be quite expensive, i.e. **Trattoria del Vecchio Pozzo** *Restaurant of the Old Well* would be fully decorated to give an 'Olde Worlde' atmosphere.

8 IN ALBERGO
At the hotel

In this Unit you will learn how to:

■ ask for a room
■ give the dates you require it for
■ ask for full or half-board
■ ask for and give details of mealtimes
■ respond to a request for means of identification

Dialogo 1 Ha una camera, per favore? *Have you got a room, please?*

Roberto asks **il direttore** for a room with a shower (**doccia**).

(a) How does **il direttore** ask: 'Single or double?'

Direttore	Buonasera. Dica!
Roberto	Ha una camera, per favore?
Direttore	Come la vuole? Singola o doppia?
Roberto	Singola con doccia.
Direttore	Per quanto tempo?
Roberto	Per una notte.
Direttore	Sì. Ha un documento?
Roberto	Ho il passaporto. La colazione è compresa nel prezzo?
Direttore	No. È a parte.

(b) How does **Roberto** ask: 'Is breakfast included in the price?

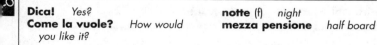

Dica! *Yes?*		**notte** (f) *night*	
Come la vuole? *How would you like it?*		**mezza pensione** *half board*	

Dialogo 2 Abbiamo due camere all'ultimo piano
We have two rooms on the top floor

Il sig. Conti is booking in advance: he wants a room with a double bed and private bath.

(a) How does he say: 'From the 26th of July to the 9th of August'?

Direttore Una camera a un letto o una camera a due letti?

Sig. Conti Una camera matrimoniale con bagno: dal 26 luglio al 9 agosto.

Direttore Vediamo un po'… Abbiamo due camere all'ultimo piano. Una piccola con balcone, e una grande.

Sig. Conti La camera grande è tranquilla?

Direttore Molto tranquilla e dà sul mare.

Sig. Conti La camera grande, allora. A che ora è il pranzo?

Direttore La colazione è dalle 7.00 alle 9.30. Il pranzo dalle 12.00 alle 2.00 e la cena dalle 7.30 alle 10.00.

camera a un letto	*single room*	**dà**	(from **dare**) *looks out over*
camera a due letti	*twin-bedded*	**vedere**	*to see*
room		**vediamo un po'**	*let's have a look*
camera matrimoniale	*double*	**tranquillo/a**	*quiet*
bedroom			

(b) What are the words for breakfast, lunch and dinner in Italian?

 Dialogo 3 Mezza pensione o pensione completa?
Full or half board?

 (a) How long does **la signora Marini** want the room for?

Direttore Mezza pensione o pensione completa?

Sig.ra Marini Mezza pensione per due persone per una settimana.

Direttore Sì, va bene. Avete il passaporto?

Sig.ra Marini No. Non l'abbiamo. Abbiamo la patente di guida.

Direttore La patente va benissimo.

Sig.ra Marini La vuole ora…? Un attimo… Ah…! Eccola!

Direttore Ed ecco le chiavi, signora. Camera 408. Gli ascensori e i gabinetti sono là in fondo. Il parcheggio è dietro l'albergo.

pensione completa	full board	ora	now
una settimana	a week	la chiave	key
la patente di guida	driving	gabinetto	toilet
licence		dietro	behind

(b) How does she say: 'We have a driving licence. Here it is.'?

Dialogo 4 C'è l'acqua calda e l'acqua fredda
There's hot and cold water

(a) How does **il signor Marini say**: 'The luggage is in the car'?

Sig. Marini   C'è l'acqua anche in camera?

Direttore   Certo, signore. In tutte le camere, c'è l'acqua calda e l'acqua fredda.

Sig. Marini   I bagagli sono nella macchina. Li porto sopra.

Direttore   Non si preoccupi! Li prende il ragazzo. Lo chiamo subito.

Sig. Marini   Grazie.

Direttore   Se qualche volta non volete fare il bagno nella piscina, c'è la nostra spiaggia privata con gli ombrelloni e le sedie a sdraio.

Attenzione! Notice that **i bagagli** *luggage* is plural in Italian.

Li porto sopra.	I'll take them upstairs.	la nostra spiaggia privata	our
Non si preoccupi!	Don't worry.	private beach	
qualche volta	sometimes	ombrellone (m.)	beach umbrella
fare il bagno	to bathe, go swimming	sedia a sdraio	deck-chair

(b) How does **il direttore** say: 'I'll call him immediately'?

Dialogo 5 Può svegliarmi?   *Can you wake me up?*

(a) How does **la segretaria** say: 'At 6 o'clock on the dot'?

Pippa   Può svegliarmi domani mattina alle sei?

Segretaria   Certamente, signorina. Camera 307, vero?

Pippa   Sì. La camera che dà sulla terrazza.

Segretaria   Va bene. Domani mattina alle sei in punto la chiamo io personalmente. Non si preoccupi!

Pippa   Grazie, molto gentile.

(b) How does **Pippa** say: 'The room that looks out over the terrace'?

Dialogo 6 Lavoro solo d'estate *I only work in summer*

Il cameriere explains that tourists come especially in the month of August.

(a) How does **il cliente** say: 'So many tourists'?

Cliente	Impossibile parcheggiare! Vengono sempre tanti turisti qui?
Cameriere	Sempre. Specialmente nel mese di agosto.
Cliente	Lavora molto, allora!
Cameriere	D'estate, sì. Moltissimo! Ma si guadagna bene!
Cliente	A che ora incomincia a lavorare la mattina?
Cameriere	Presto. Comincio alle sei e finisco verso l'una, le due di notte.
Cliente	Però, d'inverno è tutto chiuso!
Cameriere	Esatto. Lavoro solo d'estate da maggio a ottobre.
Cliente	E già. D'inverno non viene nessuno da queste parti!

Vengono (from **venire**) **... tanti turisti..?** *Do so many tourists come..?*	**però** *however, but*
guadagnare *to earn*	**d'inverno, d'estate** *in winter,*
(in)cominciare a *to start, begin to*	*in summer*
presto *early*	**esatto** *that's right, precisely*
	da queste parti *to these parts*

(b) How does **il cameriere** say: 'I begin at six and finish at about one'?

Pronuncia

I mesi dell'anno: gennaio, febbraio, marzo, aprile, maggio, giugno, luglio, agosto, settembre, ottobre, novembre, dicembre

Le stagioni dell'anno: l'inverno, la primavera, l'estate, l'autunno

Spiegazioni

1 Ho il passaporto *I've got a passport*

Attenzione! Notice the use of **il/la**, the definite article, where in English we say *a/an*:

ha *il* passaporto, *la* patente   *Have you got a passport,*
  di guida, *la* macchina?   *a driving licence, a car?*

2 Data e stagioni *Date and seasons*

Like the days, the months start with small letters: **ottobre, novembre, dicembre,** ecc.

Quanti ne abbiamo (oggi)?   *What's the date (today)?*
(Ne abbiamo) 10.   *(It's) the 10th.*

Ordinary numbers are used for the date:

il due marzo, il cinque luglio   *2nd of March, 5th of July*

However, for the first of the month you must use **il primo** *(first)*:

Oggi è il primo giugno;   *Today is the first of June*;
il primo maggio.   *the first of May.*

Note that *on* is not expressed, as in the following example:

Ci vediamo il tre agosto.   *See you on the 3rd of August.*
Lo vedo sabato.   *I'll see him on Saturday.*

With months **in** or **a** is used:

in/a giugno, in/a settembre, ecc.   *in June, in September, etc.*

But with months beginning with a vowel, **in** is used: **in aprile**, **in agosto**.

Note in the table below how *in spring*, *in summer*, etc. is expressed and how **di** often becomes **d'** before words beginning with a vowel: **d'estate**, **d'inverno**.

	d'inverno		winter
	d'estate	*in*	summer
in	**autunno**		autumn
	primavera		spring

In primavera andiamo   *In spring we go to the country.*
  in campagna.
D'estate va al mare o   *In summer he goes to the seaside*
  in montagna.   *or the mountains.*
In autunno ricomincia   *In autumn he starts working again.*
  a lavorare.

3 Dare *to give*, **venire** *to come*

Both these verbs are irregular:

Present tense	**dare** *(to give)*		**venire** *(to come)*	
(io)	**do**	*I give, am giving*	**vengo**	*I come, am coming*
(tu)	**dai**	*you give, are giving*	**vieni**	*you come, are coming*
(lui, lei)	**dà**	*he/she gives, is giving*	**viene**	*he/she comes, is coming*
(noi)	**diamo**	*we give, are giving*	**veniamo**	*we come, are coming*
(voi)	**date**	*you (pl.) give, are giving*	**venite**	*you (pl.) come, are coming*
(loro)	**danno**	*they give, are giving*	**vengono**	*they come, are coming*

4 Nel, nella *in the;* **sulla** *on the*

In *in* also combines with the definite article (**il, la,** ecc.) to mean *in the*. When this happens **in** becomes **ne**. **Nel** is therefore the contracted form of **in + il,** and **nella** of **in + la.** The pattern is then exactly the same as **del, della,** ecc. (Unit 6, p. 68): **nel, nello, nella, nell', nei, negli, nelle.**

Le chiavi sono nella borsa.	*The keys are in the bag.*
La macchina è nel garage.	*The car is in the garage.*

Su *on* contracts in the same ways as **a** *at, to.* Just as **a + il** becomes **al**, **su + il** becomes **sul**:

La camera dà sul mare.	*The room look out over the sea.*
I guanti sono sulla sedia.	*The gloves are on the chair.*

5 *Object pronouns* lo, la, li, le

lo	*him, it*	**li**	*them* (masc. pl.)
la	*you, her, it*	**le**	*them* (fem. pl.)

Lo, la, li, le, are called object pronouns and usually precede the verb:

Compro il libro.	*I'll buy the book.*
***Lo* compro.**	*I'll buy it.*
Compro i libri.	*I'll buy the books.*
***Li* compro.**	*I'll buy them.*
Compro la rivista.	*I'll buy the magazine.*
***La* compro.**	*I'll buy it.*
Compro le riviste.	*I'll buy the magazines.*
***Le* compro.**	*I'll buy them.*

Look at the first two examples above and see how the following question and answer are based on them:

Quando compra il libro?	*When will you buy the book?*
***Lo* compro domani.**	*I'll buy it tomorrow.*

Ora tocca a te! See if you can fill in the blanks for the rest on your own:

Quando compra ____ libri?	**Quando compra ____ riviste?**
____ compro stasera.	**____ compro subito.**
Quando compra ____ rivista?	**Quando paga ____ conto?**
____ compro stamattina.	**____ pago adesso.**

In negative sentences put **non** before the pronoun.

Conosci Gino? No. Non lo conosco. *Do you know Gino? No, I don't (know **him**).*

Lo, la (singular only) become **l'** before a vowel or '**h**':

Dove aspetti Anna?	*Where are you waiting for Anna?*
L'aspetto a casa.	*I'm waiting for **her** at home.*
Apro la porta. L'apro.	*I'll open the door. I'll open **it**.*

But (plural) Apro **le** finestre. **Le** apro. *I'll open the windows. I'll open **them**.* When you address a man or a woman formally use **la** for **you**:

La ringrazio, dottor Bertini,	*I thank **you**, Dr Bertini,*
del suo gentile pensiero.	*for your kind thought.*
La disturbo, signora?	*Am I disturbing **you**, Madam?*
Mi conosce?	*Do you know **me**?*
Sì. La conosco.	*Yes. I know **you**.*

6 Eccola! *Here it is!*

Ecco combines with object pronouns to mean *here he/she/it is, here they are*.

Dov'è Maria? Eccola!	*Where is Mary? Here **she** is!*
Dov'è Pietro? Eccolo!	*Where is Peter? Here **he** is!*
Dove sono i libri? Eccoli!	*Where are the books?* *Here **they** are!*
Dove sono le valigie? Eccole!	*Where are the suitcases?* *Here **they** are!*

7 Qualche volta *sometimes, occasionally*

Qualche means *a few* or *some* and is always followed by a singular noun, which must be countable (compare to **un po' di** p. 81).

Vengo con qualche amico.	*I'll come along with some friends.*
Ho qualche libro sull'Italia.	*I've got some books on Italy.*
Guarda spesso la televisione?	*Do you often watch television?*
La guardo qualche volta.	*I watch it occasionally.*

8 A che ora incomincia a lavorare? *At what time do you start working?*

When a verb follows **incominciare**, use **a** + infinitive.

Incominciare and **cominciare** both mean *to start* or *to begin*.

Incomincio a capire.	*I'm beginning to understand.*
Il bambino comincia a parlare.	*The baby is beginning to speak.*
Quando incominci a fare **i bagagli?**	*When do you start packing?*

Come si dice in italiano?

How to:

1	ask for a room	**Ha una camera/singola/ doppia/matrimoniale?**
2	give the dates you require it for	**Dal primo … al dieci, ecc. Da lunedì a giovedì, ecc.**
3	ask for full or half-board	**Pensione completa/ mezza pensione.**
4	ask for and give details about mealtimes	**A che ora è la colazione/ il pranzo/la cena? Dalle … alle …**
5	respond to a request for means of identification	**Ha un documento? Ho il passaporto/la patente di guida.**

Attività

1   What sort of hotel accommodation are these three people asking for?
Tick the appropriate places on the grid, and fill in the days or dates in
English.

(a) **Direttore**   Prego?
   Signore   Ha una camera singola?
   Direttore   Con bagno?
   Signore   La preferisco con doccia.
   Direttore   Per quanto tempo?
   Signore   Da giovedì a lunedì. Pensione completa.

(b) **Direttore**   Sì?
   Signora   Vorrei una camera dal venticinque giugno al
         quattro luglio.
   Direttore   Singola o doppia?
   Signora   Una camera matrimoniale con bagno. Pensione
         completa.

(c) **Direttore**   Dica!
   Signorina   Ha una camera a due letti dal nove maggio?
   Direttore   Per quante notti?
   Signorina   Per dieci notti. Mezza pensione.

Direttore	Fino al diciannove?
Signorina	Sì. Esatto.
Direttore	Con bagno?
Signorina	No, con doccia.

	🧽	🧽🧽	🛏	🚿	🛁	✗	½✗	**from**	**to**
(a)									
(b)									
(c)									

🧽 **camera singola** 🧽🧽 **camera doppia** 🛏 **camera matrimoniale**

🚿 **doccia** 🛁 **bagno** ✗ **pensione completa** ½✗ **mezza pensione**

2 Eccolo, eccola, ecc.

In a frenzy of last-minute packing, your friend asks you where one or two items are. Find them for him and answer with the appropriate pronoun as in the example:

Esempio: Dov'è la patente di guida?
      You **Eccola!**

(a) Dov'è il passaporto?   (e) Dove sono le chiavi?

(b) Dov'è la borsa?   (f) Dov'è la pianta (*map*)?

(c) Dov'è l'indirizzo dell'albergo? (g) Dov'è il giornale?

(d) Dove sono i biglietti?   (h) Dov'è l'orologio?

3 Answer these questions, using pronouns and translating the English as in the example.

Esempio: Conosce Pietro? Sì. ____*well*.
      Sì. Lo conosco bene.

(a) Conosce Luisa? Sì. _____ *very well.*

(b) Conosce le mie cugine? Sì _____ *fairly well.*

(c) Quando vede Anna? _____ *at about 8 o'clock.*

(d) Quando invita Luigi? _____ *today.*

(e) Invita qualche volta i suoi amici? _____ *often.*

(f) Quando guarda la televisione? _____ *after dinner.*

(g) Conosce l'Albergo Cesare? Sì. _____ *well.*

(h) Vede Carlo domani? No. _____ *this evening.*

4   Select each contracted preposition from the box below once only and
     fill in the gaps.

(a) I passaporti sono _____ studio.   (e) Il vino è _____ bicchiere.
(b) Il ghiaccio è _____ acqua.   (f) Le chiavi sono _____ borsa.
(c) I pigiami sono _____ letto.   (g) I vestiti sono _____ valigie.
(d) Gli ombrelloni sono _____   (h) Non c'è sale _____ spaghetti.
     spiaggia.

> **nel   nello   nella   nell'**
> **nelle   negli   sul   sulla**

5   Answer the questions using the first person of **venire**. If the question
     is addressed to more than one person, as in the 2nd example, answer
     with the 1st person plural.

Esempio: Viene in macchina? ... autobus.

         No. Vengo in autobus.

         Venite in autobus? ... piedi.

         No. Veniamo a piedi.

(a) Viene in aereo? ... **macchina.**
(b) Viene in metropolitana? ... **piedi.**
(c) Viene in macchina? ... **aereo.**
(d) Venite in autobus? ... **metropolitana.**
(e) Venite a piedi? ... **bicicletta.**

6   Read the following passage in which **Anna** is talking about herself
     and note how all the information can be extracted from the table on
     the opposite page:

**Abito a Milano. Lavoro in una banca commerciale. La mattina
esco alle otto meno un quarto. Incomincio a lavorare alle otto e
mezza. Finisco di lavorare alle cinque. Torno a casa alle sei meno
un quarto. Il sabato non lavoro. Vado al mare con mia sorella.**

Dove abita?	Dove lavora?	A che ora esce la mattina?	A che ora incomincia a lavorare?	A che ora finisce?	A che ora torna a casa?	Dove va il sabato?
Anna: Milano	banca commerciale	7.45	8.30	5.00	5.45	al mare sorella
Maria: Terni	agenzia di viaggi	8.15	9.00	6.00	6.45	in montagna marito
I sig.ri Spada: Napoli	istituto di lingue	7.20	8.00	1.00	1.40	in campagna genitori*

* **i nostri genitori** *our parents*; **i loro genitori** *their parents*

(a) Write similar passages, first saying what **Maria** would say about herself, and then what **i signori Spada** would say about themselves (**Abitiamo, ecc. ...**)

(b) Write contrasting statements about **Anna** on the one hand and **i signori Spada** on the other. Start like this: **Anna abita a Milano, ma i signori Spada abitano a Napoli**.

7   **Ora tocca a te!** You are booking rooms in a hotel.

Direttore	Buongiorno.
You	*Good morning. Have you got two rooms for 10 days?*
Direttore	Per quante persone?
You	*For four people.*
Direttore	Abbiamo due camere al terzo piano.
You	*With private bath?*
Direttore	Una con bagno, l'altra con doccia.
You	*Yes. That's fine. Is there a restaurant in this hotel?*
Direttore	No. C'è solo il bar.
You	*Is there a restaurant nearby?*
Direttore	C'è la 'Trattoria Monti' in piazza.

✳ Informazioni

1 Alberghi e pensioni   *hotels and guest houses*

Although **pensioni** have the reputation of being more modest establishments than **alberghi**, there is no clearcut dividing line. Many **pensioni** offer excellent value and are often family run. In regional brochures both **alberghi** and **pensioni** are now listed together, according to price and the facilities they offer.

2 Other accommodation

Ostelli per la gioventù *Youth Hostels*, **Campeggi** or **Camping** *Camp sites*, **Villaggi turistici** *Holiday Villages* and **Agriturismo** *Farm holidays* offer a variety of accommodation to suit all pockets. There are also **Case religiose di ospitalità**, hospitality offered by religious bodies, though you may find that in these you probably have to be in earlier at night.

The Italian State Tourist Office (**ENIT**) provides information about travel and accommodation in Italy. Regional brochures are available there. Address: 1 Princes St, London W1R 8AY (Tel: 0171 408 1254).

Look at this table from a hotel guide and find out how to say in Italian:

(a) Credit cards are accepted.
(b) Pets are accepted.
(c) a tennis court

♣♣ Parco giardino dell'esercizio

🐕 Si accettano piccoli animali domestici

▦ Sala congressi

👫 Accettazione gruppi

👪 Baby sitting

🄲 Accettazione carta di credito

P Parcheggio custodito

🚗 Autorimessa dell'esercizio

🚙 Trasporto clienti

🏃 Campo da tennis

What do these signs mean?

(d)

(e)

9 | AL TELEFONO
On the phone

In this Unit you will learn how to:

■ ask to speak to someone on the phone
■ ask someone to repeat themselves/speak louder
■ ask whether you have the wrong number
■ ask whether someone is in and answer accordingly
■ ask whether you can leave a message or call back later
■ ask and grant permission to enter a room

Dialogo 1 Pronto? Chi parla? *Hello, who's speaking?*

The secretary is on the phone with **l'avvocato** (lawyer) **Ferri**, who wishes to speak to **il dottor Fini**.

(a) How does **la segretaria** ask: 'Have you got an appointment?'

Segretaria Pronto? Chi parla?
Avvocato Sono l'avvocato Ferri. Vorrei parlare con il dottor Fini.
Segretaria Io sono la segretaria. Il dottore è occupato: è in riunione. Ha un appuntamento?
Avvocato No, signorina. Ma è urgente. Urgentissimo.
Segretaria Un momento, avvocato… Le passo il dottor Fini.
Avvocato Grazie.
Segretaria Prego.

---

in riunione *in a meeting*

(b) How does **la segretaria** say: 'I'll pass you to Dr Fini'?

Dialogo 2 In un ufficio *In an office*

Mr Cioffi asks to speak to the firm's Director, but on being told by the Secretary that he is at the Head Office (**la sede centrale**), he decides to wait until the Director comes back.

(a) How does **la segretaria** say: 'Come in'?

Sig. Cioffi   Permesso?
Segretaria   Avanti!
Sig. Cioffi   (*not hearing her*) Permesso... Posso entrare?
Segretaria   Avanti! Avanti! Prego, si accomodi!
Sig. Cioffi   Vorrei parlare con il direttore.
Segretaria   Mi dispiace, il direttore non c'è. È alla sede centrale. Se vuole, può parlare con me.
Sig. Cioffi   No. Devo parlare con lui personalmente.
Segretaria   Allora, deve tornare più tardi.
Sig. Cioffi   Più tardi non posso. Devo andare a Milano per affari. A che ora ritorna il direttore?
Segretaria   Fra venti minuti. Vuole aspettare qui? Prego, si accomodi! Posso offrirle un caffè?
Sig. Cioffi   Grazie. Molto gentile.
Segretaria   Prego. Si figuri!

Permesso? Posso entrare?
   May I come in?
il direttore non c'è   *the Director is out*

Prego, si accomodi!   *Please, sit down!*
per affari   *on business*

(b) How does **la segretaria** say: 'Can I offer you a coffee?'

Dialogo 3   C'è Luisa?   *Is Luisa in?*

(a) How does **Roberto** say: 'I'm afraid she's out'?

Ida   Pronto? C'è Luisa?
Roberto   No. Mi dispiace, non c'è.
Ida   C'è Carla?
Roberto   Sì. C'è. Un attimo. La chiamo.
Carla   Pronto...!
Ida   Ciao, Carla! Sono io, Ida.
Carla   Ciao, Ida!

(b) How does **Roberto** say: 'Just a minute. I'll call her.'?
(c) How does **Ida** say: 'It's me.'?

Dialogo 4 **La segreteria telefonica** *The answer-phone*

  Il nostro ufficio è chiuso. Dopo il segnale acustico, si prega di lasciare il nome, il numero di telefono e un breve messaggio. Sarete contattati al più presto. Grazie.

il segnale acustico *the beep*	**si prega di ...** *please ...*
si prega di lasciare il nome	**al più presto** *as soon as possible*
please leave your name	
sarete contattati *you will be*	
contacted	

Pronuncia

Puoi venire più tardi? Non può partire? Vuol ripetere il suo nome?

Spiegazioni

1 *The irregular verb* **potere** *to be able*

Present tense	**potere** *to be able*		
(io) **posso** *I am able, I can*	**(noi)** **possiamo** *we are able, we can*		
(tu) **puoi** *you are able, you can*	**(voi)** **potete** *you (pl.) are able, you can*		
(lui, lei) può *he/she is able, he/she can*	**(loro)** **possono** *they are able, they can*		

Verbs that follow **potere** must be in the infinitive.

Use **potere** to:

(i) ask for or give permission (this could take the form of a polite request):

Posso fumare?	*Can/may I smoke?*
Le posso fare una domanda?	*Can/may I ask you a question?*
Può assaggiare il vino se vuole.	*You can taste the wine if you like.*

(ii) say whether you are able or unable to do something:

(Non) possiamo venire domenica.	*We are (un)able to come on Sunday.*

(Non) posso arrivare prima   *I'm (un)able to arrive before*
delle undici.   *eleven.*

2 Le passo ... Posso offrirle ...

'I'll pass you Dr Fini' means *I'll pass Dr Fini to you.* **To you** in this case
is the indirect object and is expressed by **le** in Italian. Both object
pronouns (see Unit 8, p 92) and indirect object pronouns usually precede
the verb. However, with **potere, dovere, volere** and **sapere** you have a
choice. You may put the pronouns before these verbs, or attach them to
the infinitive that follows, from which you take off the final **-e: Posso
offrirle = posso offrir(e) + le.** Some other common verbs that take an
indirect object are: **dare** *to give,* **parlare** *to speak,* **scrivere** *to write,*
presentare *to introduce* and **telefonare** *to phone.*

Le telefono dopo.   *I'll phone you later.*
Un momento! Le do il numero   *One moment! I'll give you*
di telefono di Anna.   *Anna's phone number.*
Le posso offrire qualcosa da
bere?   *May I offer you something*
Posso offrirle qualcosa da   *to drink?*
bere?

Notice how in the last example **le** can either precede **posso** or follow the
infinitive.

3 Permesso ...? Avanti!   *May I ...? Come in!*

In the second dialogue **il signor Cioffi** says **Permesso?** to ask whether he
may come in. **Avanti!** *Come in!* is the normal response. **Permesso** is also
used when you wish someone to move aside to let you pass – in crowded
places, buses, etc.: **Permesso!** *Excuse me, please.* In this case the
response is **Prego!**

4 C'è, non c'è   *He/she's in, he/she's out*

A frequent use of **c'è** is to indicate whether someone is in or not. Notice
how it is used in the negative and in questions:

C'è il dottor Bassani?   *Is Dr Bassani in?*
Mi dispiace. Non c'è.   *No. I'm afraid he's out.*

5 Con me, con lui   *With me, with him*

Notice the use of **me** and **te** with prepositions. The other subject pronouns remain unchanged:

Paolo viene con te o con me?	*Is Paul coming with you or me?*
Perchè non vieni con noi?	*Why don't you come with us?*
Andiamo con loro!	*Let's go with them!*

6 Più tardi   *later*

To say *later, earlier, dearer, bigger*, use **più** with adjectives or adverbs:

più presto *earlier* (adverb)
più caro/a *dearer*, **più grande** *bigger* (adjectives).

7 Personalmente   *Personally*

To form an adverb add **-mente** to the end of an adjective:

evidente	*evident*	**evidentemente**	*evidently*

adjectives ending in **-o** add **-mente** to the feminine form:

vero, ver*a*	*true*	**veramente**	*truly, really*
chiaro, chiar*a*	*clear*	**chiaramente**	*clearly*
pratico, pratic*a*	*practical*	**praticamente**	*practically*

adjectives ending in **-le** or **-re** drop their final **-e**:

faci*le*	*easy*	**facilmente**	*easily*
genera*le*	*general*	**generalmente**	*generally*
regola*re*	*regular*	**regolarmente**	*regularly*

8 Arrivederla   *Goodbye*

Arriveder*la* is a more formal way of saying **arrivederci**, but it can only be used when addressing one person. *La* is the object pronoun for *you* that we met in Unit 8, p 93.

Come si dice in italiano?

How to:

1 ask to speak to someone on the phone

Vorrei/Posso parlare con …

2 ask someone to repeat themselves/speak louder

Può ripetere/parlare più forte?

3	ask whether you have the wrong number	**Ho sbagliato numero?**
4	ask whether someone is in answer accordingly	**C'è...?** **Sì. C'è./No. Non c'è.**
5	ask whether you can leave a message or call back later	**Posso lasciare un messaggio?** **Posso richiamare più tardi?**
6	ask and grant permission to enter a room	**Permesso?** **Avanti!**

Attività

1 Listen to these two conversations and answer the questions on them.

Ho sbagliato numero? *Have I got the wrong number?*

Gianna Pronto! Ho sbagliato numero...? No?... Puoi parlare più forte, Sandro? Non sento niente. Vorrei parlare con Vincenzo.

Sandro Vincenzo non c'è. Puoi richiamare più tardi?

Gianna D'accordo. Richiamo fra mezz'ora. Ciao!

Sandro Ciao!

(a) Is **Vincenzo** in or out?

(b) What does the man (**Sandro**) ask the woman (**Gianna**)?

(c) What does she say she will do?

Tutto a posto *Everything in order*

Dott. Cervi Non c'è? ... Posso lasciare un messaggio?

Segretaria Sì, certo. Dica!

Dott. Cervi Tutto a posto. La conferenza è il dieci giugno.

Segretaria Vuole ripetere il suo nome, per cortesia?

Dott. Cervi Cervi. Il dottor Cervi. C come Capri, E come Empoli, R come Roma, V come Verona, I come Imola.

Segretaria La ringrazio, dottor Cervi. Arrivederla.

Dott. Cervi Buongiorno.

(d) When is the conference?

(e) What does the woman ask the man to repeat?

2　Fill in the blanks in the following dialogue, using **lo**, **la**, **le**.

Signore	Posso parlare con il dottor Dolci?
Segretaria	Mi dispiace, il dottore non c'è. Oggi non è in ufficio.
Signore	Dove ____ posso contattare?
Segretaria	____ chiamo io domani mattina quando il dottore è qui.
Signore	Grazie, ma non posso aspettare fino a domani. È urgente.
Segretaria	In questo caso ____ do il suo numero telefonico privato.
Signore	Grazie. Molto gentile.
Segretaria	E se il dottore telefona qui oggi, ____ richiamo io. Va bene?
Signore	D'accordo. ____ ringrazio molto, signorina.

3　Match the phrases on the right with those on the left.

(i) Posso lasciare	(a) Può telefonare verso le dieci?
(ii) Non possiamo venire adesso,	(b) un messaggio?
	(c) il suo nome, per favore?
(iii) Non vogliamo disturbare Luisa	(d) perchè è molto occupata.
	(e) perchè non ho la chiave.
(iv) Non posso uscire stasera	(f) perchè devo lavorare fino a tardi.
(v) Vuol ripetere	(g) ma possiamo venire più tardi.
(vi) Scusi, le posso	(h) fare una domanda?
(vii) Le lascio il mio numero telefonico.	
(viii) Non posso aprire la porta	

4　In the table below　✓　=　what **Elena** wants to do.
　　　　　　　　　　　!　=　what **Elena** has to do.
　　　　　　　　　　　X　=　what **Elena** can't do.

Write nine complete statements about her. Start: **Vuole ...**

(volere) ✓	(dovere) !	(potere) X
(a) telefonare ad Anna	(d) lavorare fino a tardi	(g) fumare
(b) vedere un film	(e) uscire con i suoi genitori	(h) comprare un altro vestito
(c) uscire con Carla	(f) scrivere una lettera a suo zio	(i) venire a pranzo con noi

5   Imagine you are making the following requests to your friend: how
     would you make them in Italian? (Use the **tu** form)

     (a) Can you wait here?
     (b) Can you phone for (**per**) me?
     (c) Can you pass the salt and pepper?
     (d) Can you book another room?
     (e) Can you open the door please?

6   **Ora tocca a te!** Add your side of this phone conversation (you are
     Pat Iles):

Segretaria	Pronto!
You	*Hello! May I speak to Lisa please?*
Segretaria	Lisa è in riunione.
You	*Can I leave a message?*
Segretaria	Certo. Chi parla?
You	*Pat Iles.*
Segretaria	Come si scrive?
You	*(Spell out your whole name.)*
Segretaria	E qual è il messaggio?
You	*Pat Iles cannot go to the meeting tomorrow.*

Informazioni

1 La scheda telefonica   *Phonecard*

In a few places it is still possible to use money when making outside calls,
but in most cases you need **la scheda telefonica** which you can buy
all'edicola *at the newstand* or **dal tabaccaio**.

2 In un ufficio   *In an office*

l'agenda – il calendario – la carta – il computer – la matita –
l'orologio – la penna – il quadro – la scrivania – la sedia – la
segreteria telefonica – il telefono – il telefonino

Label the items in the picture with the words from the box. Look up those
you don't know.

(a) Quanto costa questa segreteria telefonica, e per quanto tempo è garantita?

Facile

- colore bianco
- testo di annuncio su memoria digitale
- registrazione su microcassetta delle chiamate entranti
- funzione "memo" per lasciare messaggi anche da un altro telefono
- accensione e controllo a distanza

in vendita a L. 108.000 IVA inclusa (garanzia 6 mesi)

(b) Per chi è il telefono azzurro e quanto costa per telefonare?

Telefono Azzurro
Linea gratuita 19696
per i bambini

10 | LAVORO E TEMPO LIBERO
Work and spare time

In this Unit you will learn how to:

- say in what part of town you live
- talk about the type of work you do
- say what you do in your spare time
- talk about your family
- invite someone out

Dialogo 1 Leggo, scrivo, ascolto la radio   *I read, write and listen to the radio*

Marisa interviews **Carmela** in the town square. **Carmela** explains that she comes from Palermo but that she lives and works in Naples. Then **Marisa** asks her in what part of Naples she lives, what her work is and what she does in her spare time.

(a) How does Carmela say: 'I live and work in Naples.'?

Carmela   Sono di Palermo, vivo e lavoro a Napoli.
Marisa   In che parte di Napoli abita?
Carmela   Al centro. Vicino all'università.
Marisa   Che lavoro fa?
Carmela   Insegno matematica in un istituto tecnico.
Marisa   Cosa fa nel pomeriggio?
Carmela   Se ho una riunione rimango a scuola, altrimenti torno a casa. Quando ho un po' di tempo libero, gioco a tennis o esco con qualche amica.
Marisa   E la sera?
Carmela   Dipende... Leggo, scrivo, ascolto la radio, guardo la televisione, oppure se c'è un bel film, vado al cinema.

insegnare *to teach*	**altrimenti** *otherwise*
rimango (*from* **rimanere**) *I remain, stay*	**dipendere** *to depend*
	leggo (*from* **leggere**) *I read*

(b) How does **Carmela** say: 'I play tennis.'?

Dialogo 2 Io e la mia famiglia   *My family and I*

Marisa looks at a family photo of **Pietro**, **Carmela**'s colleague.

(a) How does **Marisa** ask: 'Are they your parents?'

Marisa Che bella fotografia! Chi è quel signore lì vicino alla sedia?
Pietro Sono io.
Marisa E quei signori davanti a lei, sono i suoi genitori?
Pietro Sì. Questi sono i miei genitori: mio padre, mia madre, e questi qui sono i miei nonni.
Marisa È sua sorella la signora dietro ai nonni?
Pietro No. È mia moglie, e il bambino seduto per terra è nostro figlio Alessandro.

quel	*that*	**i nonni**	*grandparents*
sedia	*chair*	**moglie** (f)	*wife*
quei	*those*	**seduto/a**	*sitting*
i genitori	*parents*	**per terra**	*on the floor*

(b) How does Pietro say: 'And these are my grandparents (here).'?

Pronuncia

Conoscere: conosco, conoscono; conosci, conosce, conosciamo, conoscete

Leggere: leggo, leggono; leggi, legge, leggiamo, leggete

Spiegazioni

1 Rimanere   *to remain, stay*

Both **rimanere** and **restare** mean *to stay* or *to remain*. **Rimanere**, however, is irregular:

Present tense	**rimanere** *to stay or remain*		
(io) rimango	*I stay, I am staying*	**(noi) rimaniamo**	*we stay, we are staying*
(tu) rimani	*you stay, you are staying*	**(voi) rimanete**	*you (pl.) stay, you are staying*
(lui, lei) rimane	*he/she stays, is staying*	**(loro) rimangono**	*they stay, they are staying*

2 Al centro   *In the centre*

You may either say **al centro** or **in centro**. We have already met expressions where **in** is used without the definite article. A few more examples are grouped here:

in	**città**	*in*	*town*
	periferia		*the suburbs*
	piazza		*the square*
	campagna		*the country*
	montagna		*the mountains*

But remember to say **al mare** *by the sea, at/to the seaside*

3 Giocare a   *to play*

To play a game is **giocare a**:

giocare a { **tennis** / **calcio/pallone*** / **rugby** / **carte** }   *to play* { *tennis* / *football* / *rugby* / *cards* }

* Lit: **un calcio** *a kick*   **un pallone** *a football*

4 Che bella fotografia!   *What a lovely photograph!*

Che in exclamations can be used with nouns or adjectives:

Che { **bello/a!** / **belli/e!** }   *How lovely! How nice!*

Che bella macchina!   *What a lovely car!*

Che peccato!   *What a pity!*

Che guaio!   *What a nuisance!*

5 Bello/a, quello/a, ecc. *lovely, that*

When **bello** *beautiful, lovely* and **quello** *that* precede the noun they qualify, they behave similarly to **nel, nello, nella, nell', nei, negli, nelle** (Unit 8, p 92):

È un bel bambino.	*He's a lovely child.*
Che bello scaffale!	*What a nice book-case/shelf!*
Quei libri sono interessanti.	*Those books are interesting.*
Quell'uomo è povero.	*That man is poor.*
Quegli appartamenti sono belli.	*Those flats are nice.*

6 I nonni *the grandparents*

Here are some additions to members of the family you have already met or may have forgotten:

i genitori parents			
(il) padre	father	**(la) madre**	mother
(il) marito	husband	**(la) moglie**	wife
(il) nonno	grandfather	**(la) nonna**	grandmother
(lo) zio	uncle	**(la) zia**	aunt
(il) cugino	cousin (male)	**(la) cugina**	cousin (female)
(il) nipote	nephew or grandson	**(la) nipote**	niece or grand-daughter

7 nostro/a, nostri/e *our*

The following table sets out all the remaining forms of the possessive adjectives *our, your, their*. They must always be preceded by the definite article, unless you are talking about *one* member of the family only (see examples, p 59): **nostro padre** *our father*, **BUT i nostri genitori** *our parents*; **vostra figlia** *your daughter*, **BUT le vostre figlie** *your daughters*.

Note that **loro** *their* never changes and that it is **always** preceded by the definite article, whether the noun is singular or plural: **il loro cugino** *their cousin*, **i loro cugini** *their cousins*.

noi	il nostro	la nostra	i nostri	le nostre	our	
voi	il vostro	la vostra	i vostri	le vostre	your (pl.)	
loro	il la i le	loro	albergo camera bagagli chiavi		their	hotel room luggage keys

La loro cugina ha una villa in montagna.	*Their cousin has a villa in the mountains.*
I vostri colleghi sono in ufficio.	*Your colleagues are in the office.*
I loro amici vengono da Roma.	*Their friends come from Rome.*

Come si dice in italiano?

How to:

1	say you live and work in a particular town	**Vivo e lavoro a …**
2	ask in what part of a town someone lives	**In che parte di … abita?**
	say in what part of a town you live	**Abito al/in centro/in periferia.**
3	say what you do in your spare time	**Leggo, scrivo, ascolto la radio…** **Gioco a tennis/a pallone/a carte…**
4	identify members of your family (from a photo)	**Questo qui è mio marito …** **Questi sono i miei genitori …**
5	invite someone out	**Vuoi venire con me?**

Attività

1 Insert the correct form of **quel, quello, quella, quell', quei, quegli, quelle** in the following sentences:

(a) Chi è ____ signore?

(b) ____ orologio è giapponese.

(c) ____ camicia costa poco.

(d) ____ istituto è grande.

(e) ____ studente è australiano.

(f) ____ appartamenti sono moderni.

(g) ____ libri sono belli.

(h) Non sono buoni ____ pomodori?

(i) ____ cartoline sono di Roma?

(j) Sono di cristallo ____ bicchieri?

2 Insert the correct form of **bel, bello, ecc.** in the following sentences:

(a) Che ____ macchina!

(b) Che ____ studio!

(c) Che ____ posto!

(d) Che ____ bambini!

(e) Che ____ albero!

(f) Che ____ spiaggia!

(g) Che ____ camere!

(h) Che ____ uccelli!

3 This is Lucia's account of what she does every day of the week.

Fill in the blanks, using each of the words in the box below once only.

(a) Lunedì ____ a casa e ____ la televisione.

(b) Martedì vado a ____ in discoteca.

(c) Mercoledì ____ al cinema con Cesare.

(d) Giovedì resto a casa a ____ a bridge.

(e) Venerdì ____ a tennis con Enrico.

(f) Sabato sera ____ di casa alle otto e vado in piazza.

(g) Domenica ____ al ristorante con i miei genitori.

---

ballare - esco - guardo - giocare - gioco - mangio - rimango - vado

---

4 Match the phrases on the right with the sentences on the left:

(i)   Non posso giocare a bridge

(ii) Non posso giocare a calcio

(iii) Non posso giocare a tennis

(iv) Non posso fare il bagno

(a) perchè non ho la racchetta.

(b) perchè non ho le carte.

(c) perchè non ho il costume.

(d) perchè non ho il pallone.

5 Cosa fanno quando non lavorano?

Imagine what each would say if asked what they do in their spare time, but do **Adamo e Ida,** and **Enzo e Rina** together. **Guido,** for instance, would start: **Vado al cinema, ...**

	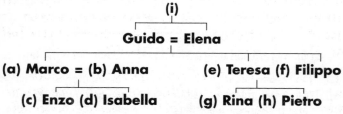 📽	📺	🎾	📖	🎵	🎭	📢
Guido	✓			✓			✓
Carla		✓	✓		✓		
Adamo e Ida	✓			✓		✓	✓
Enzo e Rina		✓	✓	✓	✓		

📽 = andare al cinema   🎵 = andare a ballare
📺 = guardare la televisione   🎭 = andare a teatro
🎾 = giocare a tennis   📢 = ascoltare la radio
📖 = leggere

6 Marco is explaining who is who in his family

(i) Continue for him, using the details from his family tree below.

(a) **Io sono Marco.**   (f) ____
(b) **Anna è mia moglie.**   (g) ____
(c) **Enzo è** ____   (h) ____
(d) ____   (i) ____
(e) ____

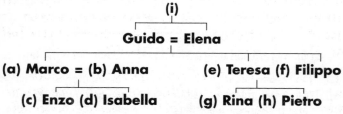

(ii) Now imagine that **Enzo** and **Isabella** are explaining the same family tree to someone else. They would start:

(a) **Marco è nostro padre.**   (f) ——
(b) **Anna è** ____   (g) ——
(c) (d) **Noi siamo i** ____   (h) ____
(e) **Teresa è** ____   (i) ____

7 **Laura** would like to go on an exchange (**fare uno scambio di ospitalità**) with Gloria, who lives in England. In this letter she gives Gloria details about herself and her family. Look up any words you don't know, then imagine you are Gloria and model your answer along the guidelines provided.

Cara Gloria,

mi chiamo Laura Valli. Ho sedici anni e vorrei studiare l'arte culinaria all'Istituto Carlo Porta di Milano. Vorrei poi continuare i miei studi negli Stati Uniti. Le lingue straniere sono molto importanti per la mia carriera, ma non conosco bene l'inglese. Leggo discretamente e capisco tutto, però non so parlare.

Ho un fratello e due sorelle. Mio fratello Mario studia medicina a Bologna. Fa il terzo anno. Le mie sorelle sono sposate. Io vivo a casa con mio padre che lavora per la ferrovia, e mia madre che è parrucchiera. Anche mia nonna vive con noi. È simpaticissima e passa molto tempo a parlare con il nostro pappagallo messicano Panchita. Abbiamo anche un bel cane Rex, e un piccolo gatto Fifì.

Vorrei fare uno scambio di ospitalità con te, se è possibile, per qualche mese. So che vuoi venire in Italia per imparare l'italiano. Il nostro villaggio non è lontano da Firenze. In Italia ci sono molte scuole e università per stranieri.

Puoi venire quando vuoi. Aspetto una tua risposta.

Un caro saluto,

Laura

Before answering Laura's letter to Gloria, look at the suggested reply, then go back to her letter and underline any words or expressions that you could use or adapt. Use the **tu** form.

Start: **Cara Laura,**

grazie della tua lettera.

Say that you are 17 and that one day you would like to work in Italy. This year you are studying Italian and French. They are two very interesting languages.

You live in a village (**villaggio**) near Brighton which is not too far from London.

Your father is an electrician (**elettricista**) and your mother works at home for an advertising agency (**agenzia pubblicitaria**).

You have a brother who works in London and a little sister who is 7 years old. Her name is Sandra and she spends a lot of time playing with your dog Rover.

You would like to go (use **venire**) to Italy in July.

End your letter: **A presto. Un caro saluto,**

Gloria

8   **Ora tocca a te!** You are **Isa**, and **Angelo** is asking you to go out dancing. Add your side of the conversation.

Angelo	Ciao, Isa!
You	*Hello!*
Angelo	Vuoi venire con me?
You	*Where?*
Angelo	A ballare.
You	*When? Now?*
Angelo	Stasera alle nove.
You	*No. This evening I can't. I have to go to the cinema with a friend.*
Angelo	Puoi venire domani? O devi uscire anche domani?
You	*Tomorrow evening I have to go to the theatre with my parents.*
Angelo	Peccato! Domenica alle otto?
You	*Sunday is fine. But I can't come before nine.*
Angelo	Alle nove va bene. Ciao, allora!
You	*Goodbye.*

✳ Informazioni

1 La scuola   *schools*

In Italy the normal school timetable starts at about 8.00/8.30 a.m. and ends at around 2.00 p.m.

2 La famiglia   *the family*

The family is still a very important unit in Italy. As food also has a significant role in Italian life, mealtimes form an integral part of Italian culture where everyone is free to join in and discuss decisions that may affect any of the individual family members. It is still the custom for children to remain in the family home until they get married unless work takes them to another town: only 15 per cent of under 25s live away from home.

It is not unusual for Italians you have just met, especially on long train journeys, to show you their family snapshots and ask personal questions. They don't mean to be indiscreet: they are generally interested in you, your family and your children.

11 | NECESSITÀ QUOTIDIANE E PREFERENZE
Daily necessities and preferences

In this Unit you will learn how to:

■ say you are hungry or thirsty
■ say what provisions you want to buy and ask for specific quantities
■ talk about your likes and dislikes
■ identify what something is made of
■ ask and state preferences

Dialogo 1 Ho sete *I'm thirsty*

Marcello and **Pippa** have been out all morning. As one of them is thirsty and the other hungry, they decide to go shopping (**fare la spesa**) and return home for lunch.

(a) How does **Pippa** say: 'I'm hungry.'?

Marcello	Senti, ho sete. Vorrei bere.
Pippa	Io, invece, ho fame. Vorrei mangiare qualcosa.
Marcello	Sai se c'è una salumeria da queste parti?
Pippa	C'è un negozio di generi alimentari a due passi da qui.
Marcello	Allora facciamo la spesa e poi torniamo subito a casa per il pranzo. Che ne dici?

qualcosa = qualche cosa *something*	**a due passi da qui** *very near here*
sai se ...? *do you know whether ...?*	**Che ne dici?** *How about it?* (Lit: what do you say about it?)
salumeria *delicatessen*	**(dici** from **dire** *to say)*
da queste parti *round here*	**senti** *listen*
negozio di generi alimentari *grocer's*	

(b) How does **Pippa** say: 'I'd like to eat something.'?

Dialogo 2 Al negozio di generi alimentari
At the grocer's

Marcello and **Pippa** are buying provisions from the **salumiere** *grocer*.

(a) How does **Pippa** ask for some rolls?

Salumiere	Cosa desidera, signora?
Pippa	Vorrei dei panini, del formaggio, del burro e della mortadella.
Salumiere	Quanto formaggio, e quanta mortadella, signora?
Pippa	Un etto di formaggio, due etti di burro, sei fette di mortadella, e sei panini.
Salumiere	Ecco, signora.
Pippa	Vorrei anche degli spaghetti e dello zucchero.
Salumiere	Quanto zucchero?
Pippa	Mezzo chilo di spaghetti e un chilo di zucchero. Poi vorrei delle uova fresche e dell'olio.
Marcello	Anche un chilo di mele e mezzo chilo di uva.
Salumiere	Subito, signore. Ecco. Desidera altro?
Marcello	No. Basta così.

dei panini	some rolls	**un chilo di**	a kilo of
del burro	some butter	**delle uova fresche**	some fresh
un etto di	100 grams of	eggs	
fetta	slice	**mele, uva**	apples, grapes

(b) How does **Pippa** ask for half a kilo of spaghetti?

Dialogo 3 Pelletteria: le piace? *leather goods shop: do you like it?*

Ada and **Simona** are choosing some leather goods. First **Simona** buys a leather handbag, **una borsa di pelle**.

(a) How does **Ada** exclaim: 'How nice this handbag is!'?

Ada	Com'è bella questa borsa! Le piace?
Simona	No. Non mi piace. È troppo grande.
Ada	Questa qui è più piccola. Va bene con i guanti.
Simona	Sì, però è troppo chiara. Non ce n'è una più scura?
Ada	Lì ce n'è una. È meno cara, ma è di plastica. Preferisce quella?

Simona	No. Preferisco questa di pelle. Quanto costa?
Ada	Costa molto.
Simona	Non importa. La compro lo stesso.

i guanti *gloves*	**quello/a** *that one*
Non ce n'è una più scura?	**La compro lo stesso.** *I'll buy it*
Isn't there a darker one?	*all the same.*
Lì ce n'è una. *There's one there.*	

(b) How does **Simona** say: 'I don't like it.'?

Dialogo 4 Le piacciono?   *Do you like them?*

Next, **Ada** would like to buy **un portafoglio** *a wallet*.

(a) How does **Ada** say: 'I like them very much.'?

Ada	Io vorrei prendere anche il portafoglio per Marco.
Simona	Di che colore lo vuole? Qui ce ne sono due molto belli. Sono più scuri della borsa. Le piacciono?
Ada	Sì. Mi piacciono moltissimo. Quanto costano?
Simona	Costano poco.
Ada	Costano poco? Allora li compro tutti e due.
Simona	Come sono eleganti quelle scarpe in vetrina! Perchè non le compra?
Ada	Perchè non ho più soldi!

ce ne sono due *there are two*	**in vetrina** *in the (shop) window*
(of them)	
Sono più scuri della borsa.	
They are darker than the handbag.	

(b) How does **Ada** say: 'Then I'll buy both of them.'?
(c) How does she say: 'I haven't any more money!'?

Spiegazioni

1 Sapere *to know;* **dire** *to say, to tell*

From now on, irregular verbs will be presented without the Italian
pronouns by the side and without the English translation: as they are

always set out in the same order you should not experience any difficulty
with the meaning.

Present tense **sapere** *to know*	**dire** *to say, to tell*
so **sai** **sa** **sappiamo** **sapete** **sanno**	**dico** **dici** **dice** **diciamo** **dite** **dicono**

2 Ho sete   *I'm thirsty*

Common expressions with **avere**, where English uses *to be*:

aver	**sete** **fame** **paura** **sonno** **ragione** **torto**	*to be*	*thirsty* *hungry* *afraid* *sleepy* *right* *wrong*	*(or to feel sleepy)*

**Ha un bicchiere d'acqua,
  per favore? Ho sete.**
	*Have you got a glass of water
	  please? I'm thirsty.*

Perchè non mangi? Non ho fame.	*Why don't you eat? I'm not hungry.*
Ho sonno. Vado a letto.	*I feel sleepy. I'm going to bed.*
No! Lui non ha torto. Ha ragione.	*No. He's not wrong. He's right.*

3 A due passi da qui   *very near here*

Notice the use of **a** for distance here: it renders the idea of *away*:

a dieci chilometri da Roma	*Ten kilometres away from Rome*
a due chilometri dall'autostrada	*Two kilometres (away) from the motorway*

4 Dei panini... *some rolls*

Di + the definite article (see Unit 6, p 68) is also used to express the idea
of *some* or *any*: **del burro** *some butter*; **della marmellata** *some jam*;
dell'uva *some grapes* (notice that **uva** is always singular).

5 Uova fresche   *fresh eggs*

Un uovo *an egg* is masculine, but the plural **uova** is feminine: **delle uova fresche**. It behaves in the same way as **un paio**, **due paia** (see Unit 4, p 46). The plural of **l'uovo** is therefore **le uova**.

6 Com'è bella questa borsa!   *How nice this handbag is!*

Like **che** (pp 112–3), **come**, **com'è**, **come sono** can be used in exclamations, but **come** must be followed by a verb:

Com'è grande!	*It's big, isn't it?* (Lit. *How big it is!*)
Come sono eleganti!	*They're elegant, aren't they?*

Come can also be used to introduce questions asking what someone or something is like:

Com'è la sua casa?	*What's your/his/her house like?*
Com'è l'amico di Pietro?	*What is Peter's friend like?*

7 Le piace? Le piacciono?   *Do you like it? Do you like them?*

Piacere (Lit: *to be pleasing to*) is used to express the idea of liking in Italian:

Mi piace.	*I like ... or I like it.*
	(Lit: *It is pleasing to me.*)
Le piace.	*You/she likes (it).*
	(Lit: *It is pleasing to you/to her.*)
Gli piace.	*He likes (it).*
	(Lit: *It is pleasing to him.*)

Mi piace **tanto questo disco!** }	*I like this record very much.*
Questo disco *mi piace* **tanto!** }	

Use the third person plural of **piacere** when more than one thing or person is liked:

Le piacciono *queste pesche*? }	*Do you like these peaches?*
Queste pesche **le piacciono**? }	(Lit. *Are these peaches pleasing to you?*)

To express dislikes use **non** before **mi piace**, **le piace**, etc:

Le ulive non mi piacciono.	*I don't like olives.*

To emphasise **non** you can use **non ... mica** or **non ... affatto** *not ... at all*:

Questa borsa non mi piace mica/affatto.	*I don't like this bag at all.*

Attenzione! **Dispiacere** means *to be sorry* or *to mind*. It is **not** the opposite of **piacere**:

Ha delle cipolle?	*Have you got any onions?*
Mi dispiace. No ne ho.	*I'm sorry, I haven't (any).*
Le dispiace tornare domani?	*Do you mind coming back tomorrow?*

Note that **a** is required

(*a*) when a name is used:

A Carlo non piace l'arte moderna. *Charles doesn't like modern art.*

(*b*) with pronouns when emphasis or contrast occurs:

Piace a me, ma non piace a te. *I like it, but you don't.*

8 Ne Some (of it)

Ne meaning *some, any, of it, (some) of it, (some) of them*, is used when quantities or numbers are involved in relation to a noun previously mentioned, and like the pronouns **lo, la, li, le**, usually precedes the verb:

Quanto burro compra?	*How much butter are you buying?*
Ne compro un etto.	*I'm buying a 100 grams (of it).*
Ha degli spiccioli?	*Have you got any small change?*
Non ne ho.	*I haven't got any.*

Although **ne** is not expressed in English it is essential in Italian.

9 Di pelle leather

To show what something is made of, use **di**:

un portafoglio di cuoio/pelle	*a leather wallet*
dei calzini di cotone	*(some) cotton socks*
una camicia di pura seta	*a pure silk shirt*
un golf di pura lana	*a pure woollen cardigan/jumper*
un anello d'oro	*a gold ring*
un bracciale d'argento	*a silver bracelet*

10 Più scuri della ... darker than ...

Di (or **di** + article) can also mean *than*. In Italian, you don't say *larger* or *smaller* but *more large, more small*, etc. Use **più ... di** (or **di** + article) to say *more ... than*, **meno ... di** (or **di** + article) to say *less ... than*:

Londra è più grande di Roma.	*London is larger than Rome.*
Maria è meno alta di Rita.	*Mary is not as tall as Rita.*
L'aereo è più veloce del treno.	*The plane is faster than the train.*

11 Tutti e due   *both (of them)*

We have seen that **tutti/e** means *all, every*:

Tutti noi.	*All of us.*
Tutti i giorni.	*Every day.*

Note also **tutti/e e** when used with numbers:

Sono tutti e due italiani.	*They are both Italian.*
Tutte e tre (le ragazze) vanno	*All three (girls) are going*
a Roma.	*to Rome.*

12 Non ho più soldi   *I haven't any more money*

The partitive article (**del, della, dei, ecc.**) is not used in negative plural expressions (see Unit 4, p. 47).

Non ha mai soldi.	*He never has any money.*
Non bevo liquori.	*I don't drink liqueurs.*

Come si dice in italiano?

How to:

1	say you are hungry or thirsty	**Ho fame. Ho sete.**
2	say what provisions you want to buy	**Vorrei del burro, dell'olio, ecc.**
	ask for specific quantities	**Vorrei un etto di burro, un litro di olio, ecc.**
3	talk about your likes and dislikes	**Le piace? Mi piace.**
		Non mi piace.
		Le piacciono? Mi piacciono.
		Non mi piacciono.
4	ask about/say what something is made of	**È di pelle? No. È di plastica.**
5	ask someone what they prefer	**Preferisce questo/a o quello/a?**
	say what you prefer	**Preferisco questo/a; quello/a.**

✅ Attività

1 Look at Mary's shopping list and, without mentioning the quantities, write down what she wants to buy. Look up any words you don't know. Start: **Maria vuol comprare *del* burro...**

> *un etto di burro*
> *due etti di formaggio*
> *due bottiglie di birra*
> *un litro di olio*
> *tre chili di spaghetti*
> *un chilo di zucchero*
> *una scatola di fiammiferi*
> *una bottiglia di acqua minerale*

2 **Lisa's** likes are marked in the table by one tick, her preferences by two ticks. Make statements about her likes and preferences.

Esempio: (a) La birra le piace, ma preferisce il vino.

Be careful with (e) and (f).

	✓	✓✓
(a)	**birra**	**vino**
(b)	**vino bianco**	**vino rosso**
(c)	**cinema**	**teatro**
(d)	**Milano**	**Firenze**
(e)	**melanzane**	**peperoni**
(f)	**libri**	**riviste**

3 Now imagine that you are **Lisa** and that somebody else is asking you the questions. Form both questions and answers.

Esempio: Le piace la birra o il vino? La birra mi piace, ma preferisco il vino.

4 When addressing a man or a woman formally use **le piace**, when addressing someone informally use **ti piace**:

Signora, le piace l'arte moderna? *Do you like modern art, (Madam)?*

Sì. Mi piace./No. Non mi piace. *Yes I do./No I don't.*
Signor Vitti, le piace il cricket? *Do you like cricket, Mr Vitti?*
Sì. Mi piace molto. *Yes, I do, very much.*
Adriano, ti piace la lingua *Adrian, do you like Italian?*
italiana?
Sì. Mi piace/No. Non mi piace. *Yes, I do./No, I don't.*

Ora tocca a te! Here you have a choice of **Mi piace molto/moltissimo; non mi piace/non mi piace molto.** Form the complete question and choose the answer that is most appropriate for you. Then check you have written **molto, ecc.** correctly.

(a) (formal) _____ la cucina italiana?
(b) (formal) _____ la musica classica?
(c) (informal) _____ lo sport?
(d) (informal) _____ il tuo lavoro?
(e) (informal) _____ il calcio?
(f) (formal) _____ gli animali?
(g) (formal) _____ i film americani?
(h) (informal) _____ le case moderne?

5 Le piace + infinitive: 'Do you like doing...?'

Ti piace guidare? *Do you like driving?*
Sì. Mi piace molto. *Yes, I do, very much.*

This time simply form the questions:

(a) (informal) _____ viaggiare?
(b) (informal) _____ leggere?
(c) (informal) _____ studiare?
(d) (formal) _____ cucinare?
(e) (formal) _____ uscire la sera?
(f) (informal) _____ andare al cinema?
(g) (informal) _____ ascoltare la radio?
(h) (informal) _____ guardare la televisione?

6   Answer these questions using **ne** in your answers, as in the example:

Esempio: Quanti biglietti deve fare?   **(1)**
              Ne devo fare uno.

(a) Quante sterline deve pagare?   (100)
(b) Quante lettere deve scrivere?   (2)

    (c) Quanti amici vuoi invitare?   (12)
    (d) Quanti francobolli devi comprare?   (9)
    (e) Quante valigie hai?   (1)
    (f) Quanti cugini ha?   (4)
    (g) Quanti caffè compri?   (7)
    (h) Quanti libri leggi?   (molti)

7   Ask the shop assistant whether she has something bigger, longer, darker, etc. using **ne** in your answer:

Esempio: Questo impermeabile è troppo corto. ____lungo.
              Ne ha uno più lungo?
              Questa scatola è troppo piccola. Non ____ grande.
              Non ne ha una più grande?

    (a) Questo vestito è troppo lungo.   ____ corto.
    (b) Questa camera è troppo piccola. Non ____ grande.
    (c) Questo cappello è troppo chiaro. Non ____ scuro.
    (d) Questa cravatta è troppo scura. ____ chiara.
    (e) Questo libro è troppo difficile. Non ____ facile.

8   Read the following passage and make comparisons between the three brothers using **più grande di …** or **più piccolo di …**

Pietro, Paolo e Lino sono tre fratelli. Pietro ha venti anni, Paolo ne ha dieci e Lino ne ha tre.

Esempio: Paolo __ Lino.
              Paolo è più grande di Lino.

    (a) Pietro __ Paolo.   (d) Pietro __ Lino.
    (b) Lino __ Paolo.   (e) Paolo __ Pietro.
    (c) Lino __ Pietro.

9   Using **più/meno veloce di** + article …, make comparisons between the speeds of the following pairs.

    (a) L'aereo __ il treno.
    (b) Il treno __ l'autobus.
    (c) La macchina __ la bicicletta.
    (d) La bicicletta __ l'autobus.
    (e) L'autobus __ la metropolitana.

10   **Alfredo** is explaining to **Gianni** what he would like to buy and why. Listen to the dialogue and answer the questions on it.

Alfredo	Vorrei comprare una nuova macchina.
Gianni	Perchè? La sua non va?
Alfredo	Va benissimo. Ma consuma troppa benzina.
Gianni	Ah, ne vuole una più economica!
Alfredo	Sì. Vorrei una macchina più economica e più veloce.
Gianni	Una macchina più piccola allora?
Alfredo	No. Le macchine piccole non mi piacciono.
Gianni	Ma quelle veloci non sono troppo care?
Alfredo	Sì, però non vorrei pagare tanto.

(a)   What would Alfredo like to buy?

(b)   Does Alfredo's car work?

(c)   Why does he mention petrol?

(d)   Does he want something faster?

(e)   Does he want something smaller?

(f)   Why? Why not?

(g)   Does Gianni think that fast cars are too cheap?

(h)   What does Alfredo not want to do?

❇ Informazioni

Mercati e negozi   *Markets and shops*

Markets are still the most popular place for buying provisions in Italy because the food there has the reputation of being fresh and cheap. Many towns have a daily market where a wide range of foodstuffs can be bought.

Below are the names of some of the shops you will see and what their vendors are called. Very often Italians use the name of the vendor rather than the name of the shop:

Vado dal farmacista or   *I'm going to the chemist* or
Vado in farmacia.   *I'm going to the chemist's (shop).*

The words in small letters are the vendors, the ones in capitals are the shops:

panettiere PANETTERIA	salumiere SALUMERIA	macellaio MACELLERIA	pasticciere PASTICCERIA	pescivendolo PESCHERIA

For ice-cream use the name of the shop: **gelateria**.
For fruit and vegetables use the name of the vendor: **il fruttivendolo**.

Here are some of the foodstuffs sold in **la salumeria**, **la macelleria** and **la pescheria**. See if you can group them under the appropriate shop:

vitello, salame, olio, trota, merluzzo, vino, maiale, olive, prosciutto, agnello, salmone, pasta, manzo, mortadella.

(a) Quanto tempo ci vuole per cuocere le pennette rigate, e quanto tempo ci vuole per cuocere gli spaghetti?
(b) Quanti grammi sono le pennette rigate?

12 CERCO CASA
I'm looking for accommodation

In this Unit you will learn how to:

- say what type of accommodation you require
- say what location you prefer
- express appreciation of the interior
- ask about the rent

  Dialogo 1 All'agenzia immobiliare *At the estate agent's*

Roberto is looking for a flat and is speaking to the estate agent (**l'agente immobiliare**).

From this point onwards the questions will be in Italian, and in **Vero o falso** correct any statements that are wrong.

(a) **Vero o falso?** Roberto cerca un appartamento in periferia.

Ag.imm.	Buongiorno! Desidera?
Roberto	Buongiorno! Cerco un appartamento di quattro camere.
Ag.imm.	Al centro o in periferia?
Roberto	Al centro. Possibilmente da queste parti.
Ag.imm.	Dunque, vediamo un po'… Ah sì! Ce n'è uno proprio vicino al Duomo. È signorile, ammobiliato, ha quattro camere, cucina, ingresso, bagno, balcone.
Roberto	Sì. Va benissimo. Qual è l'indirizzo?
Ag.imm.	Via Mirafiori 12, interno 7.
Roberto	E il numero di telefono?
Ag.imm.	86 84 52.

Ce n'è uno proprio … *There's one just …*	**cucina** *kitchen*
signorile *luxurious*	**ingresso** *entrance hall*
ammobiliato/a *furnished*	**bagno** *bathroom*

(b) Quante camere vuole Roberto?

Dialogo 2 A chi pago l'affitto?   *To whom do I pay the rent?*

The estate agent shows **Roberto** round the flat and explains that he should pay the rent to **la padrona di casa** *the landlady*, who lives on the ground floor.

(a) **Vero o falso?** La padrona di casa abita al secondo piano.

Ag.imm.	Ecco l'appartamento. Questo è l'ingresso. Di qua, prego. Da questa parte c'è il salotto.
Roberto	Che bei mobili!
Ag.imm.	Sono tutti moderni. Questa è la camera da letto. Nell'armadio c'è posto anche per le lenzuola e le coperte.
Roberto	Il balcone dà sulla strada?
Ag.imm.	No. Dà sul cortile. Qui c'è la sala da pranzo, e qui il salotto.
Roberto	E questa porta?
Ag.imm.	È la porta della cucina. Avanti, prego!
Roberto	Dopo di lei!
Ag.imm.	Grazie. Come vede, nell'appartamento ci sono tutte le comodità.
Roberto	A chi pago l'affitto?
Ag.imm.	Alla padrona di casa che abita al pianterreno.

salotto	*living/drawing room*	**cortile (m)**	*courtyard*
i mobili	*furniture*	**sala da pranzo**	*dining-room*
armadio	*wardrobe*	**pianterreno**	*ground floor*
le lenzuola	*sheets*		
coperta	*blanket*		

(b) Che cosa si paga alla padrona di casa?

Dialogo 3 Un appartamentino   *A small flat*

The landlord (**il padrone di casa**) shows a woman tenant (**inquilina**) round a small flat. **L'inquilina** first wants to know where to turn the light on.

(a) **Vero o falso?** La luce si accende vicino al citofono.

Inquilina	Dove si accende la luce?
Padr.	Qui, vicino al citofono.
Inquilina	È questo il soggiorno?

Padr.	Sì. Un attimo. Spengo. Guardi, c'è tutto: il divano, le sedie, le poltrone, lo scaffale per i libri, la televisione, il video…
Inquilina	Oh, che bella cucina! Anche il frigorifero è grande! La lavastoviglie…
Padr.	E questo è il bagno. Qui c'è la presa per il rasoio, qui la doccia e lì la lavatrice.

accendere la luce	*to turn on the light*	**poltrona**	*armchair*
citofono	*entry-phone*	**lo scaffale per i libri**	*bookshelf*
soggiorno	*living-room*	**frigorifero**	*fridge*
spegnere (la luce)	*to turn off the light* (see below)	**lavastoviglie** (f)	*dishwasher*
divano	*settee*	**presa per il rasoio**	*razor socket*
		la doccia	*shower*
		lavatrice (f)	*washing machine*

(b) Dove (esattamente) sono la televisione e la lavatrice?

Spiegazioni

1 Accendere *and* spegnere

These two verbs are also used for turning on/off the radio, television and gas. **Spegnere** is irregular. Here is the present tense:

Present tense	**spegnere** *to turn off, extinguish*
spengo	**spegniamo**
spegni	**spegnete**
spegne	**spengono**

2 Ce n'è, ce ne sono *there is… (of it, of them, etc.) there are… (of it, of them)* – see p. 69

N'è = ne + è. When **ci** precedes **ne** it becomes **ce**: **ce n'è, ce ne sono.** In the following examples notice how **uno, una, molti, ecc.** agree with the noun to which they refer: **ne** substitutes the noun (see p. 125):

Quanti piani ci sono?	*How many floors are there?*
Ce n'è un*o*. (C'è un piano.)	*There is one (of them).*
Quante camere ci sono?	*How many room are there?*
Ce n'è un*a*. (C'è una camera.)	*There is one (of them).*
Quanti negozi ci sono?	*How many shops are there?*
Ce ne sono molt*i*.	*There are lots (of them).*

(Ci sono molti negozi).

Notice also the negative construction:

C'è del latte?	*Is there any milk?*
No. *Non ce n'è.*	*No. There isn't any.*
Ci sono degli sbagli?	*Are there any mistakes?*
No. *Non ce ne* **sono.**	*No. There aren't any.*

3 Le lenzuola (sing. **il lenzuolo**) *the sheets*

This is an irregular plural like **le uova**, **le paia** (see Unit 11, p 124).

4 Dopo di lei *after you*

Although **dopo** is used by itself before a noun, it is used with **di** before a pronoun:

Il cinema è *dopo* **l'agenzia.**	*The cinema is after the agency.*
Dopo di lei!	*After you!*

5 *Uses of* **da**

Da is also used to describe the purpose of an object:

una sala da pranzo	*a dining-room*
una camera da letto	*a bedroom*
un vestito da sera	*an evening dress*
un bicchiere da vino	*a wine glass*

6 Appartamentino *small flat*

It is possible to add suffixes (special endings) to Italian nouns and adjectives in order to emphasise a particular quality or characteristic. Compare English: *statue, statuette*; *figure, figurine*.

-etto/a and **-ino/a** suggest smallness:

villetta	*small villa*	**tazzina**	*small cup, espresso cup*
casetta	*little house*	**cucchiaino**	*coffee/tea-spoon*
			(Lit: *a little* **cucchiaio**)

carino/a
bellino/a } *pretty*

7 Cercare *to look for*

Notice that **cercare** does not require a preposition to follow it as in English:

Che cosa cerca?	*What are you looking for?*
Non cerco niente.	*I'm not looking for anything.*
Cerco il dizionario.	*I'm looking for the dictionary.*

8 Verbs ending in -care, -gare, and -gere

Verbs ending in **-care** and **-gare** keep their hard 'c' and 'g' sounds throughout their conjugation. They must therefore add an 'h' before 'i'. Verbs in **-gere** do not change their spelling in this way: the 'g' sound therefore changes according to the sound following, i.e. in **leggo** and **leggono** the 'g' sound is pronounced as in 'got', but in other persons (**leggi, legge, ecc.**) as in 'ledge' (see **Pronuncia** Unit 10, p 111).

Here is the present tense of **giocare** *to play* (*a game*) and **pagare** *to pay*:

Present tense	
giocare *to play*	**pagare** *to pay*
gioco	pago
giochi	paghi
gioca	paga
giochiamo	paghiamo
giocate	pagate
giocano	pagano

Come si dice in italiano?

How to:

1 say that you are looking for a flat
   and how many rooms you require

**Cerco un appartamento
di due/di tre ..., ecc. camere.**

2 say what location you prefer

**Al centro/in periferia/da
queste parti.**

3 express appreciation of the interior

**Che bei mobili!
Che bella cucina!**

4 ask who to pay the rent to
   and answer: to the landlady

**A chi pago l'affitto?
Alla padrona di casa.**

✏ Attività

1 Here is a list of fixtures, fittings, and furniture. Look at the picture(s)
   of the rooms below and their contents, and decide which items belong
   to which room.

> ● l'acquaio ● il bidè ● la cucina ● il comodino ● il divano
> ● la doccia ● il frigorifero ● il lavandino ● la lavastoviglie
> ● la lavatrice ● il letto ● la libreria ● l'orologio ● la pianta
> ● le poltrone ● il quadro ● lo scaffale ● la scrivania
> ● le sedie ● lo specchio ● il tappeto ● la tavola ● il tavolino
> ● le tende ● il telefono ● la televisione ● la vasca da bagno
> ● il water

Group them accordingly under these rooms: **il bagno - la cucina - la
camera da letto - la sala da pranzo - il salotto - l'ingresso**

2 Look at how many rooms, etc. there are in the homes of **Anna**, **Maria**, and **i signori Spada**.

	stanze*	camere da letto	piani
Anna	4	2	1
Maria	3	1	1
i signori Spada	7	4	2

* In general, you can use either **camera** or **stanza** for room, but when you want to distinguish between a bedroom and other rooms use **camera da letto** for bedroom.

Answer the questions using **Ce n'è** or **Ce ne sono** and the number.

(a) Quanti piani ci sono nella villa dei signori Spada?
(b) Quante camere da letto ci sono nella villa dei signori Spada?
(c) Quante camere da letto ci sono nell'appartamento di Maria?
(d) Quante stanze ci sono nell'appartamento di Anna?
(e) Quante stanze ci sono nella villa dei signori Spada?

3 **Nel, nella**, etc. Link with the five objects in the left-hand column into the five most appropriate places on the right.

Esempio: Le sedie sono nel soggiorno.

(a) presa per il rasoio   salotto
(b) citofono   camera da letto
(c) frigorifero   ingresso
(d) letto   cucina
(e) divano   bagno
(f) coperte   armadio

4 Do as in **Attività 3** this time using **sul, sulla**, etc.

(a) sedie a sdraio   scaffale
(b) lenzuola   tavolino
(c) televisione   balcone
(d) libri   letto

5 Read the following and notice how the information can be extracted from the table on the opposite page:

Marco cerca un appartamento di due camere, al centro, vicino al Duomo.

	Camere	Centro o periferia?	Dove?
Marco	2	centro	Duomo
Davide	4	periferia	strada principale
Bianca	3	periferia	stazione
Lola e Rita	5	centro	ufficio

(a) Write a sentence to say what **Davide** is looking for.
(b) Write a similar sentence for **Bianca**.
(c) Write a similar sentence for **Lola e Rita**.
(d) Supposing the estate agent were to ask **Lola e Rita** what they were looking for, what would they answer?

6   In the following questions answer with **Ce n'è** (singular) or **Ce ne sono** (plural), and a number:

> **Esempio: Quanti giorni ci sono nel mese di marzo?**
> **Ce ne sono trentuno.**

(a) Quanti mesi ci sono in un anno?
(b) Quanti giorni ci sono in una settimana?
(c) Quanti giorni ci sono in un anno?
(d) Quanti minuti ci sono in un'ora?
(e) Quanti anni ci sono in un secolo?
(f) Quanti etti ci sono in un chilo?
(g) Quante lettere ci sono nell'alfabeto italiano?
(h) Quanti mesi ci sono con ventotto giorni?

7   **Marisa** is asking an inhabitant of Rome something about her flat.

Marisa   Abita a Roma, signora?
Signora   Sì. Abito vicino al Colosseo.
Marisa   In una casa moderna?
Signora   Beh… non molto moderna.
Marisa   A che piano abita?
Signora   Al quarto.
Marisa   C'è l'ascensore?
Signora   No. L'ascensore non c'è.
Marisa   Quante stanze ha?
Signora   Cinque: tre camere da letto, la sala da pranzo e il salotto. Il bagno è piccolo ma la cucina è bella grande.

(a)   Near what building does she live?
(b)   What is said about the age of the flat?
(c)   On what floor does she live?
(d)   Is there a lift in the building?
(e)   How many rooms does she say she has?
(f)   How many bedrooms does she say she has?
(g)   Which rooms are not included in her total?
(h)   What can you say about these last two rooms?

8 Piccola pubblicità   *small-ads*

The extracts below are from **piccola pubblicità** in an Italian newspaper.
First look at the **Informazioni** section, then look carefully at the
questions. See if you can understand the advertisements and give the
appropriate answers. They are written in 'telegraphic style' – only the
essential words are there.

(a) Porto Cervo (Sardegna): affittasi appartamento signorile in zona turistica.	(b) Milano: appartamenti in vendita da 2 a 5 locali.	(c) Arona in zona residenziale con parco: vendesi appartamento.
(d) Milanocase garantisce vendita immediata.	(e) Como: unica posizione villa panoramica 2 appartamenti independenti.	(f) La villa che sognate: stupenda costruzione, fronte mare Riviera dei Fiori.
(g) Cerco in giugno appartamento libero signorile in costruzione recente.	(h) Studente inglese cerca alloggio ammobiliato con scambio conversazione.	

> | **un locale**   *room* (used mostly commercially with this meaning) | **alloggio**   *lodgings* |
> |---|---|
> | **sognare**   *to dream (about)* | |

   (a)   What is being let in Sardinia?

   (b)   What are being sold in Milan?

   (c)   What is being advertised in Arona?

   (d)   What service is the firm Milanocase offering to prospective sellers?

   (e)   Describe the villa in Como.

   (f)   What makes the villa at Riviera dei Fiori so desirable?

   (g)   What is the advertiser looking for exactly? When for?

   (h)   Who is looking for what and what does he want to exchange?

Informazioni

1 Houses and flats

Although strictly speaking **appartamento** means *flat* and **casa** means *house* or *home*, since most Italians live in flats anyway, they do not make any clear distinction between the two, and usually refer to the house or flat they live in as their **casa**. The building itself is called **palazzo** or **condominio**. There is often a caretaker in charge, **il portiere**, but as costs rise, caretakers are becoming rarer, and **il citofono** is used.

In Italian newspaper advertisements you will see the words **vendesi** (from **vendere** *to sell*) and **affittasi** (from **affittare** *to let or to rent* – hence **l'affitto** *the rent*). They are a commercial way of saying **si vende** and **si affitta**. *To rent* may also be expressed as **prendere in affitto**. You will also see the expression **doppi servizi** frequently used. This means that the flat has two bathrooms: the second one might have a simpler layout with a toilet, shower and washbasin but not necessarily another bath. Often the washing machine is put in here. If you see **il box** this means a garage.

As in English, Italian names for reception rooms are subject to regional variations and changes in fashion. Generally speaking, **il salotto** would be a rather formal sitting-room (a larger one would be called **il salone**) and **il soggiorno** would combine the functions of sitting/dining room.

Most flats have balconies. In increasing order of size they are called: **il balcone**, **il terrazzo**, **la terrazza**. All three mean a lot to Italians.

Many Italians have **la seconda casa** either in the country or by the sea.

13 | VITA DI TUTTI I GIORNI
Everyday life

In this Unit you will learn how to talk about:

■ what sports you do
■ how often you do something
■ the weather
■ daily routine
■ putting a relationship on a more informal footing

 Dialogo 1 Che sport fa? *What sports do you do?*

 Giulio is talking to a journalist about his sporting activities: tennis, swimming, skiing, and jogging.

(a) **Vero o falso?** Lo sport preferito di Giulio è il nuoto.
(b) Ogni mattina si alza, si lava e si veste.

Giorn. Che sport fa durante le vacanze?
Giulio Il tennis, il nuoto e lo sci.
Giorn. Dove va a nuotare? In piscina?
Giulio D'inverno in piscina, d'estate al lago.
Giorn. Va a nuotare tutti i giorni?
Giulio No. Due volte alla settimana.
Giorn. Ma il suo sport preferito è il jogging, vero?
Giulio Eh sì. Ogni mattina appena mi alzo, mi lavo, mi vesto e via per un'ora.

durante *during*	**appena** *as soon as*
le vacanze *holidays*	**mi alzo** *I get up*
nuotare *to swim*	**mi lavo** *I wash*
piscina *swimming pool*	**mi vesto** *I get dressed*
lago *lake*	**via** *away, off I go*

(c) Dove va a nuotare d'inverno, e dove va a nuotare d'estate?

Dialogo 2   Pioggia, neve, vento, sole   *Rain, snow, wind, sun*

Giulio continues by saying that he goes jogging irrespective of the weather.

(a) **Vero o falso?** Quando corre, la pioggia fa una grande differenza per lui.

Giorn. Corre anche quando fa brutto tempo?
Giulio Pioggia, neve, vento, o sole, non fa nessuna differenza per me.
Giorn. Si sente stanco dopo un'ora di corsa, immagino!
Giulio No. Non mi sento affatto stanco. Anzi, per me il jogging è anche un modo per rilassarmi.

correre *to run*		**corsa** *running*	
fa brutto tempo *the weather's bad*		**non affatto** *not at all, not in the least*	
si sente stanco? *do you feel tired?*		**anzi** *on the contrary*	
		rilassarsi *to relax*	

(b) Giulio corre solo quando fa bel tempo?
(c) Si sente molto stanco dopo il jogging?

Dialogo 3   Un giorno qualunque   *Just an ordinary day*

Aldo and **Rita**, a husband and wife who work in their own bookshop, are in the middle of an interview about a typical day of theirs. Rita interrupts to offer the journalist a drink.

(a) **Vero o falso?** Rita offre un caffè al giornalista.
(b) La mattina lei e suo marito si alzano tardi.

Rita   Un bicchier di vino?
Giorn. No, grazie. Non bevo. Dunque… a che ora vi alzate la mattina?
Aldo   Di solito ci alziamo presto: alle sei.
Giorn. Come mai alle sei? Cosa fate in piedi così presto?
Rita   Prima di tutto facciamo il caffè.
Aldo   Senza un buon caffè non ci svegliamo.
Rita   Mentre facciamo colazione, mettiamo un po' in ordine la casa e ci prepariamo, è già ora di uscire.

di solito *usually*	**svegliarsi** *to wake up*
Come mai? *How is that?*	**mettere in ordine** *to tidy*
in piedi così presto *up so early*	**prepararsi** *to get ready*
prima di tutto *first of all*	**già** *already*

(c) Rita e Aldo si alzano alle dieci?

 Dialogo 4   Lavoriamo insieme *We work together*

Aldo explains that he deals with the sales and his wife deals with the book-keeping (**la contabilità**).

(a) **Vero o falso?** A mezzogiorno Aldo e sua moglie mangiano a casa.

Giorn. Lavorate tutti e due?
Rita Sì. Lavoriamo insieme nella nostra libreria.
Aldo Io mi occupo della vendita dei libri e mia moglie si occupa della contabilità.
Giorn. A mezzogiorno mangiate fuori?
Rita No. Torniamo a casa per il pranzo. Pranziamo verso le due.
Aldo Dopo pranzo ci riposiamo un po' e poi torniamo insieme al negozio.
Giorn. E la sera, cenate tardi?
Rita Sì. Piuttosto tardi. Non ceniamo mai prima delle nove.

libreria *book-shop*	**riposarsi** *to rest*
occuparsi *to look after*	**piuttosto** *rather*

(b) La sera, cenano presto?

 Dialogo 5   Diamoci del tu! *Let's use **tu***

Remo, who is much older than **Rina**, gets acquainted with her and puts the relationship on a more informal footing by suggesting the use of the familiar form **tu** (*you*) instead of the more formal **lei**.

(a) **Vero o falso?** Rina studia matematica.
(b) Si laurea a maggio.

Remo	Quindi, è qui per motivi di studio. Che cosa studia?
Rina	Medicina.
Remo	Che anno fa?
Rina	L'ultimo anno. Mi laureo a giugno.
Remo	Ah, c'è tempo per gli esami! Cosa fa di bello stasera?
Rina	Nulla. Resto a casa a studiare.
Remo	Non è stufa di studiare?
Rina	Un po'. E lei, cosa fa?
Remo	Ma, Rina, diamoci del tu!
Rina	E tu, cosa fai?
Remo	Niente d'interessante. Perchè non vieni da me? Possiamo fare quattro chiacchiere, mangiare un piatto di spaghetti, e poi magari andare ad un concerto. Che ne dici?

---

mi laureo   *I'm graduating*
Cosa fa di bello?   *Are you doing anything interesting?*

stufo/a di   *fed up with*
fare quattro chiacchiere   *to have a chat*

(c)   Che anno fa all'università Rina?

Spiegazioni

1 *Reflexive verbs*

In English we say 'he washes' whether a person is washing himself or something else. In Italian you must make a distinction: **si lava** (from **lavarsi** reflexive verb) *he washes (himself)*; **lava** (from **lavare**) **la maglietta** *he washes the T shirt*. In the dictionary, reflexive verbs are recognisable by **-si** (*oneself*) at the end of the infinitive. The final **'e'** of the infinitive (**lavar**e) is dropped and **lavare** *to wash* becomes **lavarsi** *to wash (oneself)*; (**vestire**) **vestirsi** *to dress oneself, to get dressed*.

The pronouns **mi, ti, si, ci, vi, si**, precede the verb and correspond to *myself, yourself*, etc.

Present tense		**lavarsi** *to wash (oneself)*	
(io)	**mi lavo** *I wash (myself)*	**(noi)**	**ci laviamo** *we wash (ourselves)*
(tu)	**ti lavi** *you wash (yourself)*	**(voi)**	**vi lavate** *you wash (yourselves)*
(lei)	**si lava** *you (formal) wash (yourself)*		
(lui, lei)	**si lava** *he/she washes (himself/herself)*	**(loro)**	**si lavano** *they wash (themselves)*

The other reflexive verbs that have appeared in this Unit are: **alzarsi** *to get up*; **laurearsi** *to graduate*; **occuparsi** *to deal with*; **prepararsi** *to prepare*; **rilassarsi** *to relax*; **riposarsi** *to rest*; **sentirsi** *to feel*; **svegliarsi** *to wake up*; **vestirsi** *to dress*.

2 Andare + *infinitive*   *to go ...-ing*

Andare a + infinitive express the idea of *to go and do something*:

D'estate *va a* **nuot*are*.**	*In summer he goes and swims (i.e. he goes swimming).*
D'inverno *andiamo a* **sci*are*.**	*In winter we go skiing.*
Vado a far*e* il **biglietto.**	*I'll go and buy the ticket./ I'm going to buy the ticket.*
Vado a **mang*iare*.**	*I'm going to eat.*

3 Due volte alla settimana   *twice a week*

The idea of frequency is expressed by **a** + definite article:

Quante volte	*al* giorno *alla* settimana *al* mese		mangia (li)? prende l'autobus? lavora? viene qui?
How many times a	day week month	do you	eat (there)? take a bus? work? come here?

4 Ogni   *every*

Ogni means *every*, but is followed by the singular except when followed by a number:

Ogni giorno; ogni sera.	*Every day; every evening/every night.*
Ogni cinque minuti; ogni due giorni.	*Every five minutes; every two days.*

5 Nessuno/a   *Not ... any ...*

Nessuno is always singular, and before a noun is used like **un, uno, una, un'**:

nessun libro; nessuno sbaglio	*no book; no mistake*
Non esercita nessuna professione.	*He doesn't practise any profession.*
Non ho nessuna voglia di andare al cinema.	*I've no wish to go to the pictures.*

6 Sentirsi   *to feel*

This verb is used (reflexively) to describe how one feels:

| **Come si sente? Mi sento stanco/bene/male.** | *How do you feel? I feel tired/well/ill.* |

7 Fa brutto tempo   *The weather is bad*

To ask what the weather is like, the verb **fare** is used in the following expressions:

Che tempo fa?					
	Fa	**freddo**	*What's the weather like?*	*It's*	cold
		caldo			hot
		bel tempo			fine
		brutto/cattivo tempo			bad weather

But notice:

Che tempo fa?	**C'è il sole.**	*It's*	sunny
	Tira/c'è vento		windy
	Piove		raining
	Nevica		snowing

8 Un bicchier(e) di vino   *A glass of wine*

Un bicchiere *a glass* can be shortened to **un bicchier** before **di**. You can either say **un bicchiere di vino** or **un bicchier di vino**.

| Vorrei **un bicchier(e) d'acqua.** | *I would like a glass of water.* |

E *and*, **a** *at, to* can add 'd' before words beginning with a vowel:

| Giorgio **e(d)** Anna vanno **a(d)** Amalfi. | *George and Anne are going to Amalfi.* |

9 Cosa fa di bello stasera?   *Are you doing anything interesting tonight?*

A friendly way of asking what people are doing. Note how **di** + adjective is used in parallel expressions: **C'è qualcosa *di* nuovo?** *Is there anything new?*

	d'**interessante**		*interesting*
	di **bello**		*nice*
(Non c'è)	*di* **speciale**	*(There's) nothing*	*special*
niente	*di* **rilevante**		*important*
	di **strano**		*strange*
	di **male**		*wrong*

10 Diamoci del tu   *Let's use tu*

This expression (Lit. *let's give each other **tu***) is said when passing from the **lei** form to the more familiar **tu** form. Remember also to use the possessive **tuo/a, ecc.** for *your* and not **suo/a, ecc.**

Devi uscire con i tuoi amici?   *Have you got to go out with your friends?*

11 Bere   *to drink*

Here is the present tense of the irregular verb **bere** *to drink*. The only irregularity is the stem: **bev-**. Otherwise it is conjugated like any other **-ere** verb:

bevo, bevi, beve, beviamo, bevete, bevono

12 Rilassarmi   *to relax (myself)*

As we have seen on p. 145, reflexive verbs add **-si** at the end of the infinitive after taking away the final vowel: **divertirsi** *to enjoy oneself* = **divertire** + **si**. Similarly, **-mi, -ti, -ci, -vi** can be added to the end of the infinitive: **divertirmi, divertirti, divertirci, divertirvi**. This is often seen with **potere, volere, dovere**, where there is a choice:

Devo lavarmi or **Mi devo lavare.**   *I must/have to wash (myself).*
Dobbiamo divertirci or   *We must enjoy ourselves.*
  Ci dobbiamo divertire.

Come si dice in italiano?

1	ask about and say what sports you do	**Che sport fa? Il nuoto, lo sci, il tennis, il jogging.**
2	ask about and say how many times a day, a week, a month, etc.	**Quante volte al giorno, alla settimana, al mese ... ? Una volta, due volte al/alla ...**

3	ask about and describe the weather	**Che tempo fa? Fa bel tempo, fa brutto tempo, c'è il sole, piove, ecc.**
4	talk about your daily routine	**La mattina mi sveglio, mi alzo … mi vesto … faccio colazione …**
5	put a relationship on a more informal footing	**Diamoci del tu!**

Attività

1 Che cosa fa? La giornata di Pietro   *Peter's day*
(See overleaf.)

Describe what **Pietro** does in each of the pictures on page 149, using each verb in this list once: **andare a letto, alzarsi, cenare, far(e) colazione, guardare la televisione, lavarsi, leggere il giornale, svegliarsi, tornare a casa, uscire di casa** and give the times.

2   Continue these sentences, using the same verb as in the first part, but in the first person, as in the example:

Esempio: Il mio amico si chiama Roberto, ma io ____ Gianni.
**   Il mio amico si chiama Roberto, ma io mi chiamo**
**   Gianni.**

(a)   Cesare si riposa la domenica, ma io ____ il sabato.
(b)   Lui si diverte a sciare, ma io ____ a nuotare.
(c)   Giovanni si sveglia alle otto meno un quarto, ma io ____ alle sette.
(d)   Cesare si alza alle otto, ma io ____ alle nove.
(e)   Ugo si lava nel bagno, ma io ____ in cucina.
(f)   Francesca si veste nella camera da letto, ma io ____ nel bagno.
(g)   Gl'italiani si riposano dopo pranzo, ma noi non ____ di pomeriggio.

3 Alzarsi, svegliarsi, ecc.

Gino, who is described here, has Bohemian habits:

Gino non *si sveglia* mai prima delle otto. Non *si alza* mai presto. Non *si lava* mai con l'acqua fredda. Non *si veste* mai prima di mezzogiorno.

Imagine you are **Gino** and describe yourself: **Non mi sveglio mai, ecc.**

4   Here is a list of reflexive verbs in the infinitive: **alzarsi** to get up; **cambiarsi** to get changed; **divertirsi** to enjoy oneself; **lagnarsi** to complain; **riposarsi** to rest; **ubriacarsi** to get drunk. Select each of them once to complete the following sentences. Make sure that you use the same person of the verb as in the first part of the sentence.

(a)   Se siamo stanchi, ____
(b)   Se non vogliamo andare a teatro con lo stesso vestito, ____
(c)   Se sono a letto e devo uscire, ____
(d)   Se bevo troppo vino, ____
(e)   Se vado a una festa, ____
(f)   Quando il servizio non è buono, (io) ____

5   **Rosa** and **Isa** have habits verging on delinquency. Column 1 shows what they always do (**sempre**) and Column 2 shows what they never

do (**non … mai**). Make sentences from each pair of words, starting like this: **Si alzano sempre tardi e non fanno mai colazione.** Note that **sempre** and **mai** go immediately after the verb.

sempre	non … mai
alzarsi tardi	fare colazione
giocare a carte	lavorare
uscire	studiare
guardare la televisione	leggere
parlare	ascoltare
prendere l'autobus	andare a piedi
cominciare	finire

6 Read the following passage about **Olga**, looking up any words you don't know. Then answer the questions on it using **lo, la, li, le** or **l'** (object pronouns).

Ogni mattina Olga prende un cappuccino al bar. Poi passa per la salumeria e prende un po' di mortadella e di salame per il pranzo. Al ritorno va prima in panetteria e compra sei panini e infine passa per l'edicola per prendere il giornale e aspettare la sua amica.

(a) Dove prende Olga il cappuccino?

(b) Dove prende la mortadella?

(c) Dove compra i panini?

(d) Dove compra il giornale?

(e) Dove aspetta la sua amica?

7 Che tempo fa?

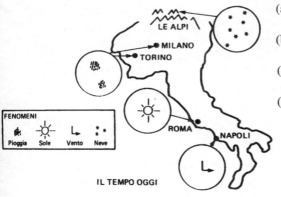

(a) Che tempo fa sulle Alpi?

(b) Che tempo fa a Milano e a Torino?

(c) Che tempo fa a Roma?

(d) Che tempo fa a Napoli?

8   **Ora tocca a te!** Here, you are a journalist interviewing **Pina**, owner
     of a restaurant.

You   *But don't you ever rest, Madam?*
Pina   Beh, con un ristorante è difficile riposarsi. La sera andiamo
           a letto molto tardi, e la mattina ci alziamo molto presto.
You   *How many hours a day do you work?*
Pina   Dieci, dodici, qualche volta anche quattordici ore.
You   *You work hard!*
Pina   Ma mi riposo durante le vacanze.
You   *How many times a year do you go on holiday?*
Pina   Due volte.
You   *When? In summer?*
Pina   No. D'estate è impossibile. Abbiamo troppi clienti. Andiamo
           in primavera e in autunno.
You   *Where do you go?*
Pina   Vado in Svizzera con mia figlia. Andiamo a sciare.
You   *Do you like skiing?*
Pina   Sì, molto. Lo sci è il mio sport preferito.

✳ Informazioni

1 La laurea   *university degree*

Most Italian students live at home: they go to the nearest university.
Laurearsi is to get one's degree and **un laureato/una laureata** are,
respectively, *a male graduate* and *a female graduate*. Italian universities
are open to all who have passed their final secondary school exams. Each
student receives **il libretto**, a document which combines a student
identity card with a record of all exams taken. It entitles the student to use
the university library (**biblioteca**) and refectory (**mensa**). Normal degree
courses last four years, but one or two, such as Engineering and Medicine,
take longer. Although graduates may take more than the stipulated time to
complete their courses, they have to pay **la tassa di fuoricorso** (a special
supplement) to do so.

All graduates are entitled to be called **dottore: dottore in legge** *Doctor
of Law*, **dottore in medicina, ecc.** *Doctor of Medicine, etc.*

2 Lo sport

COSA FANNO?

a)

b)

c)

d)

e)

f)

14 | VORREI UN'INFORMAZIONE
I'd like some information

In this Unit you will learn how to:

■ ask and give directions
■ ask how frequent the buses are
■ obtain what you need in a post office
■ follow instructions

Dialogo 1 Come si fa per andare a ...? *How do you get to ...?*

Il signor Pozzi is enquiring about the way to the central post office. He asks to go to **Via Garibaldi** and is told to go straight ahead. However...

(a) **Vero o falso?** La Posta Centrale è in Via Garibaldi.

Sig. Pozzi	Scusi, sa dov'è Via Garibaldi?
Passante	Certo, signore. Vada sempre dritto. In fondo a questa strada giri a destra. Che numero cerca?
Sig. Pozzi	Il 122.
Passante	Ah, no. Il numero 122 non esiste. Dove deve andare?
Sig. Pozzi	Alla Posta Centrale.
Passante	Ma la Posta Centrale è in Piazza Garibaldi. Prenda l'autobus fino a Via Roma e poi cambi.

in fondo a	*at the end of*	**fino a**	*up to*
girare	*to turn*	**esistere**	*to exist*

(b) Il signor Pozzi parla con un amico?

Dialogo 2 Ogni quanto tempo passano gli autobus? *How often do the buses pass?*

The passer-by now tells him how to reach the 48 bus stop.

(a) **Vero o falso?** La fermata del 48 è dopo la stazione.

Sig. Pozzi	Ogni quanto tempo passano gli autobus?
Passante	Per Via Roma ogni dieci minuti circa.
Sig. Pozzi	E che numero devo prendere?
Passante	Il 48. Vada fino all'incrocio. Per attraversare la strada passi per il sottopassaggio. La fermata è dopo il ponte.
Sig. Pozzi	Ho capito. E poi come si fa per andare a Piazza Garibaldi?
Passante	È semplice. A Via Roma prenda il 56 e scenda al capolinea. La posta è a pochi passi dall' ultima fermata.
Sig. Pozzi	Molto gentile, grazie.
Passante	Prego, per carità!

Ogni quanto tempo ...?	*How often ...?*	**sottopassaggio**	*underpass*
		semplice	*simple*
incrocio	*crossroads*	**il capolinea**	*terminus*
attraversare	*to cross*	**per carità**	*not at all!*

(b) Cosa deve fare il signor Pozzi al capolinea?

Dialogo 3 Alla posta *At the post office*

At the post office **il Sig. Pozzi** first asks for a telegram form.

(a) **Vero o falso?** Il sig. Pozzi deve andare allo sportello Nº 3 per fare il telegramma.

Sig. Pozzi	Un modulo per telegramma, per favore.
Impiegata	Per i telegrammi deve andare allo sportello Nº 3. Desidera altro?
Sig. Pozzi	Devo fare una raccomandata e un vaglia.
Impiegata	Sì. Scriva nome, cognome e indirizzo del mittente dietro la busta. Vuole la penna?
Sig. Pozzi	No, grazie. Ce l'ho.

modulo	*form*	**mittente** (m.)	*sender*
lo sportello	*counter/window*	**busta**	*envelope*
raccomandata	*registered letter*	**penna**	*pen*
vaglia (m.)	*postal order*		

(b) Che cosa deve scrivere il sig. Pozzi dietro la busta della raccomandata?

🔊 Dialogo 4 Faccia presto! *Be quick!*

(a) **Vero o falso?** La Posta Centrale apre alle due.

Sig. Pozzi	Ecco fatto! Va bene così?
Impiegata	Sì. Così va bene. Ecco il resto, signore … e questa è la ricevuta.
Sig. Pozzi	E per il pacco?
Impiegata	Sportello N⁰ 9. Vuole spedirlo oggi? Faccia presto, perchè chiude alle 14.00.
Sig. Pozzi	Dov'è la buca delle lettere, per cortesia?
Impiegata	Eccola! Là in fondo. È per le sue cartoline? Non è necessario imbucarle. Può lasciarle a me.
Sig. Pozzi	Grazie mille.
Impiegata	Prego.

Ecco fatto!	*There you are!*	**spedire**	*to send, dispatch*
ricevuta	*receipt*	**buca delle lettere**	*letter-box*
pacco	*parcel*	**imbucare**	*to post (in a box)*

(b) Qual è l'ultima cosa che il sig. Pozzi vuol sapere dall'impiegata?

Spiegazioni

1 L'imperativo *imperative* **lei** *form*

Scusi, **vada**, **prenda** and **giri** are the imperative (**lei** forms) of **scusare**, **andare**, **prendere** and **girare**, and are used when telling someone to do something.

Regular **-are**, **-ere** *and* **-ire** *verbs*

To form the imperative (**lei** form) take off the **-are**, **-ere** and **-ire** endings of the infinitive and add the following endings:

-are add **-i**		
Infinitive	*Imperative* (**lei**)	
aspett -are	aspett**i**!	*wait!*
guard -are	guard**i**!	*look!*
attravers -are	attravers**i**!	*cross!*

For verbs ending in **-iare** (as with the **tu** form p. 34) do not double the final **-i**: **Cambi! Mangi! Cominci!**

-ere and **-ire** add **-a**		
prend -ere	prend**a**!	*take!*
scriv -ere	scriv**a**!	*write!*
scend -ere	scend**a**!	*get off!*
apr -ire	apr**a**!	*open!*
sent -ire	sent**a**!	*listen!*

Aspetti alla fermata dell'autobus!   *Wait at the bus stop.*
Scriva il suo nome e cognome!   *Write your first name and surname.*
Apra la porta e chiuda la   *Open the door and close the*
  finestra, per favore!   *window, please.*

To form the negative put **non** before the verb:

Non passi di qua! È pericoloso!   *Don't go this way. It's dangerous.*
Non attraversi qui!   *Don't cross here.*

2 Object pronouns with the imperative lei form

Object pronouns precede the verb in the imperative (**lei** form):

La casa è bella: *la* compri!   *The house is nice: buy it!*
Il vino è ottimo: *l'*assaggi!   *The wine is excellent: taste it!*

3 Imperative lei irregular forms

The stem for the imperative **lei** irregular form is obtained from the first person singular of the present tense. Change the **-o** ending (from the first person singular) into **-a**.

Infinitive		*1st person singular present*	*Imperative*
dire	*to say*	**dico**	**dica!**
andare	*to go*	**vado**	**vada!**
spegnere	*to turn/switch off*	**spengo**	**spenga!**
finire	*to finish*	**finisco**	**finisca!**
leggere	*to read*	**leggo**	**legga!**
salire	*to get on, to go upstairs*	**salgo**	**salga!**

Ora tocca a te! Write down the imperative (**lei**) form of these irregular verbs (you have met the present tense of all of them in previous units): **bere**, **fare**, **pulire** *to clean* (like **capire**), **uscire**, **venire**.

4 *Imperative of* noi *and* voi *forms*

The first person plural of the imperative (*let us*) is exactly the same as the first person plural (**noi**) of the present tense (Unit 7, p 79):

Usciamo stasera?	*Are we going out tonight?*
Sì. *Usciamo!*	*Yes. Let's (go out).*
Vediamo un po'!	*Let's have a look.*

The **voi** (*you* plural) form is also the same as the present tense:

Aspettate alla fermata del pullman!	*Wait at the coach stop.*
Prendete un gelato!	*Have an ice cream.*
Venite con me!	*Come with me.*

5 Telegramma, telegrammi

Like **il cinema** in Unit 6, p 67 **il telegramma** is masculine. In fact, all nouns ending in **-ma** are masculine except for (**la**) **mamma** *mummy*. Their plurals end in **-i**:

Vuol fare due telegrammi? *Do you want to send (Lit. make) two telegrams?*

Likewise: **il programma** *programme* beomes **i programmi**; **il tema** *theme* becomes **i temi**; **il sistema** *system* becomes **i sistemi**; **il problema** *the problem* becomes **i problemi**.

Ci sono **molti problemi sociali e politici**. *There are many social and political problems.*

Il cinema, however, does not change in the plural: **i cinema**.

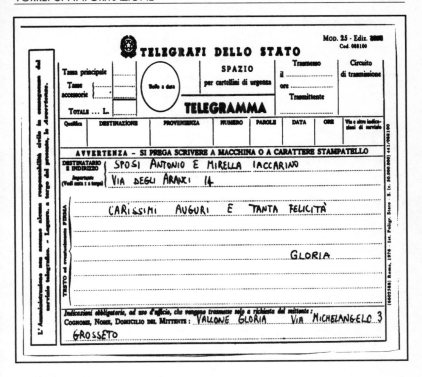

(a) Why was this telegram sent?
(b) Where does the sender live?

6 Ce l'ho   *I've got it*

When someone asks you whether you have something or not, the question is **Ce l'ha?** *Have you got it?* When you want to answer *I have/haven't got it*, you use (**Non**) **ce l'ho**. **Ce** has no meaning.

Ha il mio indirizzo?	*Have you got my address?*
Sì. *Ce l'ho.*	*Yes, I have (got it).*
Paolo ha il dizionario?	*Has Paul got the dictionary?*
No. *Non ce l'ha.*	*No, he hasn't (got it).*

7 Irregular verbs

Present tense	
salire *to go up, get on*	**togliere** *to take off*
salgo	tolgo
sali	togli
sale	toglie
saliamo	togliamo
salite	togliete
salgono	tolgono

Come si dice in italiano?

How to:

1 ask directions   **Sa dov'è ...?/Come si fa**
                                         per andare ...?

   give directions   **Vada/giri/prenda/continui ...**

2 ask and say how frequent the   **Ogni quanto tempo passano gli**
   buses are   **autobus? Passano ogni ...**

3 obtain what you need in a   **Sportello N⁰ ... Un modulo ...**
   post office

4 understand and follow instructions. **Scriva nome, cognome, indirizzo...**

Attività

In these **attività** use the **lei** form of the imperative.

1 Form questions about how to get to the places in the plan overleaf
   and answer them, using the example as a model.

   Esempio: (a) Come si fa per andare alla piscina? Prenda la prima
   traversa a sinistra.

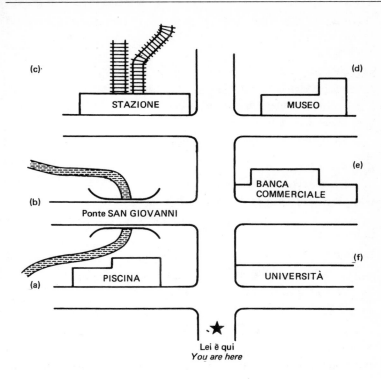

2 What are the instructions on these road signs?

   (a) **girare**   (b) **andare**   (c) **girare**

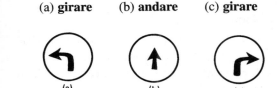

3 Read this text, then give the directions. Start: **Per andare al Duomo prenda …**

   Per andare al Duomo si deve prendere la prima strada a destra e andare sempre dritto fino a Via Firenze. In fondo a Via Firenze si deve girare a sinistra, scendere giù per Via Nazionale, e attraversare il ponte San Giovanni. Dopo il ponte si deve prendere la seconda traversa che è Via Veneto. In fondo a Via Veneto c'è una piazza: il Duomo è lì.

4   Tell someone to do what is being asked. (You are given the place.)

Esempio: Dove devo parcheggiare?   (in piazza)

**   Parcheggi in piazza!**

(a)   Dove devo aspettare?   (alla stazione)
(b)   Dove devo prenotare?   (all'agenzia)
(c)   Dove devo leggere?   (qui)
(d)   Dove devo pulire?   (dappertutto)
(e)   Dove devo venire?   (a casa)
(f)   Dove devo pagare?   (alla cassa)

5   Someone is asking permission to do something. You urge them to do it, using the object pronoun + imperative.

Esempio: Posso mangiare questi spaghetti?

**   Sì, sì. Li mangi!**

(a)   Posso mangiare queste lasagne?
(b)   Posso bere questo vino?
(c)   Posso aprire la finestra?
(d)   Posso fare i biglietti?
(e)   Posso prendere la sua macchina?
(f)   Posso prenotare l'albergo?

 6   On the next page is a plan of part of the centre of **Trento** *Trent*, a town in the mountainous **Dolomiti** *Dolomite* region of Northern Italy. You are going to hear three sets of instructions given to three different people. Each one is starting from **Piazza Duomo**, where the cross is, facing **Fontana del Nettuno** ① *the Fountain of Neptune,* and is asking how to get to a different place. As you hear the directions given to each person, follow them on the map and find out where each one wants to go.

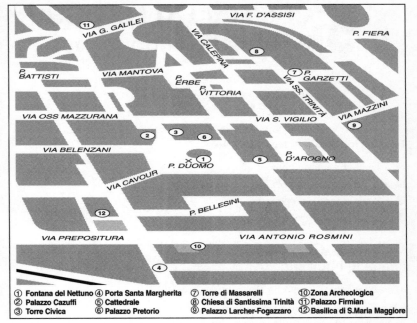

① Fontana del Nettuno ④ Porta Santa Margherita ⑦ Torre di Massarelli ⑩ Zona Archeologica
② Palazzo Cazuffi ⑤ Cattedrale ⑧ Chiesa di Santissima Trinità ⑪ Palazzo Firmian
③ Torre Civica ⑥ Palazzo Pretorio ⑨ Palazzo Larcher-Fogazzaro ⑫ Basilica di S.Maria Maggiore

(a) Vada verso Palazzo Cazuffi che è a sinistra e Torre Civica che è a destra. Subito dopo la torre giri a destra. Prenda la prima traversa a sinistra. Dopo pochi passi, a destra, trova la piazza che cerca.

(b) Vada in Via Cavour. Prenda la prima strada a sinistra e continui fino all'incrocio di Via Prepositura e Via Antonio Rosmini. Il monumento che vuole è davanti a lei.

(c) Attraversi la piazza. Dopo Torre Civica giri a destra e vada fino in fondo a Via San Vigilio. Poi giri a sinistra e continui lungo Via Santissima Trinità. In fondo alla strada c'è la chiesa che cerca.

✳ Informazioni

I beni culturali *the cultural heritage* is the responsibility of a special ministry: **Il Ministero dei Beni Ambientali e Culturali**. Italians take very great pride in their monuments and it is rare to find a town which does not have some work of art or architecture to display. **Trento** is an excellent example of a historically important town.

15 | COS'HAI FATTO OGGI?
What did you do today?

In this Unit you will learn how to:

■ ask what someone has done or did
■ ask someone to report information
■ ask what (has) happened
■ answer similar questions

Dialogo 1 Cos' hai fatto di bello?   *Have you done anything interesting?*

a) **Vero o falso?** Elena ha mangiato a casa.

Elena   Hai dormito fino a tardi oggi?
Fabrizio Eh, sì, perchè stanotte ho dormito male.
Elena   Oh, mi dispiace!
Fabrizio Ma tu, cos'hai fatto di bello?
Elena   Nel pomeriggio ho fatto una bella passeggiata e stasera ho mangiato in una rosticceria con il mio ragazzo.
Fabrizio Avete mangiato bene?
Elena   Benissimo! Ed abbiamo bevuto una bottiglia di Barbera.

hai dormito? (from **dormire**)
  did you sleep?
stanotte *last night*
male *badly*
fare una passeggiata   *to go for a walk*

ho mangiato (from **mangiare**)
  I ate
abbiamo bevuto (from **bere**)
  we drank

(b) Elena ha bevuto il vino, il liquore o l'acqua minerale?

Dialogo 2 Cos'hai fatto oggi? *What did you do today?*

A husband returns home late to find his sick wife worried but feeling better.

(a) **Vero o falso?** Il marito ha perso il treno.

Moglie Come mai così tardi? Cos'è successo?

Marito Non è successo niente. Scusa, cara. Ho perso l'autobus. Ho dovuto aspettare venti minuti alla fermata. Tu, piuttosto, come ti senti?

Moglie Adesso sto meglio, grazie.

Marito Cos'hai fatto oggi?

Moglie Ho dormito quasi tutto il giorno.

come mai...? *why, how is that?*	**ho perso** (from **perdere**) *I missed*
così tardi *so late*	**Come ti senti?** *How do you feel?*
Cos'è successo? (from **succedere**) *What's happened?*	**sto meglio** *I'm better*
	quasi *almost*

(b) La moglie sta bene adesso?

Dialogo 3 Che cosa ti ha detto? *What did he tell you?*

She tells her husband what the doctor said: she needs a little rest.

(a) **Vero o falso?** La moglie ha chiamato il medico.

Marito Hai visto il medico?

Moglie Sì. L'ho chiamato stamattina.

Marito E che cosa ti ha detto?

Moglie Ha detto che ho bisogno soltanto di un po' di riposo. Nulla di grave.

Marito Meno male! Ti ha dato delle medicine?

Moglie No. Non mi ha dato niente.

Hai visto (from **vedere**) **il medico?** *Did you see the doctor?*	**ho bisogno ... di** *I need*
	soltanto *only*
l'ho chiamato (from **chiamare**) *I called him*	**nulla di grave** *nothing serious*
	Ti ha dato ...? *Did he give you ...?*
stamattina *this morning*	**meno male!** *thank goodness!*

b) Il medico ha visitato il marito?

◎ Spiegazioni

1 *Perfect tense*

In Italian the perfect tense is used to express something that happened or has happened in the past. It is formed by using the present tense of **essere** or **avere** + past participle. In this Unit we shall deal with those verbs which form their perfect tense with **avere**. These constitute most verbs in Italian.

Formation of past participle

To form the past participle of regular verbs, change the infinitive endings as follows:

Infinitive			Infinitive	Past participle	
-are	into	**-ato:**	**parlare**	**parlato**	*spoken*
-ere	into	**-uto:**	**vendere**	**venduto**	*sold*
-ire	into	**-ito:**	**finire**	**finito**	*finished*

Ho parlato $\begin{cases} I \ spoke \\ \\ I \ have \ spoken \end{cases}$ **Ho venduto** $\begin{cases} I \ sold \\ \\ I \ have \ sold \end{cases}$ **Ho finito** $\begin{cases} I \ finished \\ \\ I \ have \ finished \end{cases}$

Note in the table below that the last vowel of the past participle does not change: **ho parlato** *I spoke/I have spoken*, **ho dormito** *I slept/I have slept*, **abbiamo parlato** *we spoke/we have spoken*, **abbiamo**, **dormito** *we slept/we have slept*.

Perfect tense		**parl -are**	*to speak*
(io)	**ho**	**parlato**	*I spoke, I have spoken*
(tu)	**hai**	**parlato**	*you spoke, you have spoken*
(lei)	**ha**	**parlato**	*you (formal), spoke, you have spoken*
(lui, lei)	**ha**	**parlato**	*he/she spoke, he/she has spoken*
(noi)	**abbiamo**	**parlato**	*we spoke, we have spoken*
(voi)	**avete**	**parlato**	*you spoke, you have spoken*
(loro)	**hanno**	**parlato**	*they spoke, they have spoken*

Perfect tense		vend -ere	to sell
(io)	**ho**	**vend*uto***	I sold, I have sold
(tu)	**hai**	**vend*uto***	you sold, you have sold
(lei)	**ha**	**vend*uto***	you (formal) sold, you have sold
(lui, lei)	**ha**	**vend*uto***	he/she sold he/she has sold
(noi)	**abbiamo**	**vend*uto***	we sold, we have sold
(voi)	**avete**	**vend*uto***	you sold, you have sold
(loro)	**hanno**	**vend*uto***	they sold, they have sold

Perfect tense		fin -ire	to finish
(io)	**ho**	**fin*ito***	I finished, I have finished
(tu)	**hai**	**fin*ito***	you finished, you have finished
(lei)	**ha**	**fin*ito***	you (formal) finished, you have finished
(lui, lei)	**ha**	**fin*ito***	he/she finished, he/she has finished
(noi)	**abbiamo**	**fin*ito***	we finished, we have finished
(voi)	**avete**	**fin*ito***	you finished, you have finished
(loro)	**hanno**	**fin*ito***	they finished, they have finished

Whereas in English we can say *I spoke, I have spoken, I did speak*, in Italian you **must** use the present tense of **avere** and say **ho parlato, hai parlato, ecc.** – that is, you must say *I have spoken, I have eaten* and **not** *I spoke, I ate, etc.*

Hai venduto la macchina?	*Did you sell/have you sold your car?*
Hai dimenticato la chiave?	*Did you forget/have you forgotten your key?*
Non ho potuto venire.	*I couldn't/I haven't been able to come.*
Ho dovuto lavorare.	*I had to/I've had to work.*
Ho venduto la casa.	*I sold/I have sold the house.*

Irregular past participles

Here is a list of some of those most frequently used:

Infinitive		Past participle		Infinitive		Past participle	
accendere	to light	**acceso**	lit	**mettere**	to put	**messo**	put
aprire	to open	**aperto**	opened	**perdere**	to lose, miss	**perso**	lost
bere	to drink	**bevuto**	drunk	**prendere**	to take	**preso**	taken
chiedere	to ask	**chiesto**	asked	**rispondere**	to reply	**risposto**	replied
chiudere	to close	**chiuso**	closed	**rompere**	to break	**rotto**	broken
dire	to say, tell	**detto**	said, told	**scrivere**	to write	**scritto**	written
fare	to do, make	**fatto**	made, done	**togliere**	to take off	**tolto**	taken off
leggere	to read	**letto**	read	**vedere**	to see	**visto**	seen

Cos'ha detto?	*What did you say?*
Ho visto Mirella.	*I saw Mirella.*

Initially, your most important task is to be able to recognise some of these past participles. When you need to use any of them, consult the table.

2 Con il mio ragazzo   *with my boyfriend*

Notice that **ragazzo**, apart from meaning *boy*, means *boyfriend*. Similarly, **la mia ragazza** is *my girlfriend*.

3 Aver bisogno di   *to need*

Need or necessity is expressed by **aver bisogno di** (Lit. *to have need of*)

Ho bisogno soltanto di un po' di riposo.	*I only need a bit of rest.*
Siamo contenti così. Non abbiamo bisogno di niente.	*We are happy as we are. We don't need anything.*

4 *The perfect tense with some expressions of time*

You will find the expressions below useful when you are talking about the past:

L'ho visto	**ieri** **l'altro ieri***	**mattina pomeriggio sera**	*I saw him*	*yesterday* *the day before yesterday*	*morning afternoon evening*
	la settimana scorsa il mese scorso l'anno scorso			*last week last month last year*	
	molto tempo poco tempo pochi giorni alcune settimane cinque minuti	**fa**		*a long time a short while a few days some weeks five minutes*	*ago*

* It is possible to say **l'altro ieri mattina/pomeriggio/sera** for *the day before yesterday in the/morning/afternoon/evening*.

5 Stanotte

This word means *last night* or *tonight*, depending on the context. If the verb is in the past **stanotte** must be *last night*:

Stanotte non ho chiuso occhio.   *Last night I didn't sleep a wink.*

6 Non mi ha dato niente *He didn't give me anything*

Mi, **ti**, **ci**, **vi** are also object pronouns. Besides meaning *myself*, *yourself*, etc. (see Reflexive verbs, Unit 13, p 145), they mean *me*, *you*, *us*, and usually precede the verb:

Ida non	*mi* *ti* *ci* *vi*	**capisce**	*Ida doesn't understand*	*me.* *you* (informal). *us.* *you* (pl).

When object pronouns precede the verb they are called unstressed pronouns.

When pronouns are used with prepositions (*con* **me**, *da* **te, ecc.**) they are called stressed pronouns.

7 Sto meglio *I'm better*

Notice these expressions with **stare** describing one's state of health:

Come sta? (Sto) ⎰ bene ⎱ *How are you? (I'm)* ⎰ well ⎱
⎰ male ⎱   ⎰ ill ⎱
⎰ meglio ⎱   ⎰ better ⎱
⎰ peggio ⎱   ⎰ worse ⎱

The present tense of **stare** is exactly like that of **dare** (Unit 8, p. 91):

sto   stai   sta   stiamo   state   stanno

Attenzione! stare *in* **piedi** *to stand* but **andare** *a* **piedi** (see p. 59).

8 Ha detto che ... *He said that ...*

Che *that, which, who, whom*. In English it can sometimes be omitted. In Italian it must always be expressed:

Questo è il libro *che* **devo comprare.** *This is the book (that) I have to buy.*

So *che* **non è vero.** *I know (that) it isn't true.*

La ragazza *che* **inviti è fidanzata.** *The girl (whom) you're inviting is engaged.*

Come si dice in italiano?

 How to:

1 ask someone what they have
    done or did
    say what you have done or did

**Cos'hai fatto? Ho dormito,
ho mangiato, ho bevuto, ho fatto
una passeggiata, ecc.**

2 ask someone to report information
    give the information

**Cosa ti ha detto?
(Mi) ha detto che...**

3 ask about what someone
    gave or has given you
    say what they gave you

**Cosa ti ha dato?
Mi ha dato ...**

4 ask what (has) happened

Cos'è successo?

✔ **Attività**

1 **A, B, C** and **D** are saying how they spent their evening. Can you fill in
   the gaps by listening to their accounts? (If you do not have the audio,
   you will find the verbs you need, jumbled up in the box below.)

A Ho _____ alla lettera di mio fratello che vive in America ed _____
   in ordine la mia camera.

B _____ degli amici a casa. _____ insieme, poi abbiamo _____ tutta
   la notte.

C Io e il mio ragazzo _____ un programma molto interessante in
   televisione.

D Mio cugino mi _____ da Milano. _____ un'ora al telefono a parlare
   con lui e con mio nipote.

**abbiamo visto - ho passato - ha chiamato - abbiamo bevuto -
risposto - ho messo - ho invitato - giocato a bridge**

---

2 Match the words on the right with those on the left:

   (i)   Hai letto   (a) la telefonata?
   (ii) Ho dormito   (b) un sacco di soldi.
   (iii) Hai risposto   (c) il gas?
   (iv) Hai fatto   (d) molto bene.
   (v)   Ho rotto   (e) alle sue domande?
   (vi) Hai spento   (f) l'affitto.

(vii)	Ha pagato	(g)	il giornale?
(viii)	Ho speso	(h)	il bicchiere.

3 In the following sentences fill the blanks, choosing between **mi** and **ti** according to the sense. Be careful to distinguish between verbs in the first person, and those in the second person (informal).

(a) Dove sei? Non _____ vedo.

(b) Cosa dici? Non _____ sento.

(c) Scusa, chi sei? Non _____ conosco.

(d) Sono qui. Non _____ vedi?

(e) Come? Non _____ capisco.

(f) Quando _____ inviti a cena?

(g) Allora, _____ accompagni?

(h) Va bene. _____ aspetto davanti al teatro.

4 Below are extracts from postcards you have received from friends in Italy. Tell someone you know what each of them has been doing. For instance, (a) would start: **Vittoria ha …**

(a)

.... Ieri ho visto
il Papa in
Piazza San
Pietro....
Saluti da Roma
        Vittoria

(b)

Firenze
... Ho comprato una
villa fra Siena e
Firenze ...
Un caro saluto
        Gino

(c)

Viareggio
...Finalmente ho aperto
un'agenzia immobiliare! ...
Quando vieni in Italia?
Roberto

(d)

Diano Marina
......Abbiamo
fatto molti
bagni...
Un abbraccio
Renzo e Mara

(e)

Sanremo
......Abbiamo
giocato alla
roulette e abbiamo
perso......
A presto!
Ada e Lino

(f)

Verona
......Ieri sera abbiamo
visto l'Aida.
Stupenda!......
Molti baci
Federico e Anna

(g)

```
Venezia
......Abbiamo preso la
gondola tutti i
giorni......
Bacioni e abbracci
        Sandro e Carla
```

5 **Ora tocca a te!** Write your own card from **Bari**:

'I've seen so many interesting things. Greetings from Bari.'

6 Below you will see what **Mara** decided to do last Monday. However, she only managed to do the things that are ticked. A cross means that she never got round to doing them. Say in Italian what she did and didn't do.

(a) pranzare dai suoi genitori ✓

(b) chiamare l'elettricista ✗

(c) guardare il programma 'TV 7 Speciale' ✓

(d) pulire la casa ✗

(e) pagare l'affitto ✗

(f) giocare a tennis con Marco ✓

(g) portare la macchina dal meccanico ✓

(h) scrivere una cartolina a sua zia Maria ✓

7 **Ora tocca a te!**

You   *Did you do anything interesting today?*

Olga   Ho lavorato tutto il giorno.

You   *Didn't you see your boyfriend?*

Olga   Sì. All'ora di pranzo.

You   *Did you eat together?*

Olga   Sì. In una elegante trattoria in Via Manzoni.

You   *So why aren't you happy?*

Olga   Perchè ho dovuto pagare io per il pranzo.

✳ Informazioni

1   When Italians send postcards they usually write two or three words only, or simply a greeting, some examples of which are given here.

Affettuosi saluti - Un caro pensiero - Un forte abbraccio - Un bacione

They are most unlikely to mention the weather.

2   **Barbera** is a dry red wine from the Piedmont and Lombardy regions in Northern Italy. Other reds include **Bardolino** and **Valpolicella** from the Veneto region, and **Chianti** from Tuscany. **Frascati** from Rome, **Soave** from **Veneto** and **Orvieto** from **Umbria** are among the better-known white wines. It should be borne in mind that wine, which is relatively cheap and plentiful in Italy, and bread, are essential components of any family meal.

16 LE PIACE VIAGGIARE?
Do you like travelling?

In this Unit you will learn how to:

■ ask someone whether they have (ever) been to …
■ say where you have lived, worked and were born
■ say how long ago
■ say how long you have been doing something

Dialogo 1 Quando è venuto in Inghilterra? *When did you come to England?*

An interview with an Italian immigrant who came to England 20 years ago.

(a) **Vero o falso?** L'immigrato ha lavorato prima a Londra.

Giornalista	Quando è venuto in Inghilterra?
Immigrato	Venti anni fa.
Giornalista	È vissuto sempre a Londra?
Immigrato	No. Quando sono arrivato, sono andato a lavorare a Bedford.
Giornalista	Si trova bene in Inghilterra?
Immigrato	Abbastanza bene. Ma ogni tanto sento la nostalgia dell'Italia.
Giornalista	Quanto tempo è rimasto a Bedford?
Immigrato	Tre anni. Dopo sono venuto ad abitare a Londra.

È vissuto ...? (from **vivere**) *Have you lived ...?*
trovarsi bene *to be happy*
abbastanza *fairly*

ogni tanto *every now and then*
sento la nostalgia *I feel homesick*
è rimasto ...? (from **rimanere**) *did you stay ...?*

(b) Dov'è andato ad abitare dopo tre anni?

Dialogo 2 Le è piaciuta l'Italia?   *Did she like Italy?*

The immigrant is asked whether he has ever returned to his birthplace.

(a) **Vero o falso?** L'immigrato è tornato in Italia molte volte.

Giornalista	È mai tornato nel suo paese nativo?
Immigrato	Sì. Ci sono tornato con mia moglie molte volte.
Giornalista	Sua moglie è italiana?
Immigrato	È di origine italiana, ma è nata a Liverpool.
Giornalista	Le è piaciuta l'Italia?
Immigrato	Sì. Le è piaciuta molto. Infatti speriamo di ritornarci quest'anno.

paese nativo	*birthplace*	**sperare di**	*to hope to*

(b) Dove spera di ritornare con sua moglie?

Dialogo 3 Incontro in Sicilia   *Meeting in Sicily*

Sandro is surprised to meet his friend **Marcello** in Sicily.

(a) **Vero o falso?** Sandro è in Sicilia da una settimana.

Sandro	Chi si vede! Che sorpresa!
Marcello	Ciao, Sandro! Da quanto tempo sei qui?
Sandro	Da una settimana. E tu?
Marcello	Sono appena arrivato. Sono partito stamattina col treno delle 10.40 (dieci e quaranta) e sono arrivato un'ora fa.
Sandro	È la prima volta che vieni in Sicilia?
Marcello	No. Ci sono venuto nel '97.
Sandro	Ti piace di più Agrigento o Siracusa?
Marcello	Non sono mai stato nè ad Agrigento, nè a Siracusa.

Chi si vede! *Look who's here!*		**non sono mai stato nè ... nè ...**	
Da quanto tempo sei qui? *How long have you been here?*		*I've never been either to ... or ...*	

(b) Con quale treno è partito Marcello?

Dialogo 4 Sei mai stato in Sardegna? *Have you ever been to Sardinia?*

Sandro wants to offer **Marcello** a coffee but his friend has to dash off.

(a) **Vero o falso?** Marcello non è mai stato in Sardegna.

Sandro   ... E la Sardegna? Sei mai stato in Sardegna?
Marcello   Purtroppo no. Lo so che c'è tanto da vedere anche lì.
Sandro   Posso offrirti un caffè?
Marcello   No, grazie. Devo scappare.
Sandro   Così presto?
Marcello   Purtroppo sì. Mi dispiace.
Sandro   Allora ti accompagno.

(b) Perchè Marcello non accetta il caffè?

purtroppo	*unfortunately*	**così presto**	*so soon*
tanto da vedere	*so much to see*	**accompagnare**	*to accompany*

Spiegazioni

1 *Perfect tense (continued)*

In this Unit we shall deal with verbs that form their perfect tense with **essere** – that is, most intransitive verbs, all reflexive verbs, and the verb **essere** itself. To form the perfect tense use the present tense of **essere** (**sono, sei, è, siamo, siete, sono**) and the past participle (Unit 15, p 166–7), which must be treated as an adjective: it must agree with the subject.

Sono tornato.	*I have returned (m.s.)*
Sono tornata.	*I have returned (f.s.)*
Siamo tornati.	*We have returned (m.pl.)*
Siamo tornate.	*We have returned (f.pl.)*
Roberto *è* and*ato* in Italia.	*Robert went/has gone to Italy.*
Lucia *è* and*ata* negli Stati Uniti.	*Lucia went/has gone to the United States.*
I signori Cortese *sono* and*ati* all'estero.	*Mr and Mrs Cortese went/have gone abroad.*
Le ragazze sono and*ate* a scuola.	*The girls went/have gone to school.*

Id*a* non è and*ata* in Germania.   *Ida did not go/has not gone to Germany.*

The past participle of **essere** *to be* is **stato**. Here is the perfect tense:

(io)	sono stato/stata	I have been
(tu)	sei stato/stata	You have been
(lui/lei)	è stato/stata	He/she has, you have been
(noi)	siamo stati/state	We have been
(voi)	siete stati/state	You have been
(loro)	sono stati/state	They have been

Note that the past participles of **stare** and **essere** are the same: **stato**.

The most common verbs which form their perfect tense with **essere** are listed below:

Regular			
andare	to go	**sono andato/a**	I went, I have been
arrivare	to arrive	**sono arrivato/a**	I arrived, I have arrived
entrare	to enter	**sono entrato/a**	I entered, I have entered.
partire	to leave	**sono partito/a**	I left, I have left
tornare	to return	**sono tornato/a**	I returned, I have returned
uscire	to go out	**sono uscito/a**	I went out, I have gone out
Irregular			
essere	to be	**sono stato/a**	I have been
nascere	to be born	**sono nato/a**	I was born
rimanere	to stay, /remain	**sono rimasto/a**	I (have) stayed/remained
venire	to come	**sono venuto/a**	I came, I have come
vivere*	to live	**sono vissuto/a**	I live, I have lived

* **Vivere** also forms the perfect tense with **avere: ho vissuto**.

In future units, other verbs forming the perfect tense with **essere** will be shown with an asterisk as follows: **salire*** *to go up, to get on* (*a bus, train, etc.*)

Remember that when you have a masculine and feminine noun together (**Ugo e Maria**) the past participle must be **masculine plural**:

Ugo e Maria *sono* andati al cinema.   *Hugh and Mary have gone to the cinema.*

2 Venti anni fa   *Twenty years ago*

Fa expresses the idea of *ago* in English.

Il treno è partito cinque minuti *fa.*	*The train left five minutes ago.*
Siamo arrivati un'ora *fa.*	*We arrived an hour ago.*

3 Ci sono tornato...   *I returned there...*

Ci can mean *here, there, us.* The context will make it clear. It behaves like an unstressed pronoun: it comes before the verb or is attached to an infinitive. **Ci + è** is normally contracted to **c'è** (see Unit 6, p 69).

È mai stato a Firenze?	*Have you ever been to Florence?*
Sì. Ci sono stato diverse volte.	*Yes, I've been there several times.*
C'è stato il mese scorso.	*He was there last month.*
Spero di andarci l'anno prossimo.	*I hope to go there next year.*

4 È nata a...   *She was born in...*

When someone asks you where you were born, remember to answer with the present tense of **essere: Sono nato/a**   *I was born* (see Unit 5, p 60).

5 Le è piaciuta l'Italia?   *Did she like Italy?*

Note that **piacere**, when used impersonally (third person only) also forms its perfect with **essere** and behaves like an adjective:

Le *è* piaci*uto lo* spettacol*o*?	*Did you like the show?*
Le *è* piaci*uta la* most*ra*?	*Did you like the exhibition?*
Le *sono* piaci*uti i* quadr*i*?	*Did you like the pictures (i.e. paintings)?*
No. *Non mi sono piaciuti.*	*No, I didn't like them.*

6 Speriamo di ritornarci...   *We hope to return there...*

To hope to is expressed by **sperare di + infinitive** in Italian:

Spero di **rivederla al più presto.**	*I hope to see you again as soon as possible.*

7 Da quanto tempo sei qui?   *How long have you been here?*

Da quanto tempo requires the present tense when the activity continues into the present:

| *Da* quanto tempo *conosci* Marco? | *How long have you known Mark?* |
| *Lo conosco da* un anno. | *I have known him for a year.* |

| *Da* quanto tempo *studia* l'italiano? | *How long have you been studying Italian?* |
| *Studio* l'italiano *da* tre mesi. | *I've been studying Italian for three months.* |

8 Nel '98   *in '98*

In + definite article is used because **anno** *year* is understood. The '19' is often omitted in speech.

9 Ti piace di più ...?   *Do you prefer ...?*

Piacere di più can be used instead of **preferire**. **Di più** (*more* or *most*) is at the end of a phrase instead of **più**:

| La musica classica *mi piace di più*. | *I like classical music more.* |
| È quello che lavora *di più*. | *He is the one who works most.* |

10 Nè ... nè   *(n)either ... (n)or*

Note that this expression, like the ones in Unit 7, p 81, requires the double negative, unless **nè** comes at the beginning of the sentence:

Non vado *nè* a Firenze *nè* a Roma.	*I'm not going either to Florence or Rome.*
Non conosco *nè* lui *nè* lei.	*I know neither him nor her.*
Nè Carlo *nè* Pietro vanno all'università.	*Neither Charles nor Peter goes to university.*

In the last example note that Italian requires a verb in the plural.

11 Lo so che ...   *I know that ...*

Lo is used with **sapere** even when there is no definite object:

Dov'è Carlo? Non *lo so*.	*Where's Carlo? I don't know.*
Sai il mio indirizzo? Sì. *Lo so*.	*Do you know my address? Yes. I do (know it).*
Come *lo sai*?	*How do you know?*

12 Col treno   *by train*

Col = con + il. Coi = con + i. These contractions are optional:

Vado a Firenze col/con il direttore.	*I'm going to Florence with the director.*
Parlano *coi/con i* ragazzi.	*They are speaking to the boys.*

Con + article may be used with means of transport instead of **in**:

Ci vado *con l'*autobus/*con la* metropolitana.	*I'm going there by bus/by tube.*

Come si dice in italiano?

How to:

1	ask someone whether they have (ever) been to …	**È (mai) stato/a in Sardegna?**
		… a Roma?
	and say where you have been	**Sono stato/a in …/a …**
2	say where you (have) lived	**Ho vissuto/Sono vissuto/a …**
3	say where you were born	**Sono nato/a …**
4	say how long ago something happened	**due/dieci/venti anni fa**
5	say how long you have been (here)	**Sono (qui) da cinque minuti/da un'ora, ecc**.
	say how long you have been waiting	**Aspetto da mezz'ora, ecc.**

Attività

1   In the left-hand column you will see what **Alberto** generally does every day of the week. Say what he did on that particular day last week, using the words in the right-hand column.

Esempio: Generalmente il lunedì va al cinema.
(Ma) lunedì scorso è andato a teatro.

	Generalmente	**La settimana scorsa**
(a)	Il lunedì va al cinema.	a teatro
(b)	Il martedì cena presto.	tardi

(c) Il mercoledì studia molto.   affatto
(d) Il giovedì lavora fino alle sei.   dieci
(e) Il venerdì mangia a casa.   fuori
(f) Il sabato gioca a carte.   scacchi
(g) La domenica dorme fino
      alle dieci.   mezzogiorno

---

scacchi   *chess*

---

2   Imagine you are **Alberto** and say what you did last week on Monday,
    Thursday and Sunday.

3   Write about the people in columns (b), (c), (d) and (e), using **Pietro
    Rossi** in column (a) as your model.

(a)	(b)	(c)	(d)	(e)
Pietro Rossi	**Paolo Nuzzo**	**Mirella Perrone**	**I signori Caraffi**	**Anna e Silvia**
È nato nel '70.	'69	'57	'58	'71
È stato in America per dieci anni.	Austria 2	Francia 1	Spagna 12	Grecia 6
È andato a Boston.	Vienna	Parigi	Barcellona	Atene
Poi è tornato in Italia.	Italia	Sicilia	Sardegna	Roma

4   Read this passage carefully and answer the questions on it as though
    you were **Anna**, using **ci** in every reply. Use the same verbs as in the
    questions.

Esempio: (a) È mai stata all'estero?
                     Sì. Ci sono stata molte volte.

Anna è stata all'estero molte volte. In aprile è andata in Italia con
Marcello. È ritornata a Pisa nel mese di agosto. Poi è andata a Firenze
in macchina con la sua amica Francesca.

(a)   È mai stata all'estero?
(b)   Quando è andata in Italia con Marcello?
(c)   Quando è ritornata a Pisa?
(d)   Com'è andata a Firenze?
(e)   C'è andata con sua sorella?

5   Answer the following questions, using the appropriate pronouns and the period of time in brackets, as in the example.

Esempio: Da quanto tempo Lucia aspetta l'autobus?   (5 minuti)
L'aspetta da cinque minuti.

(a)   Da quanto tempo Sandro non vede sua sorella?   (2 anni)
(b)   Da quanto tempo Marcello conosce Sandra?   (molti anni)
(c)   Da quanto tempo suona il violino Francesca?   (9 anni)
(d)   Da quanto tempo Mirella studia l'Italiano?   (6 mesi)
(e)   Da quanto tempo non vedono Roberto?   (molto tempo)
(f)   Da quanto tempo Anna e Roberto aspettano
        il treno?   (poco tempo)

6   Make a statement from the two sentences given, using **fa**, as in the example.

Esempio: Sono le dieci. Sandro è andato in banca all nove e un
quarto.
Sandro è andato in banca tre quarti d'ora fa.

(a)   Sono le undici. Mara è andata a fare la spesa alle nove.
(b)   È l'una. Sergio è venuto a pranzo a mezzogiorno.
(c)   Sono le sette e mezza. Mario è tornato dal lavoro alle sei.
(d)   Sono le undici e mezza. Carlo è andato a letto alle undici.
(e)   Sono le cinque e mezza. Filippo è uscito alle cinque e venti-
        cinque.

7   **Ora tocca a te!** You are being interviewed by a journalist who is asking you where you have been and what you have done in Italy.

Giornalista	Va mai in Italia?
You	*Yes, I go there almost every year.*
Giornalista	Dov'è stato l'anno scorso?
You	*I went to Venice and Verona.*
Giornalista	È rimasto molto tempo a Verona?
You	*Two evenings. For the opera.*
Giornalista	È andato con amici?
You	*No. I prefer to travel alone.*
Giornalista	Ma parla benissimo! Sono italiani i suoi genitori?
You	*Yes. And … I studied Italian at university.*
Giornalista	Dove? In Italia?
You	*First in Italy, then at the University of London.*

Giornalista	Quanto tempo fa?
You	*Two years ago.*

✳ Informazioni

1 Paese

Italians refer to the place they came from as **il mio paese**. Generally speaking, **paese** means *village* or *small town* and has no exact equivalent in English. **Il mio paese nativo** or **natale** would be *my native village* or *my birthplace*. **Paese** may also mean *country*, but in this case it is often written with a capital **'P'**: **L'Italia è un bel Paese**. *Italy is a beautiful country.*

In che parte d'Italia si trovano Palermo, Taormina e Siracusa?

17 TANTE COSE DA FARE!
So many things to do

In this Unit you will learn how to:

■ say that you have already done something
■ say that you have not yet done it
■ ask someone how much they paid for something
■ say how much you paid for something

Dialogo 1 Quando vai a fare la spesa? *When are you going to do the shopping?*

A mother asks her daughter whether she has bought everything.

(a) **Vero o falso?** Marisa è andata al supermercato con la mamma.

La mamma	Quando vai a fare la spesa, Marisa?
Marisa	L'ho già fatta, mamma! Sono andata al supermercato con Valeria.
La mamma	Hai preso tutto?
Marisa	Sì. Pane, burro, latte, uova, biscotti…
La mamma	Ma, hai comprato il pesce per stasera?
Marisa	Sì. L'ho comprato. Ne ho preso mezzo chilo.
La mamma	E dove l'hai messo? Non lo vedo.
Marisa	L'ho messo in frigorifero con l'altra roba.
La mamma	Ah brava, Marisa! Grazie.

l'ho già fatta (from **fare**) *I've already done it*		**hai preso …?** (from **prendere**) *did you get …?*	
l'ho messo (from **mettere**) *I put it*			

(b) Dove ha messo il pesce Marisa?

Dialogo 2 Il regalo per Sandro, l'avete preso? *Have you got Sandro's present?*

Franco asks **Sonia** and **Daniele** whether they have done everything that needed doing.

(a) **Vero o falso?** Daniele e Sonia hanno comprato un portafoglio per Sandro.

Franco	Avete comprato le cartoline?
Sonia	Sì. Le abbiamo pure scritte.
Franco	Quante ne avete comprate?
Daniele	Dodici. Ne abbiamo mandata una anche alla vicina di casa.
Franco	Il regalo per Sandro, l'avete preso?
Sonia	Sì. Gli abbiamo comprato una cravatta di seta pura. Eccola qua! Ti piace?
Franco	È veramente elegante! Quanto l'avete pagata?
Daniele	Parecchio.
Franco	I posti per il concerto di domani sera, li avete prenotati?
Sonia	No. Non li abbiamo ancora prenotati. Non abbiamo avuto tempo.

pure	*also, as well*	**parecchio**	*quite a lot*
mandare	*to send*	**prenotare**	*to book*
vicina di casa	*neighbour*	**non ... ancora**	*not yet*
gli abbiamo comprato	*we have bought (for) him*		

(b) Perchè non hanno prenotato i posti per il concerto?

Dialogo 3 L'ho spento (from spegnere) *I've turned it off*

Adriano discovers that **Cesare** has pulled the plug out...

(a) **Vero o falso?** Cesare ha spento il videoregistratore.

Adriano	Oddio! Che hai fatto, hai rotto il videoregistratore?
Cesare	No. L'ho spento. Ho tolto la spina perchè devo usare l'aspirapolvere.

oddio! *oh dear!*		**togliere la spina**	*to pull the plug*
Hai rotto (from **rompere**) **il**		*out*	
videoregistratore? *Have you*		**aspirapolvere** (m.)	*vacuum cleaner*
broken the video recorder?			

(b) Che cos'ha fatto Cesare per spegnere il videoregistratore?

Spiegazioni

1 *Agreement of the past participle*

When the perfect tense is formed with **avere**, and is preceded by **lo, la, li, le, l'** (direct object pronouns) or **ne**, the past participle must change its final vowel to agree with them.

> **Avete compra*t*o *le* cartoline?**   *Have you bought the postcards?*
> **Sì. *Le* abbiamo pure scrit*te*.**   *Yes, we have written them as well.*
> **... e *ne* abbiamo manda*t*a un*a* ...**   *... and we've sent one to ...*

As we have seen, **lo** and **la** (i.e. singular only) normally become **l'** before a vowel or '**h**' (Unit 8, p 93). **L'** can therefore be masculine or feminine and in the perfect tense you can tell which it is by the ending of the past participle:

Lo + ho becomes **l'ho**. **Lo ho letto** therefore becomes **L'ho letto** *I have read it.*

La ho letta therefore becomes **L'ho letta** *I have read it.*

> **Ha let*t*o il libr*o*?**   *Have you read the book?/*
>   *Did you read the book?*
> **Sì. *L'ho* let*t*o.**   *Yes, I've read it/Yes, I read it.*
> **Ha let*t*o *la* rivist*a*?**   *Have you read the magazine/*
>   *Did you read the magazine?*
> **Sì. *L'ho* let*t*a.**   *Yes, I've read it./Yes, I read it.*
> **Gino ha let*t*o *la* letter*a*.**   *Gino (has) read the letter.*
> ***L'ha* let*t*a.**   *He (has) read it.*
> **Sara ha let*t*o il bigliet*t*o.**   *Sarah (has) read the note.*
> ***L'ha* let*t*o.**   *She (has) read it.*

The sentences below will make these agreements clearer:

Hai visto	Pietro? Maria? i ragazzi? le ragazze?	Sì.	L'ho visto. L'ho vista. Li ho visti. Le ho viste.	Have you seen	Peter? Mary? the boys? the girls?	Yes, I've seen	him. her. them. them.

Hai chiuso	il cassetto? la valigia? i cassetti? le valigie?	Sì.	L'ho chiuso. L'ho chiusa. Li ho chiusi. Le ho chiuse.	Have you closed	the drawer? the suitcase? the drawers? the suitcases?	Yes I've closed	it. it. them. them.

When there is no object pronoun, the past participle does not have to agree if the object precedes the verb. In Italian you can say either:

La rivista che ho $\left\{ \begin{array}{l} \textbf{comprato} \\ \textbf{comprata} \end{array} \right\}$ *The magazine that I (have) bought.*

2 Pane, burro, latte ...

When you have a list of nouns in Italian you don't need to use the article.

3 Il regalo ... l'avete preso?　　*Have you got the present?*

Often, especially in spoken Italian, for the sake of emphasis, both the noun and the pronoun are used as in the example above. Other examples:

I posti ... li **avete prenotati?**　　*Have you booked the seats?*
L'hai letto il giornale di oggi?　　*Did you read today's paper?*
La **carne l'ho messa nel**　　*I've put the meat in the freezer.*
　congelatore.

4 *Perfect of* dovere, potere, sapere, volere

The perfect of the above verbs may always be formed with **avere**:

　ho dovuto, avete voluto, hanno potuto, abbiamo saputo

However, when the verb that follows them has its perfect tense formed with **essere** there is a choice:

$\left. \begin{array}{l} \textbf{ho} \\ \textbf{Non} \\ \textbf{sono} \end{array} \right\}$ **potuto venire.**　　*I couldn't come.*

Abbiamo dovuto ⎱
⎰ **partire.** *We had to leave.*
Siamo dovuti ⎰

With **dovere**, **potere**, **sapere**, **volere** there is also a choice of position for unstressed pronouns (see Unit 9, p 103):

Non ho potuto far*lo.* ⎱
*L'*ho potuto fare. ⎰ *I couldn't do it.*

Devo alzar*mi* presto. ⎱
Mi devo alzare presto. ⎰ *I have to get up early.*

5 Già   *already*   Non ... ancora   *not ... yet*

Notice the position of **già** and **ancora** in the following examples:

Quando fai *la* spes*a*?   *When are you doing the shopping?*
*L'*ho *già* fatt*a*.   *I've already done it.*
Hai fatto *la* spes*a*?   *Have you done the shopping?*
*Non l'*ho *ancora* fatt*a*.   *I haven't done it yet.*

6 Eccola qua/qui

Qua/qui *here*, or **là/lì** *there*, may be added to **eccolo**, **eccola**, **ecc.** to give more precision: **Eccolo qui/là.**

7 Tanto/a, tanti/e   *so much, so many*

Notice how the above adjectives are used in the singular and plural:

Al mercato c'è tanta frutta!   *There's so much fruit in the market!*
Ho tante cose da fare.   *I've got so many things to do.*

Come si dice in italiano?

How to:

1   say you have already done   **L'ho gia fatto./L'ho già fatta.**
    something

2   say that you have not yet done it   **Non l'ho ancora fatto./**
                                        Non l'ho ancora fatta.

3   ask someone how much they   **Quanto l'ha pagato?/**
    paid for something   **Quanto l'ha pagata?**

4   say how much you paid for it   **L'ho pagato/L'ho pagata ...**

☑ Attività

1 Imagine the questions below are addressed to you and answer using **ne**, making the past participle agree.

Esempio: Quante birre ha preso? (due)
Ne ho pres*e* due.

(a) Quanti pacchi ha mandato? (uno)
(b) Quanti film ha visto? (molti)
(c) Quante lettere ha spedito? (sei)
(d) Quante cartoline ha scritto? (quattro)
(e) Quante gallerie ha visitato? (una)
(f) Quanti soldi ha speso? (molti)
(g) Quante sterline ha cambiato? (poche)
(h) Quanti caffè ha bevuto oggi? (tre)

2 You are being asked by your boss when you are going to complete a number of office tasks. With your customary efficiency you have already done everything.

Esempio: Quando paga il conto?
L'ho già pagato.

(a) Quando scrive le lettere?
(b) Quando compra i francobolli?
(c) Quando vede i signori Marelli?
(d) Quando fa le due telefonate a Parigi?
(e) Quando sbriga la corrispondenza?
(f) Quando finisce il rapporto?
(g) Quando prepara i documenti?
(h) Quando consulta l'agenda?

3 You have been working so hard at the office that domestically you have let things slide, and when your flat-mate asks you about a series of chores, you have to admit that you haven't done them yet.

Esempio: Hai preparato la cena?
No. Non l'ho ancora preparata.

(a) Hai fatto il letto?
(b) Hai pulito l'appartamento?
(c) Hai pagato l'affitto?
(d) Hai fatto la spesa?
(e) Hai comprato i giornali?
(f) Hai riparato la luce?

4   Complete the following sentences with a suitable verb in the perfect tense.

Esempio: Mario ha comprato il gelato e l'____.
Mario ha comprato il gelato e l'ha mangiato.

(a)   Ho preso una penna e ____ una lettera a Marco.
(b)   Ho comprato il giornale e l'____.
(c)   Ho acceso la radio e l'____.
(d)   Giorgio ha comprato la birra e l'____.
(e)   Anna ha preso il vestito dall'armadio e l'____.
(f)   Sono andati alla stazione ma purtroppo ____ il treno.

5   **Ora tocca a te!** You are taking on the role of a husband who can't find his passport.

Moglie	Allora, caro, partiamo?
You	*I'm not ready yet.*
Moglie	Che cosa cerchi?
You	*My passport. Where did I put it? Did you take it?*
Moglie	No. Hai guardato in macchina?
You	*Yes. I've looked. It's not there.*
Moglie	Non l'hai lasciato in banca stamattina quando hai cambiato i soldi?
You	*No. Ah... One moment... Perhaps I put it in the bedroom.*
Moglie	No. Di là non c'è. Ho pulito in tutte le camere e non ho visto niente.
You	*Didn't you by any chance put it with the other documents?*
Moglie	No, no. In borsa ho soltanto i biglietti del treno.
You	*What a nuisance! What do we do now without a passport?*
Moglie	Hai guardato nello studio?
You	*Yes. I've looked everywhere.*
Moglie	Oddio! Ed il treno parte fra mezz'ora!

▓ Informazioni

Italy produces more than 600 types of **pasta**. **Fusilli**, **rigatoni** and **fettuccine** are three of the many varieties to be found. A pasta dish is the typical first course of the average Italian family at lunch which usually takes place at about 1 o'clock. All sorts of **salse** *sauces*, especially those based on tomatoes, are used to go with the **pasta**. **Cirio** is one of the well known tomato purée brands also used for making **salsa**.

What are **Fusilli Bucati Lunghi** supposed to be ideal with?

18 CHE COSA REGALARE?
What present to give?

In this Unit you will learn how to:

- ask what present to give someone
- suggest what to get for him/her
- arrange to meet up later

Dialogo 1 Il compleanno di Renzo *Renzo's birthday*

Beatrice is discussing **Renzo's** birthday present with **Alfredo**.

When you listen to this dialogue notice where **gli** comes before the verb, and when it comes after.

(a) **Vero o falso?** Renzo usa spesso il profumo.

Beatrice Sabato è il compleanno di Renzo e non so ancora cosa regalargli.

Alfredo Perchè non gli compri un romanzo?

Beatrice I romanzi non gli piacciono.

Alfredo Puoi prendergli un profumo. Un bel profumo francese.

Beatrice Però il profumo non lo usa mai.

Alfredo Quanto vuoi spendere?

Beatrice Non troppo. E non posso neanche regalargli delle sigarette perchè non fuma.

Non so ancora cosa regalargli *I don't know what to get him yet*	**non posso neanche ...** *I can't even ...*
gli *(to) him*	**fumare** *to smoke*
romanzo *novel*	

(b) Perchè Beatrice vuol fare un regalo a Renzo?

🔊 Dialogo 2   Il problema è risolto   *The problem is solved*

(a) **Vero o falso?** Beatrice prende un nuovo stereo per Renzo.

Alfredo   Gli piace la musica?
Beatrice Mi sembra di sì. So che ha un nuovo stereo.
Alfredo   Allora il problema è risolto. Gli puoi portare una cassetta o un cd.
Beatrice Buona idea! Gli prendo un disco di musica classica.
Alfredo   Io non gli regalo nulla. Gli mando solamente una cartolina di auguri. Però sabato mattina gli telefono.

---

mi sembra di sì	*I think so*	**non ... nulla**	*nothing*
disco, cd	*record, CD*	**solamente**	*only*
cassetta	*cassette*	**auguri**	*greetings*

(b) Cosa vuol fare Alfredo sabato mattina?

🔊 Dialogo 3   L'onomastico di Carla   *Carla's name-day*

Sandra decides to get some chocolates from the patisserie, and **Livio** to buy a bunch of roses from the florist's for **Carla's** name-day.

(a) **Vero o falso?** Sandra e Livio devono sbrigarsi perchè sono invitati per l'una.

Sandra Dio mio! È già mezzogiorno! Dobbiamo sbrigarci!
Livio   A che ora dobbiamo andare a pranzo da Carla?
Sandra Siamo invitati per l'una.
Livio   Cosa le portiamo? Dei fiori?
Sandra Possiamo prenderle dei cioccolatini dal pasticciere qui di fronte. So che i dolci le piacciono molto.
Livio   Ottima idea! Le compriamo una scatola di 'Baci Perugina' ed un bel fascio di rose.
Sandra Il guaio è che non abbiamo molto tempo per andare in tutti e due i negozi.
Livio   Allora facciamo così: io vado dal fioraio mentre tu vai dal pasticciere, e poi c'incontriamo sotto il palazzo di Carla.

Dio mio!	good gracious!	**fascio**	bunch
Dobbiamo sbrigarci!	We must	**guaio**	trouble
hurry!		**mentre**	while
da Carla	at Carla's place	**fioraio**	florist's
fiore (m.)	flower	**poi c'incontriamo**	then we'll
scatola	box	meet	

(b) Cosa devono fare Livio e Sandra all'una?

Spiegazioni

1 Non so ancora cosa regalargli   *I don't know what present to give him yet.*

Sapere means *to know*. **Sapere**, not **conoscere**, must be used:

Whenever a dependent clause follows:

> *So che* **Paolo vive a Taormina.**   *I know that Paul lives in Taormina.*
> *Sai dove* **va Ida?**   *Do you know where Ida is going?*
> *Sai se* **le piace l'aglio?**   *Do you know whether she likes garlic?*

whenever an infinitive follows, in which case it means *to know how to* (i.e. *to be able*):

> **Sai guidare?**   *Do you know how to drive?/ Can you drive?*
> **Sa suonare* il pianoforte?**   *Can you play the piano?*

Potere, when contrasted with **sapere**, suggests physical capability:

> **Senza occhiali non posso leggere.**   *I can't read without glasses.*
> **Non sa leggere ancora; è troppo piccolo.**   *He can't read yet. He's too young.*

Conoscere is mainly used for knowing people, places or languages:

> *Conosci* **Carlo? Sì.** *Lo conosco.*   *Do you know Charles? Yes. I do.*
> *Conosce* **Parigi†? Sì.** *La conosco.*   *Do you know Paris? Yes. I do.*
> *Conosce* **bene lo spagnolo.**   *He knows Spanish well.*

* Use **suonare** *to play an instrument*, **giocare a** *to play a game*
† Towns are feminine in Italian

2 Regalargli   *to give him*

Indirect object pronouns (unstressed)

Singular		Plural	
mi	*(to/for) me*	**ci**	*(to/for) us*
ti	*(to/for) you* (informal)	**vi**	*(to/for) you* (pl.)
gli	*(to/for) him*	**gli**	*(to/for) them* (masc./fem.)
le	*(to/for) you/her*		

The pronouns in the box are indirect objects, i.e. where *to/for* are either expressed or understood in English. 'I give him the book' means 'I give the book to him', which in Italian becomes: **Gli do il libro**. To start with it is best to concentrate on **le** and **gli**:

Le
Gli } **parlo dopo.**   *I'll talk* { *to you/to her* / *to him* } *later/afterwards.*

Le porto la valigia.   *I'll carry the suitcase for you/her.*

Gli apro la porta.   *I'll open the door for him/them.*

Like the pronouns in Unit 17, p 187, they normally precede the verb, but both object and indirect object may come after an infinitive, in which case they are attached to it (**regalargli** stands for **regalare + gli**).

Gli vorrei telefonare.
Vorrei telefonargli. }   *I would like to phone him.*

Giorgio { **mi / ti / ci / vi / gli / le** } **dà il libro.**   *George is giving* { *me / you / us / you* (pl.) / *him/them / her/you* } *the book.*

In the *written* language (and occasionally in the spoken), *to them* is **loro** or **a loro**: it can never precede the verb and can never be attached to the infinitive.

Giorgio dà il libro *a loro*.
Giorgio dà *loro* il libro }   *George is giving them the book.*

3 Non ... neanche   *not ... even*

Neanche is the opposite of **anche**:

anch'io, anche lei; neanch'io, neanche lei.

Vengo *anch'io*	*I'm coming too.*
(Io) *non* **so cosa dire.**	*I don't know what to say.*
Neanch'io.	*Neither do I.*
Non **ci andate** *neanche* **voi?**	*Aren't you going either?*
Non **ci andiamo** *neanche* **noi.**	*We're not going either.*

4   Mi sembra/mi pare   *it seems to me*

Mi sembra is another verb used impersonally in the same way as **mi piace** (Unit 11, p 124). Both verbs require the indirect object pronoun (Note 2 p. 196).

Non *mi sembra* **il momento adatto.**	*It doesn't seem the right moment to me.*
Le pare **giusto?**	*Do you think it's fair?*
Gli piace **questo disco?**	*Does he like this record?*
I fiori *le piacciono* **molto.**	*She likes flowers a lot.*
Le piacciono **i dolci?**	*Do you like sweet things?*

When used with **sì** and **no, sembra**, like **pensare** and **credere** *to think,* must be followed by **di** and has the same meaning (*to think*).

Mi sembra   di sì. ⎫
                          ⎬ *I think* ⎰ *so.*
Penso   di no. ⎭   ⎱ *not.*

5 Solamente   *only*

Solamente, solo and **soltanto** can all be used to mean *only.*

6 Dobbiamo sbrigarci   *We must hurry*

As this reflexive verb is in the infinitive, the pronoun **ci** is attached to the end of it. **Sbrigarci** (Dialogue 3) is **sbrigare + ci** (Lit: *to hurry ourselves*).

7 Ottimo/a, meglio, migliore   *excellent, better*

Ottimo/a, an adjective, is another way of saying **buonissimo/a** *very good, excellent.* There are two words for *better*: **migliore** (adjective) and **meglio** (adverb):

Fanno degli *ottimi* affari.	*They do excellent business.*
Lei mi dà *ottime* notizie.	*You're giving me very good news.*
Questo libro è *migliore* di quello.	*This book is better than that one.*
Lo so *meglio* di te!	*I know (it) better than you do!*

Il/la migliore means *the best.*

Secondo me *il periodo migliore* per visitare l'Italia è la primavera.	*In my opinion the best time to visit Italy is spring.*
Mario e Paolo sono *i miei migliori amici.*	*Mario and Paolo are my best friends.*

Buono/a, migliore, il/la migliore therefore mean *good, better, best.*

8 C'incontriamo   *we'll meet (each other)*

Incontrarsi, apparently a reflexive verb, is used reciprocally in this context to express the idea of *each other.* We have already met **ci vediamo** used in this way: it literally means *we'll see each other.*

Here are examples of other verbs being used reciprocally:

Da quanto tempo *si conoscono* Anna e Marcello?	*How long have Anna and Marcello known each other?*

Gli (*the*) may be shortened to **gl'** but only before words beginning with **i**:

Gl'italiani *si salutano* molte volte prima di lasciarsi.	*Italians say goodbye many times before leaving each other.*
Paolo e Marisa non *si parlano.*	*Paolo and Marisa don't talk to each other.*

9 Dal fioraio   *at/to the florist's*

When used with people, **da** or **da + article** means *at/to the house of, the shop of* or *the place of*:

Vado *dal* tabaccaio.	*I'm going to the tobacconist's.*
Vai *da* Giulia?	*Are you going to Julia's (place)?*
Prima vado *dal* dottore, poi *dal* salumiere.	*First I'll go to the doctor's then to the grocer's.*
Vado *dalla* mia amica.	*I'm going to my friend's house.*
Perchè *non* vieni *da* me?	*Why don't you come to my place?*

Come si dice in italiano?

How to:

1	ask what present to give someone	**Cosa posso regalare a ...?**
2	suggest what to buy him/her	**Perchè non gli compri ...?/ le compri ...?**
3	suggest what you can get for someone	**Posso prendergli .../ prenderle ...**
4	say you will meet up later	**C'incontriamo più tardi.**

Attività

1 **È il compleanno di Adriano** *It's Adrian's birthday*. Here is a list of his friends and what they do for the occasion. Write a sentence about each on the pattern of the first example.

Esempio: Anna gli dà una cravatta.

(a) Anna (*dare*) cravatta.
(b) Renzo (*dare*) libro.
(c) Beatrice (*portare*) cd.
(d) Livio (*mandare*) cassetta.
(e) Matteo (*regalare*) profumo.
(f) Maria (*telefonare*) per fargli gli auguri.

2 Time is pressing for Rita who is being asked about when she is going to do everything she needs to do: you have to supply her answers using **gli** or **le**.

Esempio: Quando telefona a Beatrice? (domani)
           Le telefono domani.

(a)	Quando telefona a Giulia?	(stasera)
(b)	Quando telefona a Renzo?	(più tardi)
(c)	Quando telefona a Marco?	(dopo cena)
(d)	Quando scrive a Anna?	(domani)
(e)	Quando scrive a Gina?	(oggi)
(f)	Quando parla a Silvio e Eva?	(dopo la lezione)

3 You are being asked to decide which presents should go to each of your friends. Form the question you are being asked, then give your answer, attaching the object pronoun to the infinitive.

Esempio: **(a) A chi vuole dare il disco?**
            Voglio darlo a Carla.

(a) Carla: (*dare*) disco
(b) Beatrice: (*mandare*) cartolina di auguri
(c) Maria: (*regalare*) borsa di pelle
(d) Marco: (*portare*) cioccolatini
(e) Gino: (*dare*) portafoglio

4 In the following conversation, choose one of the three alternatives which fits the context. Read through the whole conversation before attempting to make your choices.

Lucia Hai il nome/francobollo/biglietto per la lettera?
Eva   No. Non ce l'ho/ce l'ha/ce l'hanno.
Lucia Perchè non la/lo/le compri?
Eva   Perchè la posta è qui/chiusa/aperta.
Lucia Ma il tabaccaio è aperto/chiuso/nuovo.
Eva   Sì. Però qui vicino non c'è un pasticciere/fioraio/tabaccaio e vorrei spedire questa lettera stasera.
Lucia Perchè vuoi spedirlo/spedire/sperdirla stasera?
Eva   Perchè domani è il compleanno di Filippo e devo mandare/mandarli/mandargli gli auguri.
Lucia A chi devi mandarli/mandargli/mandarle? Non ho capito.
Eva   A Filippo.

5 **Giorgio** and **Pina** know each other, see each other, etc. Make one statement for each pair as in this example. (There is no need to repeat **Giorgio e Pina** every time.)

Esempio: Giorgio conosce Pina. Pina conosce Giorgio.
           (Giorgio e Pina) si conoscono.

(a) Giorgio incontra Pina. Pina incontra Giorgio.
(b) Giorgio vede Pina. Pina vede Giorgio.
(c) Giorgio parla con Pina. Pina parla con Giorgio.
(d) Giorgio saluta Pina. Pina saluta Giorgio.
(e) Giorgio bacia Pina. Pina bacia Giorgio.
(f) Giorgio abbraccia Pina. Pina abbraccia Giorgio.

6 **Ora tocca a te!** You are **Carla**.

Giorgio Dove vai, Carla?
You   *First I'm going to the post-office, then I'm going to buy a present for Antonio.*

Giorgio	Perchè? È il suo compleanno?
You	*No. It's his name-day.*
Giorgio	Cosa gli compri?
You	*I don't know yet.*
Giorgio	Gli piace leggere?
You	*I don't think so.*
Giorgio	Quanto vuoi spendere?
You	*Not too much.*
Giorgio	Sai se gli piace la musica?
You	*I know he likes to listen to music when he's driving.*
Giorgio	Puoi comprargli una cassetta, allora.
You	*Excellent idea!*

▊ Informazioni

1 Un fascio di fiori

If invited to a meal it is usual to take your hostess **un fascio di fiori** *a bunch of flowers*. Beware of taking chrysanthemums, however. They are used only at funerals.

2 Baci Perugina/dolci

Baci Perugina are a trade mark for chocolates known all over Europe. **Dolci** are literally 'sweet things' and may therefore refer to sweets, cakes or biscuits. **Il dolce** (See Unit 7, p 86) is the dessert or sweet.

3 Pasticceria

A **pasticceria** sells cakes, pastries and ice cream. Many of these **pasticcerie** are like cafés where you can sit and eat cakes, etc. with a drink.

4 Tanti auguri a te! *Happy Birthday to you!* (Lit: *So many greetings to you*)

Here is the Italian version of the song *Happy Birthday to You*:

Tanti auguri a te,
Tanti auguri a te,
Tanti auguri a Renzo, (*or any other name, as appropriate*)
Tanti auguri a te.

(a) È un fascio di crisantemi?

(b) Quante candeline ci sono sulla torta?

(c) Why do you think the **baci** are called Perugina?

(d) What is **La festa della Mamma**?

19 STUDIO E LAVORO
Study and work

In this Unit you will learn how to:

■ talk about your studies and your present job
■ talk about the places you have visited and how long you stayed there
■ say that you enjoyed yourself
■ ask others similar questions

Dialogo 1 Intervista con una studentessa
Interview with a student

A journalist interviews a woman graduate who has now enrolled for a degree course in languages.

(a) **Vero o falso?** La studentessa è laureata.

Giornalista Si laurea quest'anno, signorina?

Studentessa No. Mi sono già laureata.

Giornalista E perchè frequenta l'università?

Studentessa Perchè mi sono iscritta al corso di laurea in lingue. Studio l'inglese e il russo.

Giornalista È mai stata in Russia?

Studentessa No. Non ci sono mai stata. Ma sono andata diverse volte in Inghilterra. C'è tanto da vedere!

Giornalista Conosce bene Londra?

Studentessa Abbastanza bene, almeno credo. Ci sono ritornata anche quest'anno.

Giornalista C'è andata da sola?

Studentessa No. Con mio padre e mia madre.

frequentare	*to attend*	**diverso/a**	*several*
mi sono iscritta (from **iscriversi**)		**almeno**	*at least*
I have enrolled		**laurearsi**	*to graduate*

(b) (La studentessa) è mai stata in Russia?

Dialogo 2 Preferiamo viaggiare per conto nostro
We prefer to travel on our own

When asked whether she and her parents went on a package tour (**viaggio organizzato**), she answers that they prefer to make their own arrangements.

(a) **Vero o falso?** La studentessa e i suoi genitori sono stati a Canterbury solo di passaggio.

Giornalista	Avete fatto un viaggio organizzato?
Studentessa	No, no. Noi preferiamo viaggiare per conto nostro.
Giornalista	Siete stati a Canterbury?
Studentessa	Sì. Ma solo di passaggio quando siamo ritornati da Edimburgo.
Giornalista	Vi siete fermati parecchio tempo in Scozia?
Studentessa	Una settimana solamente. Dopo i miei genitori sono andati a Londra ed io sono partita per l'Irlanda per quattro giorni.
Giornalista	E poi…?
Studentessa	E poi ci siamo incontrati a Canterbury per fare insieme il viaggio di ritorno. Ci siamo divertiti moltissimo.

---

di passaggio	*passing through*	**incontrarsi**	*to meet (each other)*
fermarsi	*to stop, stay*	**insieme**	*together*
parecchio tempo	*a long time*	**divertirsi**	*to enjoy oneself*

(b) Per quanto tempo (la studentessa) è andata in Irlanda?

Dialogo 3 Un operaio di fabbrica   *A factory worker*

A factory worker explains that he came to Milan (in Northern Italy) from Messina because there is not enough work for everybody in the South.

(a) **Vero o falso?** Marcello lavora in un negozio.

Giornalista	Da che parte dell'Italia viene?
Marcello	Da Messina. Sono siciliano.
Giornalista	Quanti anni sono che lavora a Milano?
Marcello	Una quindicina di anni.
Giornalista	Sua sorella mi ha detto che vi trovate bene qui nel nord.
Marcello	È vero. Si guadagna molto. E nella fabbrica in cui lavoriamo noi, gli operai sono trattati veramente bene. Fra

poco avremo anche l'aumento.

Giornalista Come mai vi siete trasferiti qui?

Marcello Nel sud, purtroppo, è difficile trovare lavoro per tutti.

Quanti anni sono che lavora...? *How many years have you been working...?*		**avremo l'aumento** rise	*we'll have a*
una quindicina di ... *about 15 ...*		**trattare** *to treat*	
in cui *in which*		**... vi siete trasferiti** (from **trasferirsi**)?	*... did you move?*
fra poco *shortly*			

(b) Come si trova Marcello a Milano?

Spiegazioni

1 *Perfect tense of reflexive verbs*

All reflexive verbs and most impersonal verbs (or those used impersonally) form their perfect tense (p 177–8) with **essere**.

Sì è divertito alla festa di Renzo?	*Did you enjoy yourself at Lawrence's party?*
Sì. Mi sono divertito molto.	*Yes, I enjoyed myself a lot.*
Ti sei alzata* tardi stamattina?	*Did you get up late this morning?*
No. Mi sono alzata presto.	*No, I got up early.*
Vi siete asciugati?	*Did you dry yourselves?*
Sì. Ci siamo asciugati con l'asciugamano celeste.	*Yes, we dried ourselves with the blue towel.*

Perfect tense	**fermarsi** *to stop, stay*
(io) mi sono fermato (fermata)	*I stopped, I have stopped*
(tu) ti sei fermato (fermata)	*You stopped, you have stopped* (inf.)
(lui/lei) si è fermato/fermata	*He/she/it/you stopped, he/ she has stopped/you have stopped*
(noi) ci siamo fermati (fermate)	*We stopped, we have stopped*
(voi) vi siete fermati (fermate)	*You stopped, you have stopped*
(loro) si sono fermati (fermate)	*They stopped, they have stopped*

***Alzata** *the feminine form is used because a woman is being asked the question.*

2 Per conto nostro   *On our own*

To express the idea of *one's own*, use this expression with the appropriate possessive adjective: **per conto mio** *on my own*, **per conto tuo/suo/vostro** *on your own*, etc.

Lavoro per conto mio.	*I work on my own/for myself.*
Lui lavora per conto suo.	*He works on his own/for himself.*

In Dialogue 2 **preferiamo viaggiare per conto nostro** is best rendered by *we prefer to make our own arrangements*.

3 Ci siamo incontrati   *We met*

Ci siamo incontrati comes from **incontrarsi** *to meet*. However, if you want to refer to the first time someone met, use **conoscersi**:

Si sono conosciuti **in Italia,** **l'anno dopo** *si sono incontrati* **a Parigi,** *e* **quest'anno** *si sono sposati.*	*They met (each other) in Italy, the following year they met (again) in Paris, and this year they got married.*

4 Quanti anni sono che lavora...?   *How many years have you been working...?*

This is another way of expressing: **Da quanti anni lavora?**

Both of these constructions require the present tense in Italian because the activity continues on into the present (see p 179–80):

Aspetto da **dieci minuti.** *Sono* **dieci minuti** *che aspetto.*	*I have been waiting for ten minutes.*

If the activity has ceased then **per** is used with the past:

Ho lavorato **a Roma** *per* **più** **di dieci anni.**	*I worked in Rome for more than ten years.*

5 Una quindicina   *about fifteen*

To express approximate quantities, take off the final vowel of the number and add **-ina** preceded by **una**. (Use for numbers 10, 15, 20, and then in tens up to 90):

Ha *una ventina d'*anni.	*He's about 20.*
Ci sono *una trentina* di persone.	*There are about 30 people.*
***Una quindicina di* giorni.**	*About a fortnight.*

6 In cui   *In which*

After prepositions (p. 48) **cui** replaces **che**. Notice the difference between these examples:

La casa *che* ha comprato è modernissima.	*The house that he has bought is very modern.*
La casa *in cui* abita è modernissima.	*The house in which he lives is very modern.*
Non capisco la ragione *per cui* non vuoi andarci.	*I don't understand the reason why (Lit: for which) you don't want to go there.*
Questo è l'ingegnere *di cui* ti ho parlato.	*This is the engineer I spoke to you about.* (Lit: *of whom I spoke...*)

The only time that **che** may be preceded by a preposition is in a question (direct or indirect):

A *che ora* incominci a lavorare la mattina?	*At what time do you start work in the morning?* (direct question)
Non so *a che ora* viene.	*I don't know at what time he's coming.* (indirect question)

7 È difficile trovare lavoro...   *It's difficult to find work...*

Many other adjectives can be used in this way with the infinitive:

facile *easy*;   **possibile** *possible*;   **interessante** *interesting*;
importante *important*

È facile spendere i soldi.	*It's easy to spend money.*
A quest'ora è difficile trovare un posto.	*At this time it's difficult to find a seat.*
È importante studiare.	*It's important to study.*

Come si dice in italiano?

How to:

1 ask when someone is graduating	**Quando si laurea?**
say you have already graduated	**Mi sono già laureato/a.**
2 say you (have) enrolled on a particular course	**Mi sono iscritto/a al corso di ...**

3   say that one earns a lot and that   **Si guadagna molto. Gli operai**
    the workers are well treated   **sono trattati bene.**

4   ask how long someone stayed in...   **Quanto tempo si è fermato/a**
                                        in/a ...?

    say how long you stayed   **Mi sono fermato/a una settimana,**
                                        ecc.

5   ask whether someone had   **Si è divertito? Si è divertita?**
    a good time
    say that you had a very good time   **Mi sono divertito/a moltissimo.**

☑ Attività

1   **Giorgio, Anna, Marco, Carlo** and **Filippo** all enrolled at various
    universities, and each one graduated in the subject stated, in the
    number of years given in brackets. Write a statement for each,
    modelling it on the one for **Giorgio**.

    Esempio: Giorgio si è iscritto all'università di Milano. Si è
    laureato in ingegneria in cinque anni.

    Giorgio   Milano: ingegneria (5)
    Marco   Roma: medicina (6)
    Anna   Bologna: matematica e fisica (7)
    Carlo e Filippo Napoli: legge (4)

l'ingegneria	*engineering*	**la legge**	*law*

2   **Marco** is being told what he has to do. Read through the instructions
    he is given and then imagine how he would relate what he has done,
    as in the example. (The infinitives of the verbs in bold must be put
    in the perfect tense).

    Esempio: Mi sono alzato presto...

    Devi **alzarti** presto. Devi **vestirti** subito e **fare** colazione. Devi
    comprare le sigarette dal tabaccaio all'angolo e poi **telefonare** a
    Giulio e **chiedergli** il nuovo indirizzo. Dopo devi **andare** all'ufficio
    e **dire** a Marco di non venire sabato. Al ritorno devi **prendere** i soldi
    in banca e **fare** la spesa.

3   Look at **Attività 5** in Unit 18, p 200, and imagine that you and
    Giorgio met yesterday: **Io e Giorgio ci siamo incontrati ieri**.
    Continue, but don't repeat **ieri**. Start: **Ci ...**

4 **Mario** has met his ideal companion, as you will see from what he says about her. Complete his statements using each of the following prepositions **+cui**, once only: **a/con/da/di/per**

Questa è la ragazza:

(a) ____ ti ho parlato.
(b) ____ esco.
(c) ____ ricevo tante telefonate.
(d) ____ non dormo la notte.
(e) ____ scrivo sempre.

5 **Ora tocca a te!** You and your partner are on a short summer course at the University of Perugia. You are being interviewed by a journalist and are answering his questions on behalf of both of you.

Giornalista	Siete tedeschi?
You	*No, we're English.*
Giornalista	Da quanto tempo siete qui?
You	*We've been here about a fortnight.*
Giornalista	Siete venuti in aereo?
You	*No, we came by car.*
Giornalista	E perchè siete venuti a Perugia?
You	*Because we've enrolled at the University to study Italian.*
Giornalista	Quanto tempo dura il corso?
You	*It lasts a month.*
Giornalista	Avete visitato altri posti?
You	*Not many. But last Sunday we got up early and went to Assisi.*
Giornalista	Vi siete divertiti?
You	*We enjoyed ourselves very much.*

Informazioni

Italian language schools flourish in every part of Italy, especially in the resorts, cultural and artistic centres. Overleaf is an example of what is offered at the Rimini Academy.

CULTURA E LINGUA
ITALIANA Rimini Italia

CORSI 1997
STESSE TARIFFE DEL 1996

MINI-CORSO
CORSO BASE
CORSO GENERALE
CORSO SEMI-INTENSIVO
CORSO INTENSIVO
CORSO INDIVIDUALE
CORSO "BUSINESS"
CORSI DI CULTURA
CORSI TRIMESTRALI
CORSI "A CASA DELL'INSEGNANTE"
PROGRAMMI PER GRUPPI
SETTIMANA LINGUISTICA
SEMINARI E STAGE
POMERIGGIO AL PARCO   MINICROCIERA SUL MARE ADRIATICO
A CENA SULLA SPIAGGIA

Gli studenti di questa scuola (a) dove cenano?
(b) dove vanno il pomeriggio?
(c) dove fanno la mini-crociera?

20 | COME SI SENTE?
How do you feel?

In this Unit you will learn how to:

■ say how you feel (well/unwell)
■ explain what is wrong with you (where it hurts)
■ say when you require something by
■ ask others similar questions

Dialogo 1 Non mi sento molto bene *I don't feel very well*

Una signorina asks for some aspirin because she doesn't feel very well.

(a) **Vero o falso?** La signorina prende le compresse con l'acqua.

Sig.na	Ha delle aspirine, per favore?
Signore	No. Mi dispiace, non ne ho. Perchè? Si sente male?
Sig.na	Non mi sento molto bene. Ho mal di testa e mal di gola.
Signore	Ha la febbre?
Sig.na	Penso di no. Ma ho anche il raffreddore e un po' di tosse. A che ora apre la farmacia?
Signore	Fra un'ora. Un attimo… Ho delle compresse per la gola. Le vuole con l'acqua o senz'acqua?
Sig.na	Non importa. Le prendo così, senz'acqua.
Signore	Bastano due?
Sig.na	Ne basta una, grazie. Ah … sto già meglio!

sentirsi male	*to feel ill*	**raffreddore** (m.)	*cold*
mal di testa (m.)	*headache*	**tosse** (f.)	*cough*
mal di gola (m.)	*sore throat*	**compressa**	*tablet*
febbre (f.)	*temperature*		

(b) Quante compresse prende la signorina?

🎧 Dialogo 2 Dal medico *At the doctor's*

When asked by the doctor where it hurts, **la signora** answers that her head and her legs (**le gambe**) ache. She also has a stomach upset (**disturbi allo stomaco**).

(a) **Vero o falso?** La signora ha preso un po' d'insolazione.

Medico	Dove le fa male?
Signora	Qui e qui: mi fa male la testa e mi fanno male le gambe. Ho anche dei disturbi allo stomaco.
Medico	Respiri profondamente!... Ancora... Va bene. Si rivesta!
Signora	È grave, dottore? Devo andare in ospedale?
Medico	No, no. Stia tranquilla! Non è nulla di grave. Ha preso un po' d'insolazione. Tenga! Vada in farmacia con questa ricetta. Resti a letto per un paio di giorni e prenda queste medicine.
Signora	Quante volte al giorno devo prenderle?
Medico	Tre volte. Le capsule prima dei pasti e le pillole dopo i pasti.
Signora	Grazie, dottore. Quanto le devo per la visita?
Medico	Si rivolga alla mia segretaria.

---

respirare	*to breathe in*	**insolazione** (f)	*sunstroke*
profondamente	*deeply*	**tenga!**	*here you are*
ancora	*again*	**ricetta** (f)	*prescription*
rivestirsi	*to get dressed again*	**devo** (*from* **dovere**)	*I owe*
Stia tranquilla!	*Keep calm!*	**rivolgersi**	*to ask, apply*

(b) Dove deve andare la signora con la ricetta?

🎧 Dialogo 3 Dal dentista *At the dentist's*

La signorina tells the dentist she has a toothache (**mal di denti**) and he asks her which tooth (**quale dente**) hurts.

(a) **Vero o falso?** La signora ha mal di testa.

Signorina	Buongiorno, dottore.
Dentista	Buongiorno, signorina. Mi dica!
Signorina	Ho mal di denti.
Dentista	Si accomodi! Prego, si segga qui!
Signorina	Grazie.
Dentista	Quale dente le fa male?

Signorina	Questo. Ma che guaio! Proprio ora che ho gli esami!
Dentista	Ah, sì!... Questo davanti... È cariato. Non si preoccupi!
Signorina	Deve toglierlo?
Dentista	No. no. Stia tranquilla! Le faccio una medicazione prima di piombarlo e poi le do uno spazzolino e un dentifricio speciali.

Mi dica! *Tell me (what's wrong)*
si segga! (from **sedersi**) *sit down*
proprio *just*
esame (m.) *exam*

cariato/a *decayed*
medicazione (f) *dressing*
piombare *to fill*
spazzolino *toothbrush*

(b) Che cosa le dà il dentista per lavare i denti?

Dialogo 4 Dall'ottico *At the optician's*

L'avvocato asks the optician if he can **riparare** *repair* his **occhiali** *glasses* that are broken. The optician asks if he requires them immediately.

(a) **Vero o falso?** L'avvocato non deve telefonare prima di andare a prendere gli occhiali.

Avvocato	Si sono rotti gli occhiali. Può ripararli?
Ottico	Vediamo... Sì, sì. È cosa da niente, avvocato. Li lasci qui. Le occorrono subito?
Avvocato	Mi servono per domenica.
Ottico	Ah, fra quattro giorni. Va bene. Saranno pronti senz'altro per domenica.
Avvocato	Devo telefonare prima di venire a prenderli?
Ottico	No, no. Non è necessario.
Avvocato	Grazie mille.
Ottico	Prego. Arrivederla!

---

cosa da niente *nothing serious*
Le occorrono subito? *Do you need them immediately?*
mi servono (from **servire**) *I need them*

saranno *they will be*
pronto/a *ready*
senz'altro *definitely*
prima di venire *before coming*

(b) Cosa deve riparare l'ottico?

⏱ Spiegazioni

1 Avere la febbre, mal di ...   *to have a temperature, ...*

Many expressions to do with health (**la salute**) are formed with **avere** +
the definite article or **avere** + **mal di**:

Ho	**la febbre.**	*I have*	*a temperature.*
	la tosse.		*a cough.*
	il raffreddore.		*a cold.*
	l'influenza.		*influenza.*

To say *to catch a cold*, use **prendere**:

Ho preso il raffreddore.   *I've caught a cold.*

Ho mal di	**gola.**	*I have*	*a sore throat.*
	testa.		*a headache.*
	stomaco.		*stomach ache.*
	denti.		*a toothache.*

2 Mi fa male ...   *my ... hurts*

To say something hurts, apart from the set expressions with **aver mal di**
above, you can also use **far male**, which is much more general and can
refer to all parts of the body. The indirect object pronoun (**mi**, **gli**, **le**, **ecc.**
p. 196) is used: the verb **fare** can be either singular **fa** or plural **fanno**,
depending on what hurts. Therefore:

My knee hurts becomes:
  Mi fa **male** *il ginocchio.*   (Lit: *The knee hurts to me.*)

My feet hurt becomes:
  Mi fanno **male** *i piedi.*   (Lit: *The feet hurt to me.*)

Italian does not use the possessive adjective (*my, your, etc.*) with parts of
the body or with things that are worn, unless there is ambiguity:

Mi fa **male** *la* testa.	*My head hurts, I have a headache.*
Dove ha messo *il* biglietto?	*Where did you put your ticket?*
L'ho messo in tasca.	*I put it in my pocket.*
Un momento. Prendo *il* cappotto e vengo.	*One moment. I'll get my coat and come.*

| Mi
Ti
Le
Gli | fa male | la bocca.
il braccio.
il dito.
il ginocchio.
la mano.
il naso.
l'occhio destro.
l'orecchio.
la schiena.
lo stomaco. | My
Your
Her/your
His | mouth
arm
finger
knee
hand
nose
right eye
ear
back
stomach | hurts. |

Note the feminine that ends in **-o: la mano**; plural: **le mani**. In the table below note the irregularities in the plural formation of the following parts of the body:

Singular	Plural
il braccio il dito il ginocchio	le braccia le dita le ginocchia

| Mi
Ti
Le
Gli | fanno male | le braccia.
i denti.
le ginocchia.
le mani.
i piedi. | My
Your
Her/your
His/their | arms
teeth
knees
hands
feet | hurt. |

3 Reflexive verbs: imperative 2nd person singular lei form

Reflexive verbs form their imperative (**lei** form) in the same way as other verbs (p. 156), but must be preceded by **si** (*yourself*):

Si vesta! (vestirsi)	*Get dressed!*
Va alla festa? *Si diverta!* (divertirsi)	*Are you going to the party? Enjoy yourself!*
Mi preparo in due minuti.	*It will take me 2 minutes to get ready.*
Non c'è fretta. *Si cambi* (cambiarsi) **con calma!**	*There is no hurry. Take your time to get changed.* (Lit: *Change with calm.*)

In this last example, **mi preparo** *I get ready* means literally *I prepare myself,* and **si cambi** *change yourself* (i.e. *get changed*). There are many other instances in Italian of verbs being used reflexively and non-reflexively with slightly different meanings. For instance, **mi chiamo** *my name is* (from **chiamarsi**) literally means *I call myself*, so **chiamare** is used non-reflexively *to call*.

***Chiamo* il dottore?**	*Shall I call the doctor?*
Sì. *Lo chiami*.	*Yes. Call him.*

Similarly, **mettere** and **togliere** can become **mettersi** and **togliersi** when referring to things that are worn, thereby avoiding the use of the possessive:

***Si metta* il vestito blu!**	*Put your blue suit on!*
***Si tolga* la giacca!**	*Take your jacket off!*
Perchè non *ti metti* gli occhiali?	*Why don't you put your glasses on?*

To form the negative, put **non** before the verb:

***Non* si preoccupi!**	*Don't worry!*
***Non* si asciughi con l'asciugamano verde!**	*Don't dry yourself on the green towel!*

4 Quanto le devo?   *How much do I owe you?*

Another common meaning of **dovere** is *to owe*. In Italian you owe something *to* someone and an indirect object is therefore required:

***Le devo* qualcosa?**	*Do I owe you anything?*

5 Prima di + infintive   *before …*

Prima di + infinitive expresses the English *before doing …*

Devo telefonare *prima di* venire?	*Should I phone before coming?*
Mi lasci l'indirizzo *prima di* partire.	*Let me have your address before you leave.*

6 Sedersi   *to sit down*

Si segga! *Do sit down!* is the second person singular (**lei** form) imperative of **sedersi**, which is irregular, and, as we have already seen, is formed by changing the first person singular (present tense) ending **-o** to **-a** (p. 157).

Present tense	**sedersi** *to sit (down)*
mi seggo, mi siedo	**ci sediamo**
ti siedi	**vi sedete**
si siede	**si seggono, si siedono**

7 Tenga! *Here you are!*

Tenga from **tenere** *to hold, to keep* follows the same pattern as **venire** (p. 91):

Present tense	**tenere** *to hold, to keep*
tengo	**teniamo**
tieni	**tenete**
tiene	**tengono**

8 Si sono rotti gli occhiali *the glasses broke*

As **rompere** is a transitive verb and must have an object, the reflexive form **rompersi** must be used in this case (i.e. Lit: *the glasses broke themselves*). Therefore, the perfect tense must be formed with **essere** and the past participle must agree with the subject:

Si sono rotti **gli occhiali**.	*My glasses broke.*
Si è rotta **la sedia**.	*The chair broke.*

9 Occorrono, mi servono

Occorrere and **servire** both express the idea of necessity or need: the verb agrees with the thing needed and the person becomes an indirect object:

Le serve il dizionario?	*Do you need the dictionary?*
Sì. *Mi* **serve.**	*Yes, I do (need it).*
Gli **occorre la scheda telefonica.**	*He needs a phonecard.*

Quando le $\begin{cases} \text{occorr}\textit{ono} \\ \quad\quad\quad \text{gli occhiali?} \\ \text{serv}\textit{ono} \end{cases}$ *When do you need the glasses?* (Lit. *When are the glasses necessary to you?*)

Mi $\begin{cases} \text{occorr}\textit{ono} \\ \\ \text{serv}\textit{ono} \end{cases}$ **per domenica.** *I need them for Sunday.*

Come si dice in italiano?

How to:

1	ask someone how they feel	**Come si sente?**
	express how you feel	**Mi sento bene/male/meglio, ecc.**

2	say what you are suffering from	**Ho mal di testa/mal di denti, ecc.**
		Ho la febbre/il raffreddore, ecc.
3	ask what is wrong (where it hurts)	**Dove le fa male?**
	say what is wrong with you	**Mi fa male la testa.**
		Mi fanno male le gambe, ecc.
4	ask when someone requires something	**Quando le occorre/le occorrono?**
		Quando le serve/le servono?
	say when you require it/them by	**Mi occorre per...**
		Mi occorrono per...
		Mi serve per.../Mi servono per...

☑ Attività

1   What are these boys and girls saying? Each one is describing what hurts.

Use **Mi fa male/mi fanno male ...**

Anna

Giorgio

Alessandro

Livio

Orazio

Gina

2   First check your answers to **Attività 1**, then fit them into the right sentences below, but this time using **le/gli** instead of **mi** to describe what is hurting **Anna**, **Giorgio**, ecc.

   (a)   Anna non può giocare a tennis perchè …
   (b)   Giorgio non può respirare perchè …
   (c)   Livio non può leggere il giornale perchè …
   (d)   Orazio non può camminare perchè …
   (e)   Gina non può stare in piedi perchè …
   (f)   Alessandro non può giocare a calcio perchè …

3   Complete the following sentences by selecting the most appropriate of these expressions with **avere**: **il raffreddore**, **la febbre**, **mal di denti**, **mal di testa**, **mal di gola**, **mal di stomaco**. (Use each expression only once.)

   (a)   Rita non vuole parlare troppo perchè …
   (b)   Non vuole leggere perchè …
   (c)   Vuole prendere delle aspirine, perchè …
   (d)   Non vuole mangiare molto perchè …
   (e)   Vuole telefonare al dentista perchè …
   (f)   Ha bisogno di molti fazzoletti di carta (*tissues*) perchè …

4   Choose the appropriate verb from the following to complete the sentences below. Use each once only in the imperative: **lavarsi**, **asciugarsi**, **divertirsi**, **riposarsi**, **mettersi**.

   (a)   Si metta sul letto e _____.
   (b)   Prenda l'asciugamano e _____.
   (c)   Prenda il dentifrico e lo spazzolino e _____i denti.
   (d)   Si tolga la giacca e _____il cappotto.
   (e)   Vada alla festa e _____.

5   Respond with a negative command and replace the noun with a pronoun.

   Esempio: Devo accendere la luce?
   No. Non l'accenda.

   (a)   Devo prendere le pillole?
   (b)   Devo fare i biglietti?
   (c)   Devo telefonare a Livio?
   (d)   Devo scrivere a Ida?
   (e)   Devo aprire la porta?
   (f)   Devo chiudere le valigie?

6 **Ora tocca a te!** You and **Mara** are out driving: you need a rest.

You	*I don't feel well.*
Mara	Che hai? Ti fa male la testa?
You	*No. My eyes hurt.*
Mara	Perchè non ti metti gli occhiali?
You	*Unfortunately, they're at the optician's.*
Mara	Ma posso guidare io se vuoi.
You	*Alright. In that way* I can rest a bit.*
Mara	Che ne dici di fermarci un momento in farmacia?
You	*Good idea! And then we can go and have something to drink.*
Mara	Allora prima ci fermiamo in farmacia e poi andiamo al Bar Quattro Fontane.
You	*And in that way* I can also phone the doctor.*

* *in that way* così

❈ Informazioni

In Italy, as in Great Britain, there is a **Servizio Sanitario Nazionale** *National Health Service* to which all who are in work pay contributions. Anyone coming from abroad who is unlucky enough to fall ill or have an accident is entitled to use it.

21 | PROGETTI: VACANZE, MUSICA, ARTE
Plans: holidays, music, art

In this Unit you will learn how to:

■ say when you will be taking your holidays
■ say who you will be staying with or seeing
■ say when a CD, book, etc. will come out
■ ask when an exhibition will take place
■ say that you will let someone know

Dialogo 1 Progetti per le vacanze   *Holiday plans*

Massimo, asked whether he has already had his holidays (**le ferie**), answers that he will be having them at the end of July.

(a) **Vero o falso?** Massimo non ha ancora avuto le ferie.

Giornalista	Ha già avuto le ferie?
Massimo	No. Le avrò alla fine di luglio.
Giornalista	Dove andrà a passarle? In Calabria?
Massimo	Naturalmente. Andremo dai nostri parenti.
Giornalista	Li andrà a trovare certamente tutti!
Massimo	Eh, no. Sarà impossibile vederli tutti. Ne abbiamo tanti!
Giornalista	E quando partirà?
Massimo	Fra una settimana, ai primi di agosto.

Dove andrà (from **andare)?**	**Quando partirà** (from **partire)?**
Where will you go?	*When will you leave?*
sarà (from **essere)** *it will be...*	**ai primi di** *at the beginning of*

(b) Dove andranno Massimo e sua moglie per le ferie, e da chi andranno?

Dialogo 2 Non le dà fastidio tanto sole? *Doesn't so much sun bother you?*

Massimo explains that they will stay at **Catanzaro** for the Bank Holiday and will then travel around before going back to Milan.

(a) **Vero o falso?** Il sole dà fastidio a Massimo.

Giornalista	Nel mese di agosto fa un caldo da morire. Non le dà fastidio tanto sole?
Massimo	Macchè! E poi ci siamo abituati.
Giornalista	Rimarrà per il ferragosto, immagino.
Massimo	Ah, sì. Resteremo a Catanzaro per le feste e poi andremo un po' in giro prima di ritornare a Milano.
Giornalista	Quando ricomincerà a lavorare?
Massimo	Dovrò essere sul posto di lavoro il venti agosto.

un caldo da morire	*boiling hot*	**ferragosto**	*August Bank Holiday*
macchè *not at all*		**dovrò** (from **dovere**)	*I'll have to*
essere abituato/a a	*to be used to*	**sul posto di lavoro**	*at work*
rimarrà (from **rimanere**)	*you will stay*	(Lit: *at the place of work*)	

(b) Perchè Massimo dovrà essere sul posto di lavoro il venti agosto?

Dialogo 3 Una mostra d'arte *An art exhibition*

Lucia tells **Claudio** about an important art exhibition she is working on, and hopes he will come to see it.

(a) **Vero o falso?** Lucia dovrà lavorare alla mostra per tutto il periodo dell'esposizione.

Lucia	Senti, Claudio, fra tre giorni ci sarà una mostra di arte moderna.
Claudio	Ci saranno molti quadri?
Lucia	Moltissimi, perchè è un'esposizione importante.
Claudio	Ho sentito dire che vari oggetti verranno dal Museo di Arte Moderna di New York, è vero?
Lucia	Sì, è vero. Verrai anche tu, spero!
Claudio	Si dovrà fare la fila per entrare?
Lucia	Boh...! Ma penso di sì.

Claudio	Per quanto tempo ci sarà la mostra?
Lucia	Resterà aperta due o tre mesi, credo. Ma non ne sono certa. Te lo farò sapere.
Claudio	E tu lavorerai lì durante tutto il periodo dell'esposizione?
Lucia	Eh, sì. Per forza. Ed ora, scusami Claudio, ma devo andare.
Claudio	Quando ti rivedrò un'altra volta?
Lucia	Dunque... Fammi pensare... Sì, domenica, cioè no, meglio sabato.

---

sentir(e) dire che	*to hear that*	**verranno** (from **venire**)	*they will*
te lo farò (from **fare**) **sapere**	*I'll*		*come*
let you know		**boh...!**	*I don't know*
fare la fila	*to queue up*	**rivedrò** (from **rivedere**)	*I'll see again*
oggetto	*object, thing*	**fammi pensare**	*let me think*
per forza	*I must*	**cioè**	*that is*

(b) Claudio rivedrà Lucia domenica o sabato?

Dialogo 4   **In un negozio di dischi**   *In a record shop*

Una signorina wants to know when the **Festival di Sanremo** song collection (**raccolta di canzoni**) will come out.

(a) **Vero o falso?** La signorina vuole consultare la raccolta delle ultime canzoni.

Signorina	Scusi, ha il catalogo dei nuovi dischi?
Commesso	Sì. Lo vuole consultare? Quando avrà finito, me lo riporti qui per favore. Tenga!
Signorina	Grazie. Quando uscirà la raccolta delle ultime canzoni del Festival di Sanremo?
Commesso	Il nuovo cd sarà in vendita dal primo aprile. Glielo metto da parte?
Signorina	Sì, perchè domani parto per le vacanze, e non so se sarò di ritorno in tempo per comprarlo. Immagino che andrà a ruba.
Commesso	Gliene potremo conservare uno, ma deve lasciare un deposito.
Signorina	Un deposito? Quanto?
Commesso	Il trenta per cento del prezzo.

quando avrà finito *when you've finished*	**andare a ruba** *to sell like hot cakes*
in vendita *on sale*	**Gliene potremo** (from **potere**)
trenta per cento *thirty per cent*	**conservare uno.** *We'll be*
Glielo metto da parte? *shall I put it aside for you?*	*able to put one by for you.*

(b) Che cosa deve fare la signorina dopo aver consultato il catalogo?

Dialogo 5 Gliele spediranno *They'll send them to you*

The shop assistant tells the **Signorina** that she can pay the balance when she comes to collect it.

(a) **Vero o falso?** Il commesso dà una ricevuta alla signorina.

Commesso Pagherà il resto quando verrà a ritirarlo.

Signorina Va bene, grazie. Prendo anche queste due musicassette. Quanto fa?

Commesso Le faccio il conto... Un attimo, signorina, aspetti che le dò la ricevuta per quando ritirerà il disco.

Signorina Sì, grazie. Un'ultima cosa. Sa se col disco ci saranno i testi delle canzoni? Mi interessano anche le parole.

Commesso Mi spiace, non saprei. Se non ci saranno, dovrà richiederle direttamente alla casa discografica. Gliele spediranno a casa.

ritirerà (from **ritirare**) *you will collect*	**non saprei** (from **sapere**) *I wouldn't know*
testo *text*	**richiedere** *to ask for, order*
mi spiace = mi dispiace	**casa discografica** *record company*

(b) Cosa dovrà fare la signorina se col disco non ci saranno i testi?

Spiegazioni

1 *Future tense: formation*

Change the infinitive endings **-are** and **-ere** to **-erò, -erai, -erà, ecc.**

For verbs ending in **-ire**, change **-ire** to **-irò, -irai, -irà, ecc:**

    prendere   *to take*   **prend**erò   *I shall/will take*

Attenzione! Note particularly the final accent on the **io** and **lui/lei** forms as this is where the stress falls.

Future tense

parlare *to speak*	**prendere** *to take*	**coprire** *to cover*
parlerò *I shall, will speak, etc.* **parl**erai **parl**erà **parl**eremo **parl**erete **parl**eranno	**prend**erò **prend**erai **prend**erà **prend**eremo **prend**erete **prend**eranno	**copr**irò **copr**irai **copr**irà **copr**iremo **copr**irete **copr**iranno

For **pagare** and other verbs ending in **-care** and **-gare**, an 'h' is added throughout the future tense to preserve the hard sound of the infinitive (p. 136):

    pagare   pa*gh*erò, pa*gh*erai, ecc.
    cercare   cer*ch*erò, cer*ch*erai, ecc.

Verbs ending in **-giare** and **-ciare** omit 'i' in the future tense:

    mangiare   man*g*erò, man*g*erai, ecc.
    lasciare   las*c*erò, las*c*erai, ecc.
    cominciare comin*c*erò, comin*c*erai, ecc.

2 *Future tense: irregular formation*

Here is the future tense of **avere**:

avrò *I shall have, I will have, etc.* **avrai** **avrà**	**avremo** **avrete** **avranno**

Although the future endings are always the same, the stems of some verbs appear in contracted form. Here is a list of some of the more common ones. Most appear in this unit. These verbs follow the same pattern as **avere**:

andare	to go:	andrò, andrai, andrà, andremo, andrete, andranno.
cadere	to fall:	cadrò, cadrai, cadrà, ecc.
dovere	to have to:	dovrò, dovrai, dovrà, ecc.
potere	to be able:	potrò, potrai, potrà, ecc.
sapere	to know:	saprò, saprai, saprà, ecc.
vedere	to see:	vedrò, vedrai, vedrà, ecc.
vivere	to live:	vivrò, vivrai, vivrà, ecc.

The following verbs form the future tense like **fare**:

fare	to do, make:	farò, farai, farà, faremo, farete, faranno
dare	to give:	darò, darai, darà, ecc.
stare	to stay:	starò, starai, starà, ecc.

The following verbs form their future tense with a double consonant:

bere	to drink:	berrò, berrai, berrà, berremo, berrete, berranno
rimanere	to remain, stay:	rimarrò, rimarrai, rimarrà, ecc.
tenere	to hold, keep:	terrò, terrai, terrà, ecc.
venire	to come:	verrò, verrai, verrà, ecc.
volere	to wish, want:	vorrò, vorrai, vorrà, ecc.

The future of **sedersi** *to sit, to sit down*: **mi siederò, ti siederai, si siederà, ci siederemo, vi siederete, si siederanno**.

Finally, here is the future of **essere** *to be*:

sarò *I shall, will be etc.*	saremo
sarai	sarete
sarà	saranno

3 Future tense: use

The future tense, in Italian, is used to express future time:

| *Verremo a* **prenderti alla** **stazione.** | *We'll come and collect you from the station.* |

Sometimes, as we have seen, the present tense in Italian conveys the idea of something imminent, but whenever it does so, the future may equally be used:

Lo *faccio* più tardi. } *I'll do it later.*
Lo *farò* più tardi.

Ci *penso* io } *I'll see to it.*
Ci *penserò* io.

Italian also uses the future tense in subordinate clauses introduced by conjunctions of time (*when... as soon as...*, etc.) where the future is implied.

Cosa farai *quando sarai* grande?	*What will you do when you grow up?*
***Appena arriverò* sistemerò tutto.**	*As soon as I arrive I'll fix everything.*

Fra meaning *in* and **per** meaning *by*, always refer to something about to happen. They are often used, therefore, with the future tense:

Lo *vedrò fra* una settimana.	*I'll see him in a week's time.*
Lo *finirò per* venerdi.	*I'll finish it by Friday.*

The future is also used to suggest probability or possibility:

Chi *sarà* a quest'ora?	*Who could it be at this time?*
***Sarà* Mirella.**	*It's probably Mirella.*
Chi è quel ragazzo?	*Who's that boy?*
***Sarà* il suo fidanzato.**	*It's probably her fiancè. Maybe it's her fiancè.*
Che ore sono?	*What time is it?*
***Saranno* le nove.**	*It will be about nine.*

4 Macchè! *Not at all*

Macchè is used to contradict or deny what has been said previously:

Funziona bene quest'ascensore?	*Does this lift work properly?*
***Macchè!* È sempre guasto.**	*Of course not! It's always out of order.*
Guadagni molto?	*Do you earn a lot?*
***Macchè!* Lo stipendio che prendo non mi basta neanche per vivere.**	*Certainly not! The salary I get isn't even enough for me to live on.*
Gliel'hanno regalato?	*Did they give it to you?*
***Macchè* regalato! L'ho comprato.**	*Give it to me! You're joking! I bought it.*

5 Sentire *to hear, feel*

Sentire means both *to hear* and *to feel*. **Sentir(e) dire** means *to hear that ...* and **sentir(e) parlare** *to hear of ...*

Ho sentito dire che questo film   *I hear* (Lit: *heard*) *this film is*
è buono.   *good.*
Non ne ho mai *sentito* parlare.   *I've never heard of it.*

Senti! (tu) and **senta! (lei)** are used to attract attention and correspond to
the English *Listen!* or *Excuse me!*:

Senti! Perchè non usciamo?   *Listen! Why don't we go out?*
Senta per favore! Quando parte   *Excuse me! When does the next*
il prossimo treno per Verona?   *train leave for Verona?*

6 Boh....!   *I don't know!*

This is an exclamation used when the speaker does not know or is not
sure of something.

Chi è quel signore? *Boh..!*   *Who is that man? I don't know,*
                                     goodness knows!

7 Per forza   (Lit: *by force*)

This renders the idea that something is being done of necessity, whether
you like it or not:

Devi lavorare domani?   *Do you have to work tomorrow?*
Sì, *per forza,* altrimenti mi   *Yes, I really must, otherwise I'll*
licenziano.   *get the sack.* (Lit: *they dismiss*
                                     me.)

Devi già andare?   *Have you got to go already?*
Per forza, altrimenti perderò   *Yes, I've got to, otherwise I'll*
l'aereo.   *miss the plane.*
Devo farlo *per forza.*   *I absolutely have to do it.*

8 Te lo farò sapere   *I'll let you know*

Double pronouns

We have already seen how **ci + ne** becomes **ce ne** in the expression **ce ne
sono**. Other combinations of unstressed pronouns may also be found.
Here are the principles along which they combine:

Indirect object pronouns **mi** (*to/for me*), **ti** (*to/for you*), **ci** (*to/for us*), **vi**
(*to/for you* pl.) precede direct object ones **lo, la, li, le,** and also **ne**.

They (**mi, ti, ci, vi**) become **me, te, ce, ve,** before **lo, la, li, le,** and **ne**:

Mi **dà** *il libro.*	*He gives me the book.*
Me lo **dà.**	*He gives **it to me.***
Ti **darò** *la ricevuta.*	*I'll give you the receipt.*
Te la **darò.**	*I'll give **it to you.***
Vi **presenterò** *la mia ragazza.*	*I'll introduce my girlfriend to you.*
Ve la **presenterò.**	*I'll introduce **her to you.***
Pietro **ci presterà** *la macchina.*	*Peter will lend us his car.*
Ce la **presterà.**	*He will lend **it to us.***
Quante bottiglie di vino *ci* **porterà?**	*How many bottles of wine will you bring us?*
Ve ne **porterò due.**	*I'll bring **you two** (of them).*

Indirect **gli** and **le** + object pronouns are dealt with in Unit 24, p 259.

Come si dice in italiano?

How to:

1 ask someone when they will take their annual leave; say when you will have yours

Quando avrai le ferie? Le avrò alla fine di giugno/fra una settimana/fra un mese, ecc.

2 ask someone where they will be going and say who you will be staying with or seeing

Dove andrai? Andrò dai miei genitori/da un mio amico, ecc.

3 ask when a book, record, etc., will come out; say when it will do so

Quando uscirà il libro, il disco, ecc? Uscirà il dieci marzo, il quindici maggio, ecc.

4 ask someone when an exhibition will take place; say you will let them know.

Quando ci sarà la mostra? Te lo farò sapere.

☑ Attività

1 *Future: first person*

Below is a list of things **Antonella** has to do next Saturday. Imagine you are **Antonella** and answer as in the example.

Antonella, cosa farai sabato prossimo?
Esempio: (a) Mi alzerò presto, ecc.

Sabato prossimo Antonella deve:

(a) alzarsi presto
(b) bere un bicchier(e) di latte
(c) andare al mercato a fare la spesa
(d) fare i letti
(e) pulire le camere
(f) preparare da mangiare
(g) sparecchiare (*to clear*) la tavola
(h) lavare i piatti
(i) riposarsi un po'
(j) prendere un po' di sole in terrazza
(k) andare ad aiutare sua zia nel negozio di elettrodomestici (*household appliances*)
(l) finire di lavorare verso le otto
(m) uscire con delle simpaticissime amiche

2   Answer these questions with the 3rd person plural of the future tense.

Esempio: Finiscono oggi? _____ **fra un paio di settimane.**
   No. Finiranno fra un paio di settimane.

(a) Escono subito? _____ più tardi.
(b) Restano a pranzo? _____ a cena.
(c) Vengono sabato? _____ domenica.
(d) Possono farlo adesso? _____ domani pomeriggio.
(e) Sono qui alle cinque? _____ per le otto.
(f) Lo fanno stamattina? _____ dopo pranzo.
(g) Arrivano questa settimana? _____ la settimana prossima.
(h) La costruiscono quest'anno? _____ fra tre anni. (**costruire** *to build*)

3   Replace the infinitive (in brackets) by the first person plural of the future. Start: **Fra due settimane andremo ...**

Fra due settimane (*andare*) con i nostri amici in villeggiatura. (*Stare*) al mare per una diecina di giorni e poi (*trascorrere*) una settimana in montagna dove abbiamo una piccola villetta. (*Tornare*) il quattordici agosto per passare le feste a casa. Il quindici (*dare*) un grande pranzo all'aperto: (*invitare*) tutti i nostri parenti. Nel pomeriggio (*guardare*) la processione dal balcone e poi (*andare*) un po' in giro per il paese. La sera (*sedersi*) alla pasticceria 'Roma' dove (*prendere*) il gelato e (*ascoltare*) la musica fino a mezzanotte.

andare in villeggiatura	*to go on holiday*
villetta	*small villa, cottage*

4   All the questions are addressed to you alone or to you and your partner: answer with **me** or **ce** + object pronoun + verb as in the example.

Esempio: **Chi le mostrerà le diapositive?** ____ **il professore.**
Me le mostrerà il professore.

Chi vi mostrerà le diapositive? ____ **il professore.**
Ce le mostrerà il professore.

(a) Chi le riparerà la macchina?   ____ il meccanico.
(b) Chi le cambierà le sterline?   ____ il cassiere.
(c) Chi vi prenoterà l'albergo?   ____ il nostro amico
                                             Sandro.
(d) Chi le farà il quadro?   ____ un pittore francese.
(e) Chi vi porterà il vino dall'Italia?   ____ un nostro collega.
(f) Chi le disegnerà la casa?   ____ un architetto
                                             italiano.
(g) Chi le regalerà il dizionario?   ____ mia sorella.
(h) Chi vi troverà l'appartamento a
    Rimini?   ____ nostro cugino.

5 **Ora tocca a te!** You are in a bookshop and you'd like a book about
   Italy (**sull'Italia**).

You   *I'd like a book about Italy.*
Libraio Che tipo di libro? Desidera qualcosa sulla politica o
            sull'economia?
You   *I'm really looking for a book for tourists.*
Libraio Dunque, è una guida che desidera?
You   *Yes. I'd like to do a tour of the lakes.*
Libraio Ah! Allora le serve un libro sull'Italia settentrionale!
You   *Exactly. May I see what* you have?*
Libraio Mi dispiace, ma al momento non abbiamo niente.
You   *How's that?*
Libraio Purtroppo ho venduto l'ultimo un'ora fa.
You   *Aren't you expecting any others?*
Libraio Naturalmente! Ma lei quando parte?
You   *I shall be leaving on the first of June.*
Libraio Bene. Se viene qui alla fine di maggio avrò proprio ciò che
            desidera.
You   *Can I reserve a copy now?*
Libraio Senz'altro. Mi lasci il dieci per cento di anticipo e il suo
            indirizzo. Quando il libro arriverà glielo farò sapere.

*what   **ciò che**

❈ Informazioni

1 Le feste   *Festivals*

Religious festivals are still celebrated in many Italian towns and cities. Even the smallest villages pay homage to their patron saint and in many towns each district has its own local festival. The celebrations last several days and include processions, music from local bands, sporting events and firework displays. **Le sagre** *food festivals*, celebrate agricultural produce such as **l'uva** *grapes* or **pomodori** *tomatoes*. There are also the festivals that include displays of historical pageantry such as **il Palio** in Sienna which dates back to mediaeval times.

2 Il Ferragosto

This is more or less the Italian equivalent of our August bank holiday. It takes place on 15 August. Everything closes down except in tourist resorts. Many Italians take their holidays during this period. In the South especially, the day is marked by a religious festival, **La Festa dell'Assunta** *the Feast of the Assumption*.

Where are the following events (**manifestazioni**) taking place?

MANIFESTAZIONI

A Castiglion Fiorentino: **Palio dei rioni** la terza domenica di giugno. A Cortona: **Mostra-mercato nazionale del mobile antico** in agosto - settembre. A Castiglione del Lago: **festa del lago** con sfilata di barche illuminate, in agosto; **mercato dell'antiquariato** il terzo sabato di ogni mese da aprile a settembre. A Montepulciano: **Cantiere internazionale d'arte**, con mostre d'arte e spettacoli di teatro e concerti, in luglio e agosto. A Chianciano Terme: **Mostra internazionale dei telefilm** a maggio-giugno. A Chiusi: **Estate musicale** in luglio.

Dove si deve andare per vedere: (a) **La Mostra dei mobili antichi?**

(b) **La Mostra dei telefilm?**

(c) **La festa del lago?**

22 IERI E OGGI
Then and now

In this Unit you will learn how to:

■ say where you used to work
■ say whether you liked what you were doing
■ say where you used to live
■ say what you used to do
■ ask others similar questions.

Dialogo 1 Dove lavoravi?   *Where did you use to work?*

Filippo asks **Michele** where he used to work before moving to Rome. He answers that he used to be in Turin where he worked for Fiat.

(a) **Vero o falso?** A Torino Michele abitava in periferia.

Filippo	Dove lavoravi prima di trasferirti a Roma?
Michele	Ero a Torino. Lavoravo alla Fiat.
Filippo	E non ti piaceva stare lì?
Michele	No. La vita di fabbrica non mi andava proprio.
Filippo	Abitavate in centro?
Michele	No. Avevamo un appartamento in periferia; mia moglie trovava la vita molto monotona. Non veniva mai a trovarci nessuno. E tu, cosa fai qui?
Filippo	Adesso sono impiegato in una grande società straniera. Prima lavoravo anch'io in fabbrica.
Michele	Una volta riuscivo a sopportare quel lavoro, adesso non più.

fabbrica *factory*	**sono impiegato** *I'm employed*
non mi andava (from **andare**) *didn't suit me*	**società** *company*
avevamo (from **avere**) *we used to have*	**riuscivo** (from **riuscire**) **a sopportare** *I managed to put up with/I could bear*

(b) La moglie di Michele, quando abitava a Torino, trovava la vita molto interessante?

Dialogo 2 Dieci anni dopo *Ten years later*

Two men recall when they were bachelors (**scapoli**).

(a) **Vero o falso?** Quando Nino e Dario erano scapoli non uscivano mai.

Dario Lo sapevi che abbiamo un altro bambino?

Nino No, Non lo sapevo. Rallegramenti! Ti ricordi di quando eravamo scapoli? Dicevamo sempre che non volevamo sposarci.

Dario Eh, come no! Me lo ricordo bene! Si dice sempre così finchè non si incontra la donna ideale.

Nino Che bei tempi, i tempi del liceo! Uscivamo ogni sera e facevamo sempre tardi. Ti ricordi quella notte in cui ci siamo ubriacati e abbiamo fatto il bagno nel fiume?

Dario Altrochè! Una volta si poteva passare tutta la notte fuori; allora non ci si preoccupava di niente. Si era giovani e spensierati, ma ora con i bambini…

Nino Hai ragione. E poi c'è l'età. Un tempo bevevo e mangiavo senza problemi. Ora il medico mi ha proibito di bere.

Dario Purtroppo il tempo passa per tutti, e anche la salute se ne va.

rallegramenti! *congratulations!*	**altrochè!** *you bet I do!*
come no! Me lo ricordo … *of course I remember it …*	**spensierato/a** *carefree*
	far tardi *to stay up late*
finchè non si incontra *until one meets*	**un tempo** *in the past*
ubriacarsi *to get drunk*	**la salute se ne va** *our health deteriorates*
fiume (m.) *river*	

(b) Che cosa dicevano sempre quando erano scapoli?

Dialogo 3 A colloquio per un nuovo posto di lavoro
Interview for a new job

La signora Esposito asks **Eugenio Parisi** how he heard about the new job and he answers that he learnt about it from a newspaper advert (**l'inserzione sul giornale**).

(a) **Vero o falso?** Eugenio Parisi lavorava in una banca.

Sig.ra E.	Come ha saputo di questo impiego?
Eugenio P.	Ho visto l'inserzione sul giornale.
Sig.ra E.	Che titolo di studio ha?
Eugenio P.	La maturità classica.
Sig.ra E.	Non ha fatto gli studi universitari?
Eugenio P.	Non ho potuto. Mio padre era gravemente ammalato e non poteva più mantenerci. Così mi sono impiegato in un'azienda agricola.
Sig.ra E.	Che cosa faceva lì?
Eugenio P.	Mi occupavo della produzione.
Sig.ra E.	È stato licenziato?
Eugenio P.	No. Il padrone ha venduto tutto.
Sig.ra E.	Vedrà che ora con la nostra ditta si troverà bene.

titolo di studio *educational qualifications*	**azienda agricola** *large farm, agricultural co-operative*
maturità classica *high school leaving certificate*	**impiegarsi** *to get a job*
ammalato/a *ill*	**occuparsi di** *to deal with*
mantenere *to support*	**licenziato/a** *dismissed*
	ditta *firm*

(b) Perchè non ha fatto gli studi universitari?

Dialogo 4 Sa suonare? *Can you play an instrument?*

(a) **Vero o falso?** Bruno sa suonare il pianoforte.

Antonio	Da quanto tempo suona il pianoforte?
Bruno	Da quando ero piccolo. E lei, sa suonare?
Antonio	Una volta suonavo la chitarra. Adesso non suono più.
Bruno	Che tipo di musica suonava?
Antonio	Soprattutto musica rock.
Bruno	Era professionista?
Antonio	No. Ero dilettante.

chitarra	*guitar*	**il/la professionista**	*professional*
una volta...	*once...*	**il/la dilettante**	*amateur*
soprattutto	*above all*		

(b) Nel passato anche Antonio suonava il pianoforte?

Spiegazioni

1 *Imperfect tense: formation*

Take off the **-are**, **-ere** and **-ire** from the infinitive and add the appropriate endings.

Infinitive	*Imperfect*	
parl-*are*	**parl** *-avo*	*I was speaking, I used to speak, I spoke, etc.*
vend-*ere*	**vend** *-evo*	*I was sellling, I used to sell, I sold, etc.*
fin-*ire*	**fin-***ivo*	*I was finishing, I used to finish, I finished, etc.*

Imperfect tense		
parlare	**vendere**	**finire**
parlavo	**vendevo**	**finivo**
parlavi	**vendevi**	**finivi**
parlava	**vendeva**	**finiva**
parlavamo	**vendevamo**	**finivamo**
parlavate	**vendevate**	**finivate**
parlavano	**vendevano**	**finivano**

The stress always falls on the last syllable but one, except in the 3rd person plural where it shifts back to the last syllable but two:

andavo, andavi, andava, andavamo, andavate, andavano.

Only **essere** does not conform to this pattern of endings:

Imperfect tense		**essere** *to be*
ero	*I was, used to be, etc.*	**eravamo**
eri		**eravate**
era		**erano**

There are a few other verbs where, although the endings conform to the regular pattern, the stem changes. Here are some of the most important ones:

Infinitive		Imperfect
bere	*to drink*	**bev**e**vo, bev**e**vi, bev**e**va, bev**e**vamo, bev**e**vate, bev**e**vano**
dire	*to say, tell*	**dic**e**vo, dic**e**vi, dic**e**va, ecc.**
fare	*to do, make,*	**fac**e**vo, fac**e**vi, fac**e**va, ecc.**
produrre	*to produce*	**produc**e**vo, produc**e**vi, produc**e**va, ecc.**

2 Imperfect tense: use

There is no exact equivalent tense in English. **Parlavo** could mean, according to the context, *I spoke, I used to speak, I was speaking* or *I would speak*. The imperfect expresses continuity or habitual action in the past, whereas the perfect tense emphasises that the action is completed.

Mentre *aspettavo* l'autobus, è arrivato un tassì.	*While I was waiting for the bus, a taxi arrived.*

In the above example the imperfect **aspettavo** describes what was already happening and could have continued to do so when the taxi arrived.

Mentre *guidavo*, mi sono accorto che non *avevo* più benzina.	*While I was driving I realised I had run out of* (Lit: *had no more*) *petrol.*

Habitual action is often expressed by *used to* or *would*:

***Uscivamo* ogni sera.**	*We used to go out every night.*
***Facevamo* sempre tardi.**	*We would always stay up late.*

Finally, it expresses a state of things in the past:

Ha detto che *abitava* a Venezia.	*He said he lived in Venice.*
In Inghilterra non *conosceva* nessuno.	*He knew nobody in England.*
In quanti *eravate*?	*How many were there of you?*
***Eravamo* in venti, ma ora siamo in dieci.**	*There were 20 of us, but now there are 10.*
Non *sapevo* che eri qui.	*I didn't know that you were here.*

It is because such verbs as **essere** and **avere** are associated with states rather than actions, that they are frequently seen in the imperfect. Other such verbs are: **volevo** (*I wanted*), **pensavo** (*I thought*), **credevo** (*I believed*) and **immaginavo** (*I imagined*).

Giorgio *voleva* sapere dove *andavi*.	*George wanted to know where you were going.*
Pensavano solo a divertirsi.	*They thought only of having a good time.*

Sometimes the tense alters the meaning of the English. Compare the use of **sapere** in the second and third dialogues:

Lo *sapevi* che ...?	*Did you know that ...?*
Come *ha saputo* di questo posto?	*How did you hear about this job?*

3 Finchè (non)   *until*

Finchè is frequently followed by **non** even when the sense is not negative:

Non uscirai *finchè non* te lo dico io.	*You won't go out until I tell you.*
Lo aspetterò *finchè (non)* verrà.	*I'll wait (for him) till he comes.*

4 Non ci si preoccupava, si era ...   *One didn't worry, one was ...*

Here is a summary of points to note when **si** *one* is used impersonally.

(a) The verb used with impersonal **si** will be plural if the noun it refers to is plural:

In questo istituto *si insegna* l'italiano.	*Italian is taught in this institute.*
In questo istituto *si insegnano* le lingue straniere.	*Foreign languages are taught in this institute.*

(b) When impersonal **si** is followed by a part of the verb **essere** and an adjective, the verb is always in the singular and the adjective in the plural:

Quando *si è giovani*, si impara presto.	*When one is young, one learns fast.*

(c) When reflexive verbs (**divertirsi, lavarsi, ecc.**) are used in the impersonal form, use **ci si** before the verb:

(lui) si diverte *he enjoys himself*	***ci si diverte*** *one enjoys oneself*
(lei) si lava *she washes (herself)*	***ci si lava*** *one washes (oneself)*

5 **Professionista**   *professional*

Nouns or adjectives ending in **-ista** may be masculine or feminine. The plural forms end in **-i** when masculine, and **-e** when feminine:

il giornalista *(male journalist)*   **i giornalisti**
la giornalista *(female journalist)* **le giornaliste**

Similarly, **il/la**: **pian*ista*, chitarr*ista*, violin*ista*, farmac*ista*, l'art*ista*,** ecc.

6 **Andarsene**   *to be off, to leave*

Andarsene is formed from the verb **andare** and **si**, which when followed by **ne**, becomes **se**. Similarly, the reflexive pronouns **mi, ti, ci, vi** become **me, te, ce, ve** before **ne**. Here is the present tense of **andarsene** in full:

(io) me ne vado	**(noi) ce ne andiamo**
(tu) te ne vai	**(voi) ve ne andate**
(lui/lei) se ne va	**(loro) se ne vanno**

It is frequently heard in conversation, and one way of rendering **me ne vado** in English would be: *I'm off.*

> **Me ne devo andare**
or **devo andarmene.**   *I must be off.*

Remember that the perfect tense must be formed with **essere**:

Poichè mi annoiavo,   *As I was bored, I left.*
  me ne sono andato.

Se ne sono andati **senza**   *They went away without even*
  neanche salutarci.   *saying goodbye.*

Here is the perfect tense illustrated in dialogue form:

Tutti se ne sono andati.   *Everybody's left.*

A   A che ora *te ne sei andato* ieri sera?
B   *Me ne sono andato* a mezzanotte.
A   Io e Luisa invece, *ce ne siamo andati* alle dieci.
B   Perchè *ve ne siete andati* così presto?
A   Perchè eravamo stanchi. Anche Ida e Gino *se ne sono andati* così tardi?
B   No. Loro *se ne sono andati* subito dopo che *ve ne siete andati* voi, perchè stamattina dovevano alzarsi presto.

Come si dice in italiano?

How to:

1	ask someone where they used to work	**Dove lavorava?**
	say where you used to work	**Lavoravo ...**
2	ask someone whether they liked what they were doing and answer	**(Non) le piaceva?** **(Non) mi piaceva.**
3	ask someone where they lived/ used to live	**Dove abitava?**
	say where you lived/used to live	**Abitavo ...**
4	ask someone what they used to do	**Cosa faceva?**
	say what you used to do	**Uscivo, bevevo, mangiavo, andavo, suonavo, ... ecc.**

Attività

1 **Luciano**, in nostalgic mood, notes the differences between life as he saw it in **Salerno**, and as he sees it in London. On the left you have to say what he used to do or what happened in Salerno (imperfect tense), on the right what happens at present.

Esempio: A Salerno: **A Londra:**

(a) *(abitare)* in un bell' appartamento   in una vecchia casa
Abitavo in un bell'appartamento.   **Abito in una vecchia casa.**

A Salerno:	A Londra:
(a) *(abitare)* in un bell'appartamento	in una vecchia casa
(b) *(fare)* così caldo	così freddo
(c) *(esserci)* tanto sole	tanta pioggia
(d) *(uscire)* ogni sera	non ... mai
(e) *(venire a trovarmi)* tante persone	non ... nessuno
(f) *(andare)* ogni domenica alla spiaggia	qualche volta in piscina
(g) *(parlare)* con tanta gente	non... con nessuno
(h) *(bere)* caffè e vino	tè e birra

2   Answer these questions, making sure you use the appropriate person of the verb in the imperfect, as in the examples.

Esempi: Perchè Franca non è uscita ieri? _____ *(piovere)*
Perchè pioveva.

Perchè non mi avete scritto? _____non *(avere)* **il tuo indirizzo.**
Perchè non avevamo il tuo indirizzo.

(a)   Perchè Franco non l'ha bevuto il caffè? _____ *(essere)* troppo forte.

(b)   Perchè sei andato dal dentista? _____ mi *(far male)* un dente.

(c)   Perchè avete comprato due biciclette? _____ *(costare)* poco.

(d)   Perchè hai cambiato lavoro? _____ dove *(essere)* prima *(dovere)* lavorare troppo.

(e)   Perchè non ha comprato la casa in Via Roma? _____ *(essere)* troppo cara.

(f)   Perchè non avete mangiato nulla? _____ non *(avere)* appetito.

(g)   Perchè hanno bevuto tutta quell'acqua? _____ *(avere)* sete.

(h)   Perchè siete andati a letto così presto? _____ *(essere)* stanchi morti.

(i)   Perchè sei andato dal medico? _____ non *(sentirsi)* bene.

(j)   Perchè Ida è andata in banca? _____ *(aver bisogno di)* soldi.

3   *Imperfect and perfect*

Gianfranco could get no peace: every time he was engaged in a task (imperfect) something happened (perfect).

Esempio: Mentre Gianfranco *(mangiare)*, *(rompersi)* **il dente.**
Mentre Gianfranco mangiava si è rotto il dente.

(a)   Mentre Gianfranco *(radersi)*, *(telefonare)* Marco.

(b)   Mentre *(scrivere)*, *(rompersi)* la penna.

(c)   Mentre *(riparare)* la macchina, *(arrivare)* Francesca.

(d)   Mentre *(cucinare)*, *(scottarsi)* la mano.

(e)   Mentre *(leggere)*, *(andarsene)* la luce.

(f)   Mentre *(guardare)* la tv, sua moglie gli *(chiedere)* di aggiustare la lavatrice.

radersi *to shave (oneself)*

4 Piccoli annunci (inserzioni)

(i) NEOLAUREATA offresi come babysitter di pomeriggio e di sera. Abita a Bergamo. Telefono: 437027

(ii) Marisa, diplomata in ragioneria, si offre per mezza giornata per lavori d'ufficio. Telefonatele nelle ore dei pasti al numero 64 30 00 6 di Venezia.

(iii) Siamo due giovani prossimi alle nozze. Vorremmo (*we would like*) prendere in affitto un appartamento, anche piccolo ma confortevole. Telefonateci al numero 48 93 12 di Pisa.

(iv) Laureato scienze politiche, trentenne, pluriennale (*of many years*) esperienza lavorativa, francese, inglese, tedesco, esamina proposte interessanti. Roma 20 14 82.

i   (a) È laureata da molto tempo?
    (b) Per quale periodo della giornata si offre come baby-sitter?
    (c) Dove vive?

ii (a) Ha il diploma di segretaria o di ragioniera?
    (b) Per quanto tempo vuole lavorare?
    (c) Quando bisogna telefonare?

iii (a) Sono già sposati i due giovani?
    (b) Vogliono comprare l'appartamento?
    (c) L'appartamento deve essere per forza grande?

iv (a) È laureato in scienze economiche e bancarie?
    (b) Quanti anni ha?
    (c) Lavora da poco tempo?
    (d) Quali lingue conosce?

5 Tutti se ne vanno *Everybody's leaving*

This dialogue contains all forms of the present tense of **andarsene**. Fill in the blanks appropriately.

Esempio: È tardi. ____ vado.
È tardi. Me ne vado.

A Ma come! Già _____ vai?
B Eh, sì. _____ devo andare.
A E Bruna? _____ va anche lei?
B No. Bruna non _____ va ancora. Però Anna e Roberto _____ vanno.
    E voi, quando _____ andate?
A Noi _____ andiamo più tardi.

6 **Ora tocca a te!** You are **il datore di lavoro** (_employer_) interviewing
a woman for a job.

You	_Where did you work when you were in Naples?_
Signora	Lavoravo in un'azienda agricola che esportava frutta in tutta Europa.
You	_But you yourself, what did you do exactly?_
Signora	Controllavo la qualità della frutta.
You	_Did you find the work difficult?_
Signora	Sì, perchè bastava un piccolo sbaglio per perdere clienti molto importanti.
You	_How long did you work in that co-operative?_
Signora	Tre anni e mezzo. Poi ce ne siamo andati a Sorrento, perchè mio padre era stanco di vivere in una grande città.
You	_Is that why you want to change your job?_
Signora	Sì, soprattutto per questo.

Informazioni

1 Torino

It is mainly due to the expansion of the **Fiat** car factory in the 1950's,
which drew workers from the whole peninsula, that Turin has become
the large industrial city it is now.

2 Lavoro

Finding work, although still rather difficult in the South and the
islands due to lack of investment, remains a problem for the whole of
Italy – hence the need for more and more qualifications.

Anche chi lavora e non
ha tempo può conseguire la

LAUREA

PRESSO QUALSIASI UNIVERSITÁ ITALIANA

*CEPU prepara agli esami di tutte le Facoltà, cura le
pratiche burocratiche, fornisce testi e dispense, garantisce
un insegnamento personalizzato attraverso lezioni tenute
da TUTOR individuali. Incontri in giorni e orari a scelta
dalle 9.00 alle 22.00. Oltre 1200 TUTOR INDIVIDUALI.*

70 CENTRI IN ITALIA.

®*CEPU* *Preparazione*
Universitaria

CHIEDI INFORMAZIONI
Numero Verde
167-011074

Via Bertola, 50/c – TORINO

Con noi il 91% supera gli esami

(a) **Secondo l'annuncio, qual è la percentuale degli studenti che
supera gli esami?**

23 | SENZA COMPLIMENTI!
No need to be polite!

In this Unit you will learn how to:

■ invite someone in, informally
■ ask someone what they were saying
■ say that you were about to …
■ ask someone to do something for you
■ tell someone there's no need to be polite

Dialogo 1 Stavamo proprio parlando di te
We were just talking about you

Angelo has heard somone ring the bell (**hanno suonato il campanello**) and **Bruna** goes to open the door to let **Gianna** in.

(a) **Vero o falso?** Quando hanno suonato, Angelo è andato ad aprire la porta.

Angelo	Hanno suonato il campanello. Vado ad aprire?
Bruna	No, Angelo, vado io. Dev'essere Gianna. Ciao Gianna! Entra! Stavamo proprio parlando di te.
Gianna	Davvero? E che cosa stavate dicendo?
Bruna	Ah...
Gianna	Sono venuta a salutarti perchè parto domani mattina presto. Disturbo?
Bruna	No, no, figurati! Vieni, cara, vieni. Entra pure!
Gianna	Grazie.
Bruna	Ma perchè stai in piedi? Siediti! Faccio il caffè!
Gianna	No, grazie. Me ne devo andare. Ho promesso alla mamma di aiutarla a fare le valigie. Ti lascio il mio indirizzo?
Bruna	Sì, sì. Stavo proprio per chiedertelo. Scrivimelo qui sopra.
Gianna	Ecco, tieni. Ed ora ti saluto.

Davvero? E che cosa stavate dicendo? *Were you? And what were you saying?*	*going to ask you for it.*
Sì, sì. Stavo proprio per chiedertelo. *Yes, do. I was just*	**promettere** *to promise* (past part: **promesso**)

(b) Cos'ha scritto Gianna per Bruna?

Dialogo 2 Ma dai, siediti! *Come on, sit down*

Bruna offers Gianna a glass of liqueur.

(a) **Vero o falso?** Bruna offre a Gianna un bicchierino di liquore.

Bruna	Ma siediti! Cosa posso offrirti? Lo prendi un bicchierino di liquore?
Gianna	No, grazie.
Bruna	Ma dai, siediti! Solo due minuti. Non fare complimenti!
Gianna	Non faccio complimenti. E poi, non bevo più. Ho anche smesso di fumare.
Bruna	Che brava! Ma oggi fa' un'eccezione. Tieni, assaggia questa Sambuca! Vedi com'è buona! Cin cin!
Gianna	Cin cin!

oggi fa' un'eccezione *today make an exception*		**assaggiare** *to taste*	
smettere di (past part: **smesso**) *to stop*		**Sambuca** *a type of liqueur* **cin cin!** *cheers!*	

(b) Gianna fuma ancora?

Dialogo 3 Che cosa facciamo da mangiare?
What shall we cook?

Romano suggests they should cook **la pastasciutta** (pasta served with a sauce).

(a) **Vero o falso?** Romano chiede a Silvio di prendergli una scatola di pomodori.

Romano	Senti, Silvio, facciamo la pasta?
Silvio	D'accordo. Fammi un favore, prendimi una scatola di pomodori!
Romano	Quale? Quella grande?

Silvio	No. Quella che hai in mano. Dammi anche l'apriscatole!
Romano	Dov'è? Lì dentro?
Silvio	Sì. Nel secondo cassetto.
Romano	Non metterci l'aglio nella salsa, però, perchè non mi piace. Falla solo con la cipolla. È cotta la pasta?
Silvio	Penso di sì. Assaggiala! Dimmi se c'è abbastanza sale! Attento! Non scottarti!
Romano	Per me va bene. Se la vuoi al dente, è pronta.

Fammi un favore!	*Could you do me a favour?*	**aglio, cipolla**	*garlic, onion*
		falla	*make it*
Prendimi una scatola.	*Get me a tin.*	**Assaggiala!**	*try it*
dammi	*give me*	**Non scottarti!**	*Don't burn yourself.*
apriscatole (m.)	*tin-opener*	**al dente**	*slightly underdone* (Lit: *to*
lì dentro	*in(side) there*		*the tooth*)

(b) A Romano piace l'aglio?

Spiegazioni

1 *Imperative:* tu, noi, *and* voi *forms*

To obtain the **tu** (familiar) form of the imperative of regular **-are** verbs, take off the **-are** from the infinitive and add **-a:**

ordin-**are** becomes **ordina**:

Ordina il secondo piatto!	*Order the second course.*
Paga il conto!	*Pay the bill.*

For most **-ere** and **-ire** verbs, the **tu** form of the imperative is the same as the **tu** form of the present tense:

(**tu**) **prendi** ... →	*Prendi il cappello e l'ombrello!*	
		Take your hat and umbrella.
(**tu**) **chiudi** ... →	*Chiudi (la porta) a chiave!*	
		Lock the door.
(**tu**) **vieni** ... →	*Vieni dentro!*	*Come inside!*
(**tu**) **corri** ... →	*Corri! corri!*	*Run! Run!*
(**tu**) **scendi** ... →	*Scendi giù!*	*Come downstairs!*

For the negative of the **tu** form use **non + infinitive:**

Alberto, *non toccare* **il quadro!**	*Albert! Don't touch the picture.*
Maria, *non parlare* **con**	*Mary! Don't talk with your*
la bocca piena!	*mouth full!*
Non cambiare **discorso!**	*Don't change the subject.*

As we saw in Unit 14, p 158 the **noi** and **voi** forms of the imperative are the same as the present tense. The negative is formed by putting **non** before the verb:

Non parlate **tutti insieme!**	*Don't all speak at once.*

2 Imperative with unstressed and reflexive pronouns

With the **lei** forms, unstressed and reflexive pronouns precede the imperative:

Mi porti **una forchetta e**	*Bring me a knife and fork.*
un coltello!	
Si segga **qui!**	*Sit (down) here.*
Non si preoccupi!	*Don't worry.*
Mi scusi **tanto, signor Sauri!**	*I'm so sorry, Mr Sauri.*

With the other forms of the imperative, the unstressed and the reflexive pronouns follow the verb and are joined to it, except in the negative where there is a choice:

Scusami **del ritardo!**	*Sorry I'm late.* (lit: *Excuse me*
	for the lateness).
Non dargli **la mancia!** or	*Don't give him a tip.*
Non gli dare **la mancia!**	
Non andarci! or *Non ci andare!*	*Don't go there.*
Accompagniamola **a casa!**	*Let's take her home.*
Sediamoci **a tavola!**	*Let's sit down to dinner*
	(at the table).
Sedetevi **qui!**	*Sit down here.*

3 Imperative tu form of fare, dire, stare, dare and andare:

(a) **fa'** *do*;   **di'** *say*;   **sta'** *stay*;   **da'** *give*;   **va'** *go*.

Da' **un'occhiata al libro!**	*Have a look at the book.*
Sta' **attento!** *Sta'* **zitto!**	*Be careful. Be quiet.*

(b) All the unstressed pronouns (including **ci**, **vi** and **ne**) except **gli**, double their initial consonants when combined with the above verbs (informal **tu**):

fa' + lo *becomes* **fallo**	***Fallo* subito!**	*Do it immediately.*
di' + mi *becomes* **dimmi**	***Dimmi* la verità!**	*Tell me the truth!*
da' + le *becomes* **dalle**	***Dalle* il cucchiaio!**	*Give her the spoon.*
va' + ci *becomes* **vacci**	***Vacci* tu!**	*You go there!*
di' + gli *becomes* **digli**	***Digli* di venire a pranzo!**	*Tell him to come to lunch.*
sta' + mi *becomes* **stammi**	***Stammi* a sentire!**	*Listen to me.*

4 *Imperative of* essere *and* avere.

essere	avere
sii (tu)!	**abbi (tu)!**
sia (lei)!	**abbia (lei)!**
siamo (noi)!	**abbiamo (noi)!**
siate (voi)!	**abbiate (voi)!**

> ***Abbiate* pazienza!**   *Be patient!*
> ***Siate* un po' più generosi!**   *Be a bit more generous!*

5 Pure

Pure may be used in the following ways:

(a) To grant permission with more conviction:

> **Posso entrare?**   *May I come in?*
> **Entri *pure*!**   *Please do.*
> **Posso fare una telefonata?**   *May I make a phone call?*
> **Sì, prego. Faccia *pure*!**   *Certainly, go ahead!*

(b) Like **anche** to mean *also*:

> **Vieni *pure* tu!**   *You come too!*

6 Quello, quella, quelli, quelle   *that one, those ones*

The above, apart from being adjectives, may also be used as pronouns meaning *the ones(s), that(one), those*. They must agree with the noun they refer to:

> **Questo rasoio non funziona:**   *This razor doesn't work.*
>   **prendi *quello* del mio ragazzo.**   *Take my boyfriend's one.*
> **Chi è quella donna?**   *Who is that woman?*

Quale? *Quella* **con gli**   *Which one? The one with the*
  occhi celesti?   *blue eyes?*
Preferisco i quadri moderni   *I prefer modern paintings to*
  a *quelli* **antichi**.   *old ones.*

7 Quello che, ciò che, quel che

In sentences such as the following, **quello che** means *what*:

  Non sa *quello che* **vuole.**   *He doesn't know what he wants.*

You could equally say:

  Non sa *ciò che* **vuole,** or **Non sa** *quel che* **vuole.**

8 In mano   *in your hand*

Here are a few more expressions with **in** where Italian uses neither the
definite article nor the possessive.

Cos'hai in $\begin{cases} \textbf{testa?} \\ \textbf{tasca?} \\ \textbf{mano?} \\ \textbf{bocca?} \end{cases}$ *What have you got* $\begin{cases} \textit{on your head?} \\ \textit{in your pocket?} \\ \textit{in your hand?} \\ \textit{in your mouth?} \end{cases}$

9 Come!   *What!*

When used alone **Come!** means *What!* It expresses surprise.

  Come! **Questa bottiglia**   *What! Is this bottle already*
    è già vuota?   *empty?*

10 Stare per + infinitive   *to be about to*

This construction renders the idea of *to be about to, to be on the point of*.
It is used in the present and imperfect:

  Lo spettacolo *sta per* **finire.**   *The performance is about to end.*
  Quando siamo usciti,   *When we went out it was*
    stava **per piovere.**   *just about to rain.*
  Stiamo per **acquistare una**   *We are on the point of buying*
    nuova casa.   *a new house.*

11 Gerund

Formation of gerund:

-**are** verbs: drop -**are** and add -**ando**
-**ere/-ire** verbs: drop -**ere/-ire** and add -**endo**

pag*are* → pag*ando*   pot*ere* → pot*endo*   fin*ire* → fin*endo*

Notice, however, these three special forms:

bere → bev*endo*   **fare** → fac*endo*   *dire* → dic*endo*

Use of gerund:

The Italian gerund corresponds to the form of the verb which, in English, ends in -*ing*.

Sbagliando **s'impara.**	*One learns by making mistakes.*

Sometimes it is best translated by *as, since, while*:

Dovendo **mantenere la famiglia, lavora molto.**	*As he has to support his family, he works hard.*
Non *avendo* **spiccioli, non mi ha dato il resto.**	*Since he didn't have any change, he didn't give me any (change).*
Andando **a teatro, ho incontrato Francesca.**	*As I was going to the theatre, I met Frances.*

Notice that the Italian gerund can never be preceded by a preposition as in English, and that its ending never changes. When object pronouns are used with a gerund, they are attached to the end of it, but when **stare + gerund** is used (see below) they precede **stare**:

Vedendo*lo arrivare* **così tardi, ho pensato che ...**	*Seeing him arrive so late, I thought that ...*

Stare + gerund stresses the time during which the action is happening:

Cosa *stai facendo*?	*What are you doing?*
Di chi *stai parlando*?	*Who are you talking about?*
Stavamo uscendo **quando è arrivato un nostro amico.**	*We were just going out when a friend of ours arrived.*
Ha cambiato i soldi? No, *li sta cambiando* **adesso.**	*Has he changed the money? No, he is changing it now.*

It is important to notice that no gerund can refer to the object of a sentence, so that if a sentence has both subject and object, the gerund must refer to the subject: **L'ho visto attraversando la strada** must mean

I saw him as I crossed the road. To say I saw him cross(ing) the road Italian uses the following two ways:

L'ho visto *attraversare* **la strada.**	*I saw him cross the road.*
L'ho visto *che attraversava* **la strada.**	*I saw him crossing the road.*

Come si dice in italiano?

How to:

1 invite someone in, informally ask them to sit down	**Vieni! Entra (pure)!** **Siediti!**
2 ask what they were saying; respond	**Cosa stavi dicendo?** **Stavo dicendo che ...**
3 say that you were about to ask ...	**Stavo per chiedere, ecc.**
4 ask someone to do something for you	**Fammi un favore, prendimi, dammi, ecc.**
5 tell someone not to stand on ceremony, there's no need to be polite.	**Senza complimenti!**

☑ Attività

1 You are **Vincenzo Alvaro's** boss. One day, at work, he does not feel very well. Tell him to do the following, using the **tu** form of the imperative as in the example.

Esempio: (a) Lasciare tutto.
          Lascia tutto!

(a) Lasciare tutto.
(b) Tornare a casa.
(c) Andare a letto.
(d) Coprirsi bene.
(e) Prendere un paio di aspirine.
(f) Chiamare il medico.
(g) Rimanere a casa per qualche giorno.
(h) Non preoccuparsi di niente.

coprirsi (like *aprire*) *to cover oneself*

2   Turn the following statements into commands or prohibitions according to the sense, using the **tu** form.

Esempio: (a) È vietato entrare. Non entrare!
             È meglio telefonare. Telefona!

(a)   È vietato fumare.
(b)   È meglio prendere l'aereo.
(c)   È inutile insistere.
(d)   È vietato parcheggiare lì.
(e)   È più conveniente andare in macchina.
(f)   È meglio portare l'ombrello.
(g)   È importante mettere la data su questo modulo.
(h)   È meglio usare la scheda telefonica.

vietato *forbidden*

3   *Prohibitions with the* **tu** *form*

You are going to tell someone not to do something. Respond to the following statements by using **non** + infinitive + direct object pronoun, choosing your verbs from the list below and using each once only.

perdere	**usare**	**prendere**	**attraversare**
pagare	**firmare**	**comprare**	**bere**

Esempio: (a) Il contratto non mi piace.
             Non firmarlo!

(a)   Il contratto non mi piace.
(b)   La macchina è guasta.
(c)   Il prosciutto è troppo caro.
(d)   Il conto è sbagliato.
(e)   L'acqua non è potabile.
(f)   Questo treno è troppo lento.
(g)   Questa strada è pericolosa.
(h)   Questi documenti sono molto importanti.

contratto	*contract*	**potabile**	*drinkable*
pericoloso	*dangerous*	**guasto**	*out of order*

4 *Commands and prohibitions:* sta', va', di', da', fa'

You are being told to tell individual children to do certain things. Follow the instructions as in the example. Join the pronouns to the imperative where necessary.

Esempio: Dica ad Alfredo di farle vedere cos'ha in mano.
Alfredo, fammi vedere cos'hai in mano!

(a) Dica a Luigi di stare zitto.
(b) Dica ad Alfredo di farle assaggiare il gelato.
(c) Dica ad Elena di andare all'altra tavola.
(d) Dica a Vittorio di darle il bicchiere.
(e) Dica a Maria di passarle il sale e il pepe.
(f) Dica a Nina di dirle cosa vuole per secondo piatto.

5   Complete as indicated, choosing between the present of **stare per** and **stare** + gerund, according to the sense, and using the appropriate person of the verb.

Esempio: Gli ospiti non si sono ancora messi a tavola?
No____ (chiacchierare)
No. Stanno chiacchierando.

(a) Posso parlare con Lucia?
     Mi spiace, ma ____ *(fare il bagno)*
(b) Che buon odore viene dalla cucina!
     Sì. Mariangela ____ *(cucinare)*
(c) Come sei bagnata Mirella!
     Sì. ____ *(piovere)*
(d) Vera avrà molto da fare in questi giorni.
     Perchè? ____ *(sposarsi)*
(e) Che rumore viene da quella radio!
     Cosa vuoi! Il gruppo 'Ragazzi del Sole'____ *(suonare)*
(f) Perchè fanno le valigie?
     Perchè ____ *(partire)*

| **un odore** | *smell* | **sposarsi** | *to get married* |
| **bagnato/a** | *soaked* | **un rumore** | *noise* |

6   In Column A you will see where people are. Match up with what they are doing in Column B, and change the infinitives to **stare** + gerund.

Esempio: Sandro è in banca. (cambiare) un assegno
Sandro è in banca. Sta cambiando un assegno.

A   B

(i) Laura è in sala da pranzo.   (a) *(chiacchierare)*

(ii) Siamo in un negozio   (b) *(cucinare)*
di abbigliamento.

(iii) I signori Ricci sono in   (c) *(fare)* la spesa
un supermercato.

(iv) Mario è in cucina.   (d) *(lavorare)*

(v) Alessandro è in ufficio.   (e) *(mangiare)*

(vi) Gli ospiti sono in salotto.   (f) *(comprare)* delle cravatte

assegno *cheque*

7 **Ora tocca a te!** Your mother is surprised to see you up so early
because she had forgotten you had an exam today.

Mamma Che fai in piedi così presto? Non sono ancora le cinque!

You *I'd like to study a bit.*

Mamma A quest'ora? Come mai?

You *But didn't you know that I've got an exam today?*

Mamma Ah, me n'ero proprio dimenticata! Ti preparo una tazza di
caffè?

You *No thanks. Go back to bed.*

Mamma Hai ancora molto da fare?

You *No, not much.*

Mamma Stai studiando tanto, è vero; fra un paio di anni però sarai
medico!

You *Yes, but only if I pass this exam. It's one of the most
difficult ones.*

Mamma Ma perchè ti preoccupi tanto?

You *Because this time I'm not sure of myself.*

Mamma Non ti preoccupare! Andrà tutto perfettamente, vedrai.

Informazioni

Senza complimenti!

You will often hear this expression when Italians are eager for you to accept
a drink or hospitality. If you don't wish to accept, you in your turn may
answer **Senza complimenti!** or **Non faccio complimenti!**

24 | HA BISOGNO DI AIUTO?
Do you need any help?

In this Unit you will learn how to:

■ ask someone to help you
■ ask someone for advice
■ ask for someone's particulars
■ ask someone to hold the line on the phone
■ ask and say whose something is

Dialogo 1 Al commissariato *At the police station*

Una signora reports the loss of her passport to the police and is told that she has to make a statement (**fare la denuncia**).

(a) **Vero o falso?** La signora è agitata perchè ha perso il passaporto.

Poliziotto	Che cosa posso fare per lei, signora?
Signora	Mi aiuti, per favore! Ho perso il passaporto.
Poliziotto	Non si agiti! Mi dica dove l'ha smarrito.
Signora	Questa mattina sono andata a visitare il Duomo e all'uscita mi sono accorta di non averlo più.
Poliziotto	Ne è sicura? Ha controllato bene?
Signora	Sì. L'ho cercato dappertutto. Che cosa mi consiglia di fare?
Poliziotto	Deve fare la denuncia.
Signora	Oddio! E come si fa?
Poliziotto	Stia tranquilla! Gliela scriviamo noi. Lei intanto si segga.

aiutare	*to help*	**controllare**	*to check*
agitarsi	*to get upset*	**gliela scriviamo noi**	*we'll write*
smarrire	*to mislay, lose*	*it for you*	
accorgersi	*to notice*		

(b) Quando si è accorta di non avere più il passaporto?

Dialogo 2 Mi dia le sue generalità! *Give me your particulars*

She gives **il poliziotto** her particulars so that he can write the statement for her.

(a) **Vero o falso?** Occorre la carta bollata per fare la denuncia.

Poliziotto	Di che nazionalità è?
Signora	Sono svizzera.
Poliziotto	Ecco la carta bollata... Mi dia le sue generalità!
Signora	Franca Pesce, nata a Lugano, il venti luglio 1970, residente a Losanna, Via San Lorenzo numero 14...
Poliziotto	... e attualmente dimorante ...
Signora	... presso mio padre, residente a Roma in Via Guiseppe Verdi, numero 6.
Poliziotto	Ecco. Ho finito. Firmi qui sotto e metta la data.
Signora	Vi mettete voi in contatto con me se lo trovate?
Poliziotto	Sì, sì. Aspetti una nostra comunicazione!

---

le generalità	*details, particulars*	**aspetti una nostra**	
dimorante	*staying at*	**comunicazione**	*we will inform*
presso	*at*		*you*
mettersi in contatto	*to get in touch*		

(b) Dov'è nata la signora e in che anno?

Dialogo 3 Un incidente *An accident*

La signora A asks to use a phone in an emergency.

(a) **Vero o falso? La signora A** Telefona all'ospedale perchè suo marito si sente male.

Signora A	Posso usare il suo telefono, per cortesia?
Signora B	Venga, faccia pure! Che cos'è successo?
Signora A	Mio marito si è sentito male per strada.
Signora B	Mi dispiace. Conosce il numero del suo medico?
Signora A	No. Mi aiuti a cercarlo, per favore.
Signora B	Si calmi, signora! Eccolo! Questo è il numero di casa e questo quello dello studio. Ma perchè non telefona all'ospedale?

Chiami il pronto soccorso!

Signora A   Sì. Forse è meglio. Pronto!... È l'ospedale?... Come?...
Cosa?... Non ho capito!... Alzi la voce!... Ah... Ho
sbagliato numero? Mi scusi!

Venga, faccia pure!   *Come in!*   **pronto soccorso**   *casualty*
   Do by all means!   *department*
sentirsi male   *to feel ill*   **Come?**   *Pardon?*
per strada   *in the street*   **alzare la voce**   *to raise one's voice*

(b)   La signora A ha chiesto alla signora B due favori. Quali sono?

Dialogo 4   Attenda in linea!   *Hold the line!*

Signora A passes the receiver to **Signora B**.

(a)   **Vero o falso?** La centralinista non capisce subito ciò che le dice la
signora B.

Signora B   Dia a me, signora! Faccio io! Pronto? Mi passi il pronto
soccorso!

Centralinista Un attimo. Attenda in linea!... Parli pure!

Signora B   Un signore sta male. Mandi subito un' ambulanza in Via
Pini.

Centralinista Va bene, ma ripeta l'indirizzo e parli più lentamente,
signora.

Signora B   Via dei Pini, 11. Accanto alla pasticceria 'La Perla'.

---

centralinista (m. or f.)   *operator*   **accanto a**   *by*

(b)   Che cosa ha fatto la signora B per chiamare l'autoambulanza?

Dialogo 5   Una stazione di servizio   *A service station*

La signora asks **il benzinaio** *pump attendant* to fill up (**fare il pieno**).

(a)   **Vero o falso?** La macchina è del benzinaio.

Benzinaio   Di chi è questa macchina? È sua, signora?
Signora   Sì. È mia.
Benzinaio   Quanti litri, signora?
Signora   Mi faccia il pieno.
Benzinaio   Normale o super?

Signora	Super. E controlli l'olio e l'acqua, per piacere.
Benzinaio	Va bene, signora. Ecco fatto! Ho controllato anche le gomme. Tutto a posto.
Signora	Grazie. Quanto le devo? Ho solo questo biglietto da cento-mila.

benzina normale	*two-star petrol*	**gomma**	*tyre*
benzina super	*four-star petrol*	**tutto a posto**	*everything in order*

(b) La signora ha chiesto al benzinaio di controllare l'olio, l'acqua e le gomme?

Spiegazioni

1 Come? *Pardon? What? Sorry?*

When you do not understand something or cannot hear properly, use either **Come?** or **Prego?**

2 Gliela scriviamo noi *We'll write it for you ourselves*

(a) **Le** (*to you/for you, to her/for her*) and **gli** (*to him/for him, to them/for them*) both become **glie**, combining with the following pronoun, **lo/la/li/le/ne**:

glielo, gliela, glieli, gliele, gliene.

The examples below illustrate how the double pronouns are used:

Hai dato l'indirizzo a Carla?	*Did you give the address to Carla?*
No. *Glielo* darò domani.	*No. I'll give **it to her** tomorrow.*
Hai dato la chiave a Mario?	*Did you give the key to Mario?*
No. *Gliela* darò più tardi.	*No. I'll give **it to him** later.*
Hai dato i moduli a Giulia?	*Did you give the forms to Julia?*
No. *Glieli* darò il mese prossimo.	*No. I'll give **them to her** next month.*
Hai dato le diapositive ai tuoi genitori?	*Did you give the slides to your parents?*
***Gliele* darò stasera.**	*I'll give **them to them** this evening.*

(b) When you use these double pronouns with the perfect tense, remember to make **lo/la/li/le/ne** agree with the past participle. Remember also that

glielo and **gliela** (singular only) both become **gliel'** before 'h': **glielo + ho dato** becomes **gliel'ho dato**.

Che bell'anello!	*What a lovely ring!*
Chi gliel'ha (glielo + ha) **regalato?**	*Who gave it to you?*
Me l'ha regalato il mio ragazzo.	*My boyfriend gave it to me.*
Che bella casa!	*What a lovely house!*
Chi gliel'ha (gliela + ha) **disegnata?**	*Who designed it for you?*
Che bei regali!	*What lovely presents!*
Chi glieli ha fatti?	*Who gave them to you?*
Che belle rose!	*What lovely roses!*
Chi gliele ha regalate?	*Who gave them to you?*

Finally, here are two examples with **ne**:

Le ha parlato dei suoi progetti?	*Did he talk to her about his plans?*
Sì. *Gliene* ha parlato ieri.	*Yes, he talked to her about them yesterday.*
Quanti dischi *gli* hai comprato?	*How many records did you buy for him?*
***Gliene* ho comprati *due*.**	*I bought him two (of them).*

3 Presso mio padre   *at my father's*

Presso is also used to mean c/o *(care of)* when you are writing an address.

4 Una nostra comunicazione

To say *of ours, of yours, of mine*, etc., Italian does not translate *of*:

Aspetto *un mio* amico.	*I'm waiting for a friend of mine.*
***Due suoi* fratelli lavorano in Germania.**	*Two of his brothers work in Germany.*

5 Stia tranquilla!   *Keep calm!*

Infinitive	Imperative
avere	**abbia!**
dare	**dia!**
essere	**sia!**
stare	**stia!**

Note these irregular forms of the imperative 2nd person singular (**lei**):

Non *abbia* paura!	*Don't be afraid!*
***Dia* una buona mancia!**	*Give a good tip!*

Sia **puntuale!**   *Be punctual!*
Stia **attento!**   *Be careful!*

6 È mia   *it's mine*

In answer to the question **Di chi è/ Di chi sono?** do not use the definite article with the possessive:

Di chi è	**quel cane?**	È *mio.*	*Whose is*	*that dog?*	*It's mine.*
	quella giacca?	È *mia.*		*that jacket?*	
Di chi sono	**questi guanti?**	Sono *suoi.*	*Whose are*	*these gloves?*	*They are his/hers/*
	queste scarpe?	Sono *sue.*		*these shoes?*	*yours.*

Come si dice in italiano?

How to:

1   ask someone to help you   **Mi aiuti, per favore!**

2   ask someone for advice   **Che cosa mi consiglia di fare?**

3   ask someone's particulars   **Mi dia le sue generalità!**

4   ask someone to hold the line
     on the phone   **Attenda in linea!**

5   ask/say whose something is   **Di chi è questo/a? È mio/mia.**

✍ Attività

1   You are supervising a group of children in a restaurant and telling them what they must and must not do.

   Esempio: Dica (a) loro di: aspettare un attimo.
   　　　　　Aspettate un attimo!

   Dica loro di:

   (a)   lavarsi le mani
   (b)   aspettare qui
   (c)   venire a tavola
   (d)   sedersi

(e) non gridare
(f) non fare troppo rumore
(g) non toccare i fiori sulla tavola
(h) bere piano piano
(i) non parlare con la bocca piena

piano piano _slowly_	**gridare** _to shout_

2 Each sentence on the right is said in response to one on the left, but
   they have got mixed up: sort out the correct pairs.

(i)	Dammi le chiavi!	(a)	Sì. Gliel'ho detto.
(ii)	Hai dato le riviste a Giulia?	(b)	Ma gliene ho già fatte tante!
(iii)	Hai detto a Stefano di venire a pranzo?	(c)	Ma te l'ho già detto cento volte!
(iv)	Perchè non me lo dici?	(d)	Ma te l'ho già dato!
(v)	Falle una fotografia!	(e)	Ma te ne ho già fatte due!
(vi)	Fammi una fotografia!	(f)	No. Non gliele ho ancora date.
(vii)	Dammi l'indirizzo!	(g)	Gliel'ho già dato.
(viii)	Dagli il caffè!	(h)	Glieli ho già dati.
(ix)	Quando gli darai i soldi?	(i)	Te le ho già date.

3 **Ho dimenticato di ...** _I've forgotten to ..._

Here is a list of things you have forgotten to do and which your friend
obligingly offers to do for you. Use double pronouns and the present
tense as in the example.

Esempio: Ho dimenticato di fare la spesa.
Non si preoccupi! Gliela faccio io.

(a) Ho dimenticato di fare i biglietti.
(b) Ho dimenticato di comprare il pane.
(c) Ho dimenticato di cambiare i soldi.
(d) Ho dimenticato di riportare i libri in biblioteca (_library_).
(e) Ho dimenticato di imbucare la lettera.
(f) Ho dimenticato di prendere il giornale.
(g) Ho dimenticato di chiudere le valigie.

4 Di chi è? *Whose is it?*

Il signor Marchi, your boss, is having a big office clean-out, and wants to know to whom various articles belong. Assume they belong to you unless you see **(R)** by the question, in which case they belong to your senior colleague, **la signora Renata**.

Esempi: **Di chi è questa penna?**   **Di chi è questo libro?**   **(R)**
         È mia.   **È suo.**

(a)   Di chi è questa fotografia? **(R)**
(b)   Di chi è questo ombrello? **(R)**
(c)   Di chi è questo cappello?
(d)   Di chi sono questi occhiali? **(R)**
(e)   Di chi sono quei documenti?
(f)   Di chi sono quelle chiavi? **(R)**
(g)   Di chi sono questi biglietti?
(h)   Di chi sono quei giornali? **(R)**
(i)   Di chi sono queste riviste?

5   Now make sure that (a), (b), (d), (f) and (h) do belong to **la signora Renata** by asking her.

Esempio: (a) È sua questa fotografia?

6   **Ora tocca a te!** You are asking for advice.

You	*I've lost my driving licence and I don't know what to do.*
Signorina	Sa dove l'ha smarrita?
You	*I'm not sure. Perhaps I left it in the car. During the night someone broke into my car and took everything.*
Signorina	Non si preoccupi! Ci sono buone possibilità di ritrovarla, perchè di solito la spediscono in Questura.
You	*What's the Questura?*
Signorina	È l'ufficio centrale di polizia. Vada lì a denunciare lo smarrimento.
You	*And do you know where it is please?*
Signorina	Certo. È in Via Mazzini.
You	*Thank you.*
Signorina	Prego. Prima di andarci però, compri dal tabaccaio un foglio di carta bollata per la denuncia.
You	*And meanwhile what do I do without a licence?*
Signorina	Per il momento può usare una copia della denuncia come documento.

❋ Informazioni

NUMERI DI EMERGENZA

Soccorso pubblico di emergenza

Nell'interesse di tutti, è consigliabile ricorrere a
questo numero soltanto in caso di reale e
incombente pericolo alle persone o di gravi calamità
e qualora non sia possibile chiamare i diversi enti
direttamente interessati.

113

Emergenza Sanitaria

118

Soccorso stradale

Automobile Club d'Italia

116

NUMERO DI PUBBLICA UTILITÀ INFORMAZIONI E
SERVIZI PROVINCIA DI ROMA

Servizio ambulanze

Civitavecchia
Ambulanze C.R.I.   **3333**

Tivoli
Ambulanze USL RM/26 **2439**

Ambulanze C.R.I.   **2008**

In caso di emergenza, per un grave incidente stradale per esempio, che
numero chiama?

25 | SCAMBIO DI OPINIONI
Exchange of opinions

In this Unit you will learn how to:

■ say you could …
■ say you ought to …
■ say you would like to …
■ say it would be necessary to …
■ ask others similar questions

Dialogo 1

Elsa and **Curzio** are in Italy and are interviewing some passers-by. They see a distinguished-looking man and approach him.

(a) **Vero o falso?** *Il Corriere della Sera, La Stampa e La Repubblica* sono giornali.

Elsa	Mi scusi, signore. Siamo due studenti della Svizzera italiana e vorremmo farle alcune domande sulla stampa italiana.
Sig. Neri	Sarò lieto di rispondervi.
Curzio	Potrebbe dirci quali sono i quotidiani più diffusi nel suo Paese?
Sig. Neri	Ho appena comprato *Il Corriere della Sera*. Sa, io sono di Milano. *Il Corriere* oltre ad essere il quotidiano della mia città, è anche uno dei più letti in Italia.
Curzio	Potrebbe mostrarmelo?
Sig. Neri	Con piacere. Se non trovo *Il Corriere*, compro *La Stampa* di Torino, o *La Repubblica* di Roma.

vorremmo	*we would like to*	**diffuso/a**	*widely circulated*
stampa	*press*	**oltre ad essere**	*besides being*
lieto/a di	*happy to*	**Potrebbe mostrarmelo?**	*Could*
potrebbe dirci	*could you tell us*	*you show it to me?*	
quotidiano	*daily paper*		

(b) Di dov'è il signor Neri, e qual è il giornale che di solito legge?

Dialogo 2 Potrebbe darci qualche informazione...?
Could you give us some information...?

(a) **Vero o falso?** Quando il signor Neri è a Napoli e non vuole avere notizie di carattere economico-finanziario, legge *Il Mattino*.

Sig. Neri	Quando sono a Napoli leggo *Il Mattino*. Se poi voglio avere notizie di carattere economico-finanziario compro *Il Sole 24 Ore*.
Elsa	Potrebbe darci qualche informazione sui settimanali più diffusi?
Sig. Neri	I settimanali di carattere politico economico culturale che io compro più frequentemente sono *L'Espresso* e *Panorama*.
Curzio	E che cosa leggono di preferenza le donne della sua famiglia?
Sig. Neri	*Grazia, Panorama*, e più o meno gli stessi giornali.
Elsa	Ci scusi per il disturbo!
Sig. Neri	Ma si figuri!

notizie (f.pl.)	*news*	**di preferenza**	*mostly*
carattere (m.)	*character*	**disturbo**	*inconvenience*
settimanale (m.)	*weekly (paper)*		

(b) *L'Espresso* e *Panorama* escono ogni mese?

Dialogo 3 La televisione: opinioni a confronto
Television: opinions compared

Ezio is asked whether he is satisfied with television programmes.

(a) **Vero o falso?** A Ezio e a Bruno non piacciono gli stessi programmi.

Giornalista	È soddisfatto dei programmi televisivi?
Ezio	Sì. Ma vedrei volentieri dei cambiamenti.
Giornalista	Potrebbe suggerirne qualcuno?
Ezio	Secondo me ci dovrebbero essere più documentari, più programmi di informazione scientifica e culturale.
Bruno	Ma che dici! Più film, più sport, più musica: ecco cosa ci vorrebbe!
Giornalista	Allora, secondo lei, la televisione dovrebbe divertire il pubblico?
Bruno	Eh, certamente! Dopo una giornata di lavoro uno vuole distrarsi.

vedrei volentieri *I'd love to see*	**ci dovrebbero essere** *there ought to be*
cambiamento *change*	
suggerirne qualcuno *to suggest some*	**ci vorrebbe** *one would need*
secondo me *in my opinion*	**divertire** *to entertain*
	distrarsi *to take one's mind off things*

(b) Secondo Ezio ci dovrebbero essere più film o più documentari?

Dialogo 4 Non sono affatto d'accordo
I don't agree at all

Bruno is for, **Ezio** is against, **le televisioni private** *independent television.*

(a) **Vero o falso?** Ezio è d'accordo col suo amico sui programmi televisivi.

Bruno Meno male che ci sono le televisioni private!

Giornalista E lei, che cosa pensa di quello che ha detto il suo amico?

Ezio Non sono affatto d'accordo. Bisognerebbe abolirle, queste televisioni private.

Giornalista Per lei, allora, quale dovrebbe essere il ruolo della televisione nella società moderna?

Ezio Dovrebbe sì divertire, ma prima di tutto informare e offrire diverse visioni del mondo.

abolire *to abolish*	**ruolo** *role*
bisognerebbe *one would need to*	**mondo** *world*

(b) Che cosa vorrebbe abolire Ezio?

Spiegazioni

1 *Conditional tense: formation*

The conditional tense for all verbs is easily formed by replacing the final -**ò** of the future with the endings in the table overleaf (in bold italics). There are no exceptions and the endings are identical for -**are**, -**ere** and -**ire** verbs.

Infinitive	Future	Conditional	
parlare	parlerò	parler	-ei
vendere	venderò	vender	-esti
sentire	sentirò	sentir	-ebbe
vedere	vedrò	vedr	-emmo
bere	berrò	berr	-este
avere	avrò	avr	-ebbero

Conditional tense	comprare		essere	
comprerei	I would buy		sarei	I would be
compreresti	you would buy		saresti	you would be
comprerebbe	you/he/she would buy		sarebbe	you/he/she would be
compreremmo	we would buy		saremmo	we would be
comprereste	you would buy		sareste	you would be
comprerebbero	they would buy		sarebbero	they would be

Note that the ending **-emmo** of the conditional (1st person plural) has 'mm' and that they must both be clearly articulated to avoid confusion with the future ending **-emo**.

Here are some examples of irregular verbs to show how easy it is to form the conditional once you know the future tense:

Future	Conditional
avrò:	**avrei, avresti, avrebbe, avremmo, avreste, avrebbero** I would have, etc.
andrò:	**andrei, andresti, andrebbe, andremmo, andreste, andrebbero** I would go, etc.
vedrò:	**vedrei, vedresti, vedrebbe, vedremmo, vedreste, vedrebbero** I would sell, etc
berrò	**berrei, berresti, berrebbe, berremmo, berreste, berrebbero** I would drink, etc.

2 Conditional tense: uses

Generally, the conditional renders *should*, *would* or *could* in Italian when these refer to the present or the future.

Prenderei **volentieri un aperitivo. E tu?**	*I'd love to have an aperitif. What about you?*
Che ne *diresti* **di una bella passeggiata?**	*What would you say to a nice walk?*
A quest'ora *sarebbe* **impossibile trovarlo in casa.**	*It would be impossible to find him at home at this time.*
Non *saprei* **dire perchè.**	*I couldn't* (Lit: *wouldn't know*) *say why.*

Note particularly the meaning of the conditional of **potere**, **dovere** and **volere**:

potrei	*I could (I would be able)*
dovrei	*I should or I ought (I would have to)*
vorrei	*I would like (I would want, wish)*
Potresti **andare a trovarla.**	*You could go and see her.*
Dovrebbe **scrivere subito.**	{ *You ought to write immediately.* { *You should write immediately.*

The conditional of **volere** and **potere** is often used for making polite requests:

Potrebbe **farmi un favore?**	*Could you do me a favour?*
Vorrei **fare una telefonata.**	*I'd like to make a phone call.*

A reflexive verb would, of course, have to be preceded by the appropriate reflexive pronoun (**mi, ti, si, ci, vi, si**): **mi divertirei, ti divertiresti, si divertirebbe, ecc.**

To form the perfect conditional tense simply use the conditional of **essere/avere** + past participle:

avrei comprato	*I would have bought*
sarei uscito/a	*I would have gone out*

3 Alcuno/a, qualcuno, nessuno   *any, someone/anyone, no-one*

Alcun, alcuno/a in the singular is used only in a negative sense:

Senza *alcun* **dubbio.**	*Without a doubt.*

In the plural **alcuni/e** means some, *a few*:

alcuni **mesi fa,** *alcuni* **giorni fa**	*a few months ago, a few days ago*

It also means *some* when *some, but not all* is implied, i.e. for contrast or emphasis. It may be used with or without a noun:

| *Alcune* notizie erano vere, *altre* false. | *Some news was true, some not* (lit; *false*). |
| *Alcuni* lo approvano, *altri* no. | *Some approve of it, others don't.* |

Qualcuno/a *one or two, some* is used only in the singular:

| **Potrebbe suggerirne** *qualcuno?* | *Could you suggest some?* |

Qualcuno is also used in the masculine singular form only and means *someone* or *anyone*:

Cerca *qualcuno?* **No.**	*Are you looking for* someone?
Non **cerco** *nessuno.*	*No. I'm* not *looking for* anyone.
Perchè non chiedi a *qualcuno?*	*Why don't you ask* someone?
C'è *qualcuno* **che vorrebbe farlo?**	*Is there* anyone *who would like to do it?*

4 Nessuno/a (Unit 13, p 146) may be used with or without a noun. It can mean *no, none, nobody, no-one, not any (one)*. It is used in the singular only:

Nessuno **l'avrebbe creduto.**	*No-one would have believed it.*
Nessuno **di noi andrà all'estero quest'anno.**	*None of us will go abroad this year.*
Non ha *nessun* **fratello.**	*He hasn't any brothers.*

5 Giorno, giornata *day*

Giorno is the day, considered as a date.

| **Lunedì è il primo** *giorno* **della settimana.** | *Monday is the first day of the week.* |
| **Che** *giorno* **è?** | *What day is it?* |

Giornata is used when referring to the duration of the day or to the weather.

Abbiamo passato una bellissima *giornata* **a Firenze.**	*We spent a very nice day in Florence.*
Che brutta *giornata*!	*What a horrible day!*
Che bella *giornata*!	*What a lovely day!*

Similarly, **mattina, mattinata**   *morning*
            sera, serata   *evening*

6 Lieto/a di + *infinitive / noun/ pronoun* *happy to...*

Some adjectives may be followed by **di** + infinitive:

Sono *stufo di* lavorare.	*I'm fed up with working.*
Sono *stanco di* aspettare.	*I'm tired of waiting.*
Sei *sicuro di* poterlo fare?	*Are you sure you can do it?*
Sono *contento di* rivederla.	*I'm pleased to see you again.*
Sono *soddisfatto di* lui.	*I'm very pleased with him.*

7 Figurarsi *to think, fancy, imagine*

Figurarsi is mainly used in exclamations:

***Figurati* che è rimasto senza un centesimo!**	*Just think of it! He hasn't a penny left!* (Lit: *he has remained without a cent.*)

Si figuri! is a polite way of saying *not at all* or *don't mention it.*

La disturbo?	*Am I disturbing you?*
Ma no, *si figuri*!	*No, not at all!*
Molto gentile, grazie!	*That's very kind of you!*
Prego, *si figuri*!	*Don't mention it.*

8 Prima, dopo *first, later*

When referring to time, **prima** means *before, first, earlier*, while **dopo** means *after(wards), later*:

Avresti dovuto dirmelo *prima*.	*You ought to have told me before.*
***Prima* vado in Francia, poi in Germania.**	*First I'm going to France, then to Germany.*
Vengo a mezzogiorno.	*I'm coming at midday.*
Se vuole, può venire *prima*.	*If you want, you can come earlier.*
È arrivato subito *dopo*.	*He arrived soon afterwards.*
Mangio *dopo*.	*I'm eating later.*

9 Bisognerebbe abolirle *you would need to abolish them*

We have already seen that unstressed pronouns have a choice of position when used with **potere/dovere/volere**:

Non *posso* trovarlo.
Non *lo posso* trovare.

With impersonal verbs such as **bisognare**, the object pronouns must be attached to the infinitive if they refer to it:

Bisogna far*lo* subito.	*It must be done at once.*
Bisogna parlar*gli*.	*It is necessary to speak to him.*
Non *mi* piace far*lo*.	*I don't like doing it.*

Come si dice in italiano?

How to:

1 ask whether someone could tell   **Potrebbe dirmi,**
    you, show, give you, do, etc.   **mostrarmi, darmi, fare, ecc?**
    say you could tell/show someone, etc.   **Potrei dirle/mostrarle, ecc.**

2 say someone ought to …   **Dovrebbe …**
    say you ought to …   **Dovrei …**

3 say someone would like to …   **Vorrebbe …**
    say you would like to …   **Vorrei …**

4 say it would be necessary to …   **Bisognerebbe …**

☑ Attività

1 Select a verb in the list below once only to complete the responses, using the first person singular of the conditional.

> **guardare – mettere – mangiare – bere – ascoltare – prendere**

(a) L'acqua? La _____ ma non ho sete.

(b) Gli spaghetti? Li _____ ma non ho appetito.

(c) Il cappotto? Lo _____ ma non ho freddo.

(d) Le aspirine? Le _____ ma non ho più mal di testa.

(e) Il concerto alla radio? L' _____ ma non ho tempo.

(f) Il programma alla *tv? Lo _____ ma devo uscire.

*pronounced **tivù**.

2 In the table opposite you are given details of what **Ada**, **Vittorio**, and **i signori Miele** would do if they had the means.

(a) Say what **Ada** would do. (**Vivrebbe, ecc.**)

(b) Pretend you are **Vittorio** and say what you would do.

(c) Say what **i signori Miele** would do.

	vivere	comprare	andare	imparare a
Ada	in città	piccolo appartamento	ogni sera a ballare	guidare
Vittorio	al mare	villa	spesso a nuotare	suonare la chitarra
I signori Miele	in montagna	casetta	ogni tanto a sciare	dipingere

casetta *small house*	**dipingere** *to paint*

3 Match up the sentences on the left with those on the right.

(i) Sono tanto stanco!

(a) Avresti dovuto assaggiarla prima di comprarla.

(ii) Perchè non me l'hai detto che non avevi i soldi?

(b) Avresti potuto romperti la testa.

(iii) Perchè non sei venuto alla festa di Sandro?

(c) No. Mi dispiace. Non saprei dirglielo.

(iv) Questo liquore è ottimo!

(d) Ti saresti divertito molto.

(v) Quest'uva non è buona.

(e) No. Dovrebbe arrivare col treno delle dieci.

(vi) Meno male che non ti sei fatto niente!

(f) Ne berrei un altro bicchierino.

(vii) È arrivato tuo nonno?

(g) Avresti dovuto riposarti un po' prima di uscire.

(viii) Scusi signore, sa dov'è il Consolato Inglese?

(h) Te li avrei prestati io.

4 *Conditional + double pronouns*

There are several things you would like to do or ought to do. Your friend would love to do them for you but … Use the conditional and the appropriate pronouns in your answer.

Esempio: Dovrei pagare il conto _____ ma sono al verde. *(I'm broke)*.
Te lo pagherei io, ma sono al verde.

(a) Dovrei portare le valigie alla stazione. _____ ma mi fa male la schiena.

(b) Dovrei portare la macchina dal meccanico. ____ ma non ho tempo.

(c) Non so fare la traduzione. ____ ma non ho il dizionario.

(d) Dovrei pulire l'appartamento. ____ ma sono stanco.

(e) Vorrei cambiare diecimila lire. ____ ma non ho spiccioli.

(f) Vorrei fare la pizza. ____ ma non ho gli ingredienti.

(g) Dovrei imbucare questa lettera. ____ ma non passo per la posta.

5 **Ora tocca a te!** You are on the phone to **Renata** and inviting her to your party.

You   *Hi, Renata! Can you come to my party this evening?*

Renata Vorrei tanto, ma sono molto impegnata in questo periodo.

You   *But what have you got to do that's so important?*

Renata Devo riordinare la casa, devo lavare, ... sono sola e devo pensare a tutto.

You   *And couldn't you do all these things at another time?*

Renata Sì, potrei, solo che oggi ritornano i miei genitori da una vacanza all'estero.

You   *But weren't they supposed to come back next week?*

Renata Sì, effettivamente, avrebbero voluto fermarsi per altri cinque o sei giorni, ma mia zia ha avuto un bambino e così hanno deciso di rientrare prima.

You   *At what time will they arrive?*

Renata Dovrebbero essere all'aeroporto alle sei, e andrò io stessa a prenderli in macchina.

You   *Anyway, if you change your mind, you can always let me know. Call me when you like.*

Renata Ti ringrazio. Se posso, verrò volentieri, magari solo per salutarti e farti gli auguri.

◼ Informazioni

NON È MAI
TROPPO TARDI
PER DIVENTARE
UN NUOVO
ABBONATO.

(a) Cos'è la RAI?
(b) Nel primo dialogo quali sono i quotidiani?

KEY TO EXERCISES

Alternative answers are marked / (e.g. **per piacere/per favore**). Words that are not strictly necessary in the answer are put in brackets: **(e) questa è Elena**. With **Vero o falso** statements, a 'V', indicates that the statement is true. Otherwise the corrected version appears.

Unit 1

Dialoghi

1 (a) Parla inglese? (b) Parlo inglese e francese. (c) Non parlo tedesco. (d) Parlo inglese. Parlo francese. Parlo tedesco. (e) Non parlo cinese. Non parlo giapponese. Non parlo russo. (f) Parla italiano? (g) (i) Gérard Dupont parla francese. (ii) Betty Warren parla inglese. (iii) Anna Muti parla italiano. (iv) Helga Weil parla tedesco. **2** (a) Scusi, l'ascensore, per favore? (b) Grazie. (c) Scusi, il telefono, per favore? **3** (a) per piacere. (b) Mi dispiace. (c) Scusi, la banca, per piacere/per favore? (d) Non lo so. (e) sinistra, stazione, ascensore, grazie, telefono. (i) La stazione è a destra. (ii) La posta è a sinistra. (iii) V. (iv) La polizia è a destra (f) Sempre dritto! the museum; the police station **4** Buongiorno, signorina Giulia! Arrivederci professore! **5** (a) Un gelato, signorina? (b) No, grazie. Sì, grazie. (c) tea; coffee; beer; espresso (d) acqua minerale. (i) Un gelato? Sì, grazie. (ii) Una pasta? No, grazie. (iii) Una limonata? Sì, grazie.

Attività

1 (b) Anna: Una birra, per favore. (c) Alfredo: Un gelato, per favore. (d) Maria: Un tè, per favore. (e) Roberto: Un cappuccino, per favore. (f) Rita: Una granita di limone, per favore. (g) Carlo: Un cioccolato, per favore. (h) Olga: Una coca-cola, per favore.
2 (b) La birra è per Anna. (c) Il gelato è per Alfredo. (d) Il tè è per Maria. (e) Il cappuccino è per Roberto. (f) La granita di limone è per Rita. (g) Il cioccolato è per Carlo. (h) La coca-cola è per Olga.

3 (a) Franco parla inglese. (b) Rita parla francese e spagnolo.
(c) Carlo parla tedesco e spagnolo. (d) Carlo parla tedesco, ma non
parla francese. (e) Non parlo spagnolo. (f) Parla francese? (g) Parlo
inglese, francese e spagnolo; non parlo tedesco.

4 Dialogo

Turista Excuse me!
You *Sì...? Prego?/Sì...?/Prego?*
Turista The post office, please.
You *È lì, a sinistra.*
Turista And the station?
You *Sempre dritto!*
Turista Thank you.
You *Prego.*

Unit 2

Dialoghi

1 (a) Ecco il Duomo! (b) il Museo Nazionale; la Banca Commerciale.
(c) Questo è il museo. **2** (a) Dopo il Consolato Americano (b) strada;
via; principale (c) Dov'è Piazza Municipio, per favore? (d) È vicino a
Via Roma. (e) Dove sono i negozi, per favore? **3** (a) (Io) prendo una
pizza e un bicchier(e) di vino. (b) Cosa prende? (c) vino rosso (d)
Un'acqua minerale con gas, per piacere. (e) Un bicchier(e) di vino
rosso, per piacere. **4** (a) Altro? (b) (E) lo zucchero! (c) Lo zucchero,
per piacere. **5** (a) **7** beers; **5** sandwiches; 1 ice cream.

Attività

2 (b) Il Ponte Vecchio: Firenze (c) Il Palazzo del Parlamento: Londra
(d) La Torre Eiffel: Parigi (e) La Torre Pendente: Pisa (f) Il Vesuvio:
Napoli (g) Il Colosseo: Roma. (h) Piazza San Marco: Venezia.
3 Dov'è il Colosseo? A Roma. Dov'è il Vesuvio? A Napoli. Dov'è la
Torre Eiffel? A Parigi. La Scala è a Milano. Il Ponte Vecchio è a
Firenze. Il Palazzo del Parlamento è a Londra. La Torre Pendente è a
Pisa. Piazza San Marco è a Venezia.
4 (a) Scusi, dov'è il Consolato Americano? (È) a sinistra dopo la
posta. (b) Scusi, dov'è Piazza Garibaldi? (È) a destra dopo la stazione.
(c) Scusi, dov'è il Duomo? (È) a destra dopo il Museo Nazionale.
(d) Scusi, dov'è l'Albergo Miramare? (È) a destra dopo Piazza
Garibaldi. (e) (Sono) a sinistra dopo la posta.
5 Drinks: la limonata, la birra, l'acqua minerale, l'aranciata, il tè.

Food: la pizza, la pasta, il formaggio, il panino, il prosciutto. Places: la banca, il Duomo, la piazza, il museo, l'albergo.
6 Marta prende il tè con latte e (con) zucchero. Filippo prende il tè con limone senza zucchero. Io prendo il tè...
7 Cos'è questo? (Questo) è un espresso. Cos'è questo? (Questo) è un gelato. Cos'è questa? (Questa) è una pasta. Cos'è questa? (Questa) è una limonata.

Unit 3

Dialoghi

1 (a) A che piano abitano i signori Nuzzo, (per favore)? **2** (a) Come si chiama? Mi chiamo Marco Russo. (b) Di dov'è? Sono di Napoli. **3** (a) Come ti chiami? (b) Io sono di Milano. (c) Che cosa fai? Sono segretaria. **4** (a) Di che nazionalità è, signorina? Sono italiana. (b) Anch'io sono italiano. (c) È greca. **5** (a) Io sono Massimo. (b) (E) questa è Elena. Piacere. (c) Quanti anni hai? Ho diciotto anni. **6** (a) Sono sposata. (b) Ha due fratelli e una sorella. (c) Quanti figli ha, signora? (d) Quanti anni hanno? (e) La bambina ha solo quattro anni.

Attività

1 Notice the omission of the letters –**i** and –**a**.
2 (a) I 12 (b) IV 47 (c) I 13 (d) III 38.
3 (a) Il professor Russo è architetto. (b) Carlo Pini è ragioniere. (c) Olga Fulvi è dentista. (d) Anna Biondi è giornalista.
4 (a) Helga è tedesca. (b) Gérard e Philippe sono francesi. (c) Juanita è spagnola. (d) Ivan e Natasha sono russi. (e) Anna e Pina sono italiane.
5 (a) Helga è di Bonn. (b) Gérard e Philippe sono di Nizza. (c) Juanita è di Barcellona. (d) Ivan e Natasha sono di Omsk. (e) Anna e Pina sono di Trento.
6 (a) Helga abita a Bonn. (b) Gérard e Philippe abitano a Nizza. (c) Juanita abita a Barcellona. (d) Ivan e Natasha abitano a Omsk. (e) Anna e Pina abitano a Trento.
7 Cara Luisa, ho diciassette anni. Sono di Siena ma abito a Lucca. Mio padre è italiano e mia madre è tedesca. Ho un fratello. Si chiama Luigi e ha diciotto anni./Mio fratello Luigi ha diciotto anni.

Unit 4

Dialoghi

1 (a) Alle otto. **2** (a) mattina, sera **3** (a) 850 lire (b)Vuole queste?

(c) È una cartolina di Roma. (d) iii (e) 3 postcards and
2 papers **4** (a) Molto gentile. (b) 9.00 – 8.00 **5** (a) Desidera? (b)
Quanto costa? (c) La camicetta è troppo cara. **6** (a) Prendo un paio di
sandali marroni. (b) Che numero?

Pronuncia

lunedì, sabato, domenica, aprono, chiudono.

Attività

1 (a) 9.30 – 1.00. (b) 3.00 – 4.00 (c) 9.00 – 2.00 (d) 9.00 – 1.30
(e) 9.00 – 7.30.
2 (a) la giacca (b) la maglietta (c) la cravatta (d) la gonna (e) i jeans
(f) i pantaloni (g) le scarpe (h) i sandali (i) il vestito (j) la camicetta
(k) i guanti (l) la camicia.
3 (a) Quanto costa la maglietta? Trentacinquemila lire. (b) Quanto
costano i pantaloni? Centoquarantamila lire. (c) Quanto costano le
scarpe? Centotrentacinquemila lire.
4 (a) Carlo compra una maglietta rossa, tre magliette gialle, una
cravatta gialla, una cravatta verde, due paia di scarpe nere, un paio di
pantaloni gialli e un paio di pantaloni verdi. (b) Ottocentomila lire
(800.000 lire).

5 Ora tocca a te!

Tabaccaio	Can I help you?
You	*Due francobolli.*
Tabaccaio	For abroad?
You	*Sì, Per la Francia.*
Tabaccaio	Anything else?
You	*Una cartolina di Roma e questo giornale.*
Tabaccaio	Then…
You	*Nient'altro. Quant'è?*
Tabaccaio	Three thousand seven hundred lire.
You	*Ecco!*

Informazioni

3 (a) closed; (b) open; (c) sales. Upim advert: a discount offer for
men's women's/children's outer wear from 17/10 to 19/11.

Unit 5

Dialoghi

1 (a) Vado a Bologna. (b) In treno. (c) Solo per dieci giorni. **2** (a) Scusi, sa dov'è la fabbrica di scarpe? (b) una fermata is a bus stop. (c)Non è lontano. **3** (a) Come si scrive? (b) Mio marito è svizzero. (c) Capisco tutto. **4** (a) Sono nata a Lucca, ma abito a Siena. (b) Quante lingue parla?

Attività

2 (a) 76 (b) 85 (c) 68 (d) 79 (e) 170 (f) 198 (g) 177 (h) 102
3 (a) ...va in ufficio in bicicletta. (b) ... va a Parigi in treno. (c) ...va a Roma in macchina. (d) ... va a casa a piedi. (e) ...vanno a scuola in autobus. (f) ... va a Milano in aereo.
4 - Dove vai, Franco? - Vado a Roma. – Come vai? – In macchina.
– Dove vai, Anna? – Vado a casa. – Come vai? – A piedi.
– Dove vai, Francesca? – Vado a Milano. – Come vai? – In aereo.
5 (a) Sono le dieci e cinque (b) È l'una meno un quarto (c) Sono le tre meno dieci (d) Sono le tre e venti (e) Sono le sei meno un quarto (f) Sono le sei e mezza (g) È mezzogiorno (h) È mezzanotte

6 Ora tocca a te!

Dirigente	Your name?
You	*Pat Brown.*
Dirigente	Brown? How do you spell it?
You	*B come Bari, R come Roma, O come Ostia, W come Washington, N come Napoli.*
Dirigente	You're English aren't you?
You	*No. Sono americano/a, ma abito a Londra.*
Dirigente	How old are you?
You	*Ho trentatrè anni.*
Dirigente	What (work) do you do?
You	*Lavoro in un'agenzia di viaggi.*
Dirigente	Do you speak French and German?
You	*Capisco tutto ma non parlo bene.*

Informazioni

2 A handbook or guide to professional careers.

Unit 6

Dialoghi

1 (a) Alle quindici e venticinque. (b) Da che binario? **2** (a) Tre posti per domani mattina. (b) expresso coffee, fast train; bank note, ticket **3** (a) È in ritardo di due minuti. (b) Il treno è in partenza dal binario nove. **4** (a) Dov'è la fermata del sessantotto? (b) Alla prossima fermata scendo anch'io. (c) per favore, per piacere, per cortesia.

Attività

1 (a) Siena, 1, seconda, 16.20, 3. (b) Roma, 2, prima, 10.40, 15. (c) Genova, 1, seconda, 23.55, 7. (d) Novara, 1, prima, 18.30, 1.
2 (a) dell' (b) agli (c) delle (d) dello (e) allo (f) degli (g) all' (h) alle (i) della (j) al.
3 i(e) ii(i) iii(g) iv(a) v(b) vi(c) vii(d) viii(f) ix(h)
4 In via Terni ci sono tre alberghi. In Piazza Dante c'è un palazzo. In Piazza Cavour ci sono quattro bar. A Roma ci sono due aeroporti.
5 (a) Pina va in banca fra un'ora. (b) Giorgio va al colloquio fra tre ore. (c) Enrico ritorna a casa fra un quarto d'ora/quindici minuti. (d) Carlo va alla discoteca fra dieci minuti. (e) Il treno arriva fra cinque minuti.
6 Ora tocca a te!

Impiegato	Yes…Can I help you?
You	*Vorrei prenotare tre posti per dopodomani, giovedì.*
Impiegato	Where to?
You	*Livorno.*
Impiegato	Do you want to leave in the morning or evening?
You	*Non c'è un treno diretto alle undici?*
Impiegato	No, but there's a fast train that leaves at midday.
You	*Va bene. Tre posti per giovedì allora. Seconda classe.*

Informazioni

(a) You travel better and you spend less. (b) They are state owned.
(c) 167-431784 (d) 24975 or 20268

Unit 7

Dialoghi

1 A(a) B(c) C(d) D(a)

2 (a) Ottima idea. **3** (a) Ma oggi è chiuso. (b) C'è un buon ristorante qui vicino? **4** (a) Tutti i giorni, eccetto il lunedì. **5** (a) C'è molta gente oggi. (b) È una specialità della casa. **6** (a) Un altro po' di vino? (b)Per me niente.

Attività

1 Antipasti: antipasto misto, coppa di gamberetti, melone con prosciutto. Primi: lasagne al forno, risotto alla milanese, spaghetti alle vongole. Secondi: bistecca alla griglia, fritto misto di pesce, pollo arrosto, sogliola alla griglia.

Contorni: fagiolini, insalata mista, patatine fritte.

Frutta – dolci: gelati misti, macedonia di frutta, frutta fresca.

Da bere: acqua minerale, vino rosso, vino bianco.

2 (a) Aldo prende un gelato alla fragola, (b) Giulia prende un gelato al limone. (c) Bruno prende un gelato al caffè. (d) Silvia prende un gelato al cioccolato. (e) I signori Lambrini prendono un tè al limone.

3 i(d) ii(h) iii(e) iv(a) v(f) vi(g) vii(c) viii(b)

4 i(b) & (d) ii(d) iii(c) because it's in a huge park in a wood. iv(d) 'You eat well and keep your figure.' v(a)&(c).

5 Ora tocca a te!

Cameriere	What are you having?
You	*(Vorrei) antipasto misto.*
Cameriere	And for the first course?
You	*Minestrone.*
Cameriere	Would you like to order the second course now?
You	*Perchè no? Cosa/che cosa mi consiglia?*
Cameriere	The fish is very good today.
You	*Non mangio pesce. Bistecca alla griglia.*
Cameriere	Certainly. And any side dishes?
You	*Prendo insalata mista e/con patatine fritte.*
Cameriere	And to drink?
You	*Mezza bottiglia di vino locale.*
Cameriere	Red or white?
You	*Meglio il vino rosso con la bistecca.*
Cameriere	Straight away.
	...
Cameriere	Everything alright?
You	*Sì. Benissimo. Un altro po' di pane, per piacere.*
Cameriere	Here you are. Anything else?
You	*No, grazie, Basta così.*

Unit 8

Dialoghi

1 (a) Singola o doppia? (b) La colazione è compresa nel prezzo? **2** (a) Dal ventisei luglio al nove agosto. (b) (la) colazione, (il) pranzo, (la) cena. **3** (a) a week. (b) Abbiamo la patente di guida...Eccola! **4** (a) I bagagli sono nella macchina. (b) Lo chiamo subito. **5** (a) Alle sei in punto. (b) La camera che dà sulla terrazza. **6** (a) tanti turisti (b) Comincio alle sei e finisco verso l'una.

Spiegazioni 5 Quando compra i libri? Li compro stasera. Quando compra le riviste? Le compro subito. Quando compra la rivista? La compro stamattina. Quando paga il conto? Lo pago adesso.

Attività

1 (a) single room, shower, full board, Thursday – Monday. (b) double room, bath, full board, 25 June – 4 July. (c) Room with twin beds, shower, half board, 9 May – 19 May.

2 (a) Eccolo! (b) Eccola! (c) Eccolo! (d) Eccoli! (e) Eccole! (f) Eccola! (g) Eccolo! (h)Eccolo!

3 (a) Sì. La conosco molto bene. (b) Sì. Le conosco abbastanza bene. (c) La vedo verso le otto. (d) Lo invito/l'invito oggi. (e) Li invito spesso. (f) La guardo dopo cena. (g) Sì. Lo conosco bene. (h) No. Lo vedo stasera.

4 (a) nello studio. (b) nell'acqua. (c) sul letto. (d) sulla spiaggia. (e) nel bicchiere. (f) nella borsa. (g) nelle valigie. (h) negli spaghetti.

5 (a) No. Vengo in macchina. (b) No. Vengo a piedi. (c) No. Vengo in aereo. (d) No. Veniamo in metropolitana. (e) No. Veniamo in bicicletta.

6 (a) Abito a Terni. Lavoro in un'agenzia di viaggi. La mattina esco alle otto e un quarto. Incomincio a lavorare alle nove. Finisco di lavorare alle 6.00. Torno a casa alle sette meno un quarto. Il sabato non lavoro. Vado in montagna con mio marito.

Abitiamo a Napoli. Lavoriamo in un istituto di lingue. La mattina usciamo alle sette e venti. Incominciamo a lavorare alle otto. Finiamo di lavorare all'una. Torniamo a casa alle due meno venti. Il sabato non lavoriamo. Andiamo in campagna con i nostri genitori.

(b) Anna lavora in una banca commerciale, ma i signori Spada lavorano in un istituto di lingue. La mattina Anna esce alle otto meno un quarto, ma i signori Spada escono alle sette e venti. Anna incomincia a lavorare alle otto e mezza, ma i signori Spada incominciano a lavorare alle otto. Anna finisce di lavorare alle cinque, ma i signori Spada finiscono di lavorare all'una. Anna torna a casa alle sei meno un quarto, ma i signori Spada tornano a casa alle due meno venti. Il sabato Anna va al mare con sua sorella, ma i signori Spada vanno in campagna con i loro genitori.

7 Ora tocca a te!

Direttore	Good morning.
You	*Buongiorno! Ha due camere per dieci giorni?*
Direttore	For how many?

You	*Per quattro persone.*
Direttore	We have two rooms on the third floor.
You	*Con bagno?*
Direttore	One with a private bath, the other with a shower.
You	*Sì. Va benissimo. C'è il ristorante in questo albergo?*
Direttore	No. There's only a bar.
You	*C'è un ristorante qui vicino?*
Direttore	There's the 'Tattoria Monti' in the square.

Informazioni

(a) Accettazione carta di credito. (b) Si accettano piccoli animali domestici. (c) (Un) campo da tennis. (d) No vacancies. (e) Dry cleaning.

Unit 9

Dialoghi

1 (a) Ha un appuntamento? (b) Le passo il dottor Fini. **2** (a) Avanti! (b) Posso offrirle un caffè? **3** (a) Mi dispiace, non c'è. (b) Un attimo. La chiamo. (c) Sono io.

Attività

1 (a) Out. (b) He asks whether she can call back later. (c) She says she will call back in half an hour. (d) 10 June. (e) His name.

2 Dove lo posso contattare? La chiamo io… Le do… La richiamo io… La ringrazio.

3 (i)(b) ii(g) iii(d) iv(f) v(c) vi(h) vii(a) viii(e)

4 (a) Vuole telefonare ad Anna. (b) Vuole vedere un film. (c) Vuole uscire con Carla. (d) Deve lavorare fino a tardi. (e) Deve uscire con i suoi genitori. (f) Deve scrivere una lettera a suo zio. (g) Non può fumare. (h) Non può comprare un altro vestito (i) Non può venire a pranzo con noi.

5 (a) Puoi aspettare qui? (b) Puoi telefonare per me? (c) Puoi passare il sale e il pepe? (d) Puoi prenotare un'altra camera? (e) Puoi aprire la porta, per piacere?

6 Ora tocca a te!

Segretaria	Hello!
You	*Pronto! Posso parlare con Lisa, per piacere?*
Segretaria	Lisa is in a meeting.
You	*Posso lasciare un messaggio?*
Segretaria	Certainly. Who's speaking?

You	*Pat Iles.*
Segretaria	How do you spell it?
You	*P come Palermo, A come Ancona, T come Torino, I come Imola, L come Livorno, E come Empoli, S come Salerno.*
Segretaria	And what's the message?
You	*Pat Iles non può andare alla riunione domani.*

Informazioni

(a) Costa 108.000 lire ed è garantita per sei mesi. (b) È per i bambini. Non costa niente./È gratuito.

Unit 10

Dialoghi

1 (a) Vivo e lavoro a Napoli. (b) Gioco a tennis. **2** (a) Sono i suoi genitori? (b) E questi qui sono i miei nonni.

Attività

1 (a) quel signore (b) quell'orologio (c) quella camicia (d) quell'istituto (e) quello studente (f) quegli appartamenti (g) quei libri (h) quei pomodori (i) quelle cartoline (j) quei bicchieri.

2 (a) bella macchina (b) bello studio (c) bel posto (d) bei bambini (e) bell'albero (f) bella spiaggia (g) belle camere (h) begli uccelli.

3 (a)...rimango a casa e guardo... (b)...vado a ballare... (c) ... vado al cinema... (d)... resto a casa a giocare a bridge. (e) ...gioco a tennis ... (f)... esco di casa... (g) ...mangio ...

4 i(b) ii(d) iii(a) iv(c)

5 Guido: Vado al cinema, leggo, ascolto la radio.

Carla: Guardo la televisione, gioco a tennis, vado a ballare.

Adamo e Ida: Andiamo al cinema, leggiamo, andiamo a teatro, ascoltiamo la radio.

Enzo e Rina: Guardiamo la televisione, giochiamo a tennis, leggiamo, andiamo a ballare.

6 I (c) Enzo è mio figlio. (d) Isabella è mia figlia. (e) Teresa è mia sorella. (f) Filippo è mio fratello. (g) Rina è mia nipote. (h) Pietro è mio nipote. (i) Guido e Elena sono i miei genitori.

II (b) Anna è nostra madre. (c) (d) Noi siamo i loro figli. (e) Teresa è nostra zia. (f) Filippo è nostro zio. (g) Rina è nostra cugina. (h) Pietro è nostro cugino. (i) Guido e Elena sono i nostri nonni.**7** Cara Laura, grazie della tua lettera. Ho diciassette anni e un giorno vorrei lavorare in Italia. Quest'anno studio l'italiano ed il francese. Sono due lingue molto interessanti. Abito/Vivo in un villaggio vicino a Brighton che non è troppo lontano da Londra. Mio padre è elettricista e mia madre lavora a casa per un'agenzia pubblicitaria. Ho un fratello che lavora a Londra e una piccola sorella che ha sette anni. Si chiama Sandra e passa molto tempo a giocare con il nostro cane Rover. Vorrei venire in Italia a luglio. A presto. Un caro saluto. Gloria.

8 Ora tocca a te!

Angelo Hi, Isa!
You *Ciao!*
Angelo Would you like to come out with me?
You *Dove?*
Angelo Dancing.
You *Quando? Adesso?*
Angelo This evening, at nine.
You *No. Stasera non posso. Devo andare al cinema con un amico/ un'amica.*
Angelo Can you come tomorrow? Or have you got to go out tomorrow too?
You *Domani sera devo andare a teatro con i miei genitori.*
Angelo Pity! Sunday at eight?
You *Domenica va benissimo. Ma non posso venire prima delle nove.*
Angelo Nine o'clock is fine. Goodbye then!
You *Ciao!*

Unit 11

Dialoghi

1 (a) (Io) ho fame. (b)Vorrei mangiare qualcosa. **2** (a) Vorrei dei panini. (b) Mezzo chilo di spaghetti. **3** (a) Com'è bella questa borsa! (b) Non mi piace. **4** (a) Mi piacciono moltissimo. (b) Allora li compro tutti e due. (c) Non ho più soldi!

Attività

1 Maria vuol comprare del burro, del formaggio, della birra, dell'olio, degli spaghetti, dello zucchero, dei fiammiferi (e) dell'acqua minerale.
2 (b) Il vino bianco le piace, ma preferisce il vino rosso. (c) Il cinema le piace, ma preferisce il teatro. (d) Milano le piace, ma preferisce Firenze. (e) Le melanzane le piacciono, ma preferisce i peperoni. (f) I libri le piacciono, ma preferisce le riviste.

3 (b) Le piace il vino bianco o il vino rosso? Il vino bianco mi piace, ma preferisco il vino rosso. (c) Le piace il cinema o il teatro? Il cinema mi piace, ma preferisco il teatro. (d) Le piace Milano o Firenze? Milano mi piace, ma preferisco Firenze. (e) Le piacciono le melanzane o i peperoni? Le melanzane mi piacciono, ma preferisco i peperoni. (f) Le piacciono i libri o le riviste? I libri mi piacciono, ma preferisco le riviste.

4 (a) Le piace…? (b) Le piace…? (c) Ti piace…? (d) Ti piace…? (e) Ti piace…? (f) Le piacciono…? (g) Le piacciono…? (h) Ti piacciono…?

5 (a), (b), (c), (f), (g), (h) Ti piace? (d), (e) Le piace?

6 (a) Ne devo pagare cento. (b) Ne devo scrivere due. (c) Ne voglio invitare dodici. (d) Ne devo comprare nove (e) Ne ho una. (f) Ne ho quattro. (g) Ne compro sette. (h) Ne leggo molti.

7 (a) Ne ha uno più corto? (b) Non ne ha una più grande? (c) Non ne ha uno più scuro? (d) Ne ha una più chiara? (e) Non ne ha uno più facile?

8 (a) Pietro è più grande di Paolo. (b) Lino è più piccolo di Paolo. (c) Lino è più piccolo di Pietro. (d) Pietro è più grande di Lino. (e) Paolo è più piccolo di Pietro.

9 (a) L'aereo è più veloce del treno. (b) Il treno è più veloce dell'autobus. (c) La macchina è più veloce della bicicletta. (d) La bicicletta è meno veloce dell'autobus.(e) L'autobus è meno veloce della metropolitana.

10 (a) A new car. (b) Yes, very well. (c) Because his car uses too much petrol. (d) Yes. (e) No. (f) He doesn't like small cars. (g) No. He thinks they are too expensive. (h) He does not want to pay all that much.

Informazioni

SALUMERIA: salame, olio, vino, olive, prosciutto, pasta, mortadella.
MACELLERIA: vitello, maiale, agnello, manzo.
PESCHERIA: trota, merluzzo, salmone.

(a) Ci vogliono cinque minuti per (cuocere) le pennette rigate, e undici minuti per gli spaghetti. (b) Sono cinquecento grammi.

Unit 12
Dialoghi

1 (a) Roberto cerca un appartamento al centro. (b) Ne vuole quattro.

2 (a) La padrona di casa abita al pianterreno. (b) Si paga l'affitto.

3 (a) V. (b) La televisione è nel soggiorno, e la lavatrice è nel bagno.

Attività

1 BAGNO: il bidè, la doccia, la vasca da bagno, il water, il lavandino.
CUCINA: la cucina, il frigorifero, la lavastoviglie, la lavatrice,
l'acquaio.
CAMERA DA LETTO: il letto, il comodino, lo scaffale.
SALA DA PRANZO: le tende, le sedie, la tavola.
SALOTTO: il divano, la libreria, le poltrone, il quadro, la scrivania, il
tappeto, la televisione.
INGRESSO: il telefono, il tavolino, la pianta, lo specchio, l'orologio.
2 (a) Ce ne sono due. (b) Ce ne sono quattro. (c) Ce n'è una. (d) Ce ne
sono quattro. (e) Ce ne sono sette.
3 (a) La presa per il rasoio è nel bagno. (b) Il citofono è nell'ingresso.
(c) Il frigorifero è nella cucina. (d) Il letto è nella camera da letto.
(e) Il divano è nel salotto. (f) Le coperte sono nell'armadio.
4 (a) Le sedie a sdraio sono sul balcone. (b) Le lenzuola sono sul letto.
(c) La televisione è sul tavolino. (d) I libri sono sullo scaffale.
5 (a) Davide cerca un appartamento di quattro camere, in periferia,
vicino alla strada principale. (b) Bianca cerca un appartamento di tre
camere, in periferia, vicino alla stazione. (c) Lola e Rita cercano un
appartamento di cinque camere, al centro, vicino all'ufficio.
(d) Cerchiamo un appartamento di cinque camere, al centro, vicino
all'ufficio.
6 (a) Ce ne sono dodici. (b) Ce ne sono sette. (c) Ce ne sono
trecentosessantacinque. (d) Ce ne sono sessanta. (e) Ce ne sono cento.
(f) Ce ne sono dieci. (g) Ce ne sono ventuno. (h) Ce n'è uno.
7 (a) The Coliseum. (b) It's not very modern. (c) On the fourth. (d) No.
(e) Five. (f) Three. (g) Bathroom and kitchen. (h) The bathroom is
small but the kitchen is nice and big.
8 (a) A luxury flat in a tourist district. (b) Two- to five-room flats.
(c) A flat in a residential district with park. (d) Immediate sale. (e) A
villa with a scenic view built as two separate flats, in a unique
position. (f) It's a superbly built dream villa, and on the seafront.
(g) He's looking for a luxury flat in a modern block that is free in
June. (h) An English student is looking for furnished accommodation
in exchange for conversation.

Unit 13

Dialoghi

1 (a) Lo sport preferito di Giulio è il jogging. (b) V. (c) D'inverno va a nuotare in piscina, d'estate (va a nuotare) al lago. **2** (a) Quando corre, la pioggia non fa nessuna differenza per lui. (b) No. Corre anche quando fa brutto tempo. (c) No. Non si sente affatto stanco. **3** (a) Rita offre un bicchiere di vino al giornalista. (b) La mattina lei e suo marito si alzano presto. (c) No. Si alzano alle sei. **4** (a) V. (b) No. Cenano piuttosto tardi. **5** (a) Rina studia medicina. (b) Si laurea a giugno. (c) Fa l'ultimo anno.

Attività

1 (a) Si sveglia alle sei e mezza. (b) Si alza alle sette. (c) Si lava. (d) Fa colazione alle otto. (e) Legge il giornale. (f) Esce di casa alle otto e mezza. (g) Torna a casa alle sei. (h) Cena alle otto. (i) Guarda la televisione. (j) Va a letto alle undici.

2 (a) …io mi riposo … (b) …io mi diverto … (c) …io mi sveglio … (d) … io mi alzo … (e) … io mi lavo … (f) …io mi vesto … (g) … noi non ci riposiamo …

3 Non mi sveglio mai … Non mi alzo mai … Non mi lavo mai … Non mi vesto mai prima …

4 (a) …ci riposiamo. (b) … ci cambiamo. (c) … mi alzo. (d) … mi ubriaco. (e) … mi diverto. (f) … mi lagno.

5 Giocano sempre a carte e non lavorano mai. Escono sempre e non studiano mai. Guardano sempre la televisione e non leggono mai. Parlano sempre e non ascoltano mai. Prendono sempre l'autobus e non vanno mai a piedi. Cominciano sempre e non finiscono mai.

6 (a) Lo prende al bar. (b) La prende in salumeria. (c) Li compra in panetteria. (d) Lo compra all'edicola. (e) L'aspetta all'edicola.

7 (a) Nevica. (b) Piove. (c) C'è il sole/fa bel tempo. (d) Tira vento/c'è vento.

Ora tocca a te!

You	*Ma non si riposa mai, signora?*
Pina	Well, with a restaurant it's difficult to rest. We go to bed very late at night, and in the morning we get up very early.
You	*Quante ore al giorno lavora?*
Pina	10, 12, sometimes even 14 hours.
You	*Lavora molto!*

Pina But I rest during the holidays.
You   *Quante volte all'anno va in vacanza?*
Pina Twice.
You   *Quando? D'estate?*
Pina No. In summer it's impossible. We have too many customers.
         We go in spring and autumn.
You   *Dove va?*
Pina I go to Switzerland with my daughter. We go skiing.
You   *Le piace sciare?*
Pina Yes, a lot. Skiing is my favourite sport.

Informazioni

2 (a) Scia. (b) Nuota. (c) Fa il jogging. (d) Gioca a calcio. (e) Gioca a
carte. (f) Gioca a tennis.

Unit 14

Dialoghi

1 (a) La Posta Centrale è in Piazza Garibaldi. (b) No. Parla con un
passante. **2** (a) La fermata del 48 è dopo il ponte. (b) Deve scendere.
3 (a) V. (b) Deve scrivere (il suo) nome, (il suo) cognome e (il suo)
indirizzo. **4** (a) La Posta Centrale chiude alle due. (b) Vuol(e) sapere
dov'è la buca delle lettere.

Spiegazioni

3 beva, faccia, pulisca, esca, venga. **5** (a) To send best wishes for their
wedding. (b) Grosseto.

Attività

1 (b) Come si fa per andare a Ponte San Giovanni? Prenda la seconda
traversa a sinistra. (c) Come si fa per andare alla stazione? Prenda la
terza traversa a sinistra. (d) Come si fa per andare al museo? Prenda la
terza traversa a destra. (e) Come si fa per andare alla Banca
Commerciale? Prenda la seconda traversa a destra. (f) Come si fa per
andare all'università? Prenda la prima traversa a destra.
2 (a) Giri a sinistra. (b) Vada sempre dritto. (c) Giri a destra.
3 …vada…giri…scenda…attraversi…prenda.
4 (a) Aspetti alla stazione! (b) Prenoti all'agenzia! (c) Legga qui!
(d) Pulisca dappertutto! (e) Venga a casa! (f) Paghi all cassa!
5 (a) … Le mangi! (b) …Lo beva! (c) …L'apra! (d) …Li faccia! (e) …
La prenda! (f) …Lo prenoti!

6 (a) Piazza Vittoria. (b) Porta Santa Margherita. (c) Chiesa di SS. (Santissima) Trinità.

Unit 15

Dialoghi

1 (a) Elena ha mangiato in una rosticceria. (b) Ha bevuto il vino. **2** (a) Il marito ha perso l'autobus. (b) No. Sta meglio. **3** (a) V. (b) No. Ha visitato la moglie.

Attività

1 A … risposto … ho messo in ordine … **B** Ho invitato … Abbiamo bevuto … giocato a bridge … **C** … abbiamo visto … **D** …ha chiamato…Ho passato …

2 i(g) ii(d) iii(e) iv(a) v(h) vi(c) vii(f) viii(b)

3 (a) Non ti vedo. (b) Non ti sento. (c) Non ti conosco. (d) Non mi vedi? (e) Non ti capisco. (f) Quando m'inviti? (g) Allora, mi accompagni? (h) Ti aspetto…

4 (a) Vittoria ha visto il Papa in Piazza San Pietro. (b) Gino ha comprato una villa fra Siena e Firenze. (c) Roberto ha (finalmente) aperto un'agenzia immobiliare. (d) Renzo e Mara hanno fatto molti bagni. (e) Ada e Lino hanno giocato alla roulette e hanno perso. (f) Federico e Anna hanno visto l'Aida. (g) Sandro e Carla hanno preso la gondola tutti i giorni.

5 Ho visto tante cose interessanti. Saluti da Bari.

6 (a) Ha pranzato dai suoi genitori. (b) Non ha chiamato l'elettricista. (c) Ha guardato il programma TV 7 speciale. (d) Non ha pulito la casa. (e) Non ha pagato l'affitto. (f) Ha giocato a tennis con Marco. (g) Ha portato la macchina dal meccanico. (h) Ha scritto una cartolina a sua zia Maria.

7 Ora tocca a te!

You	*Cos'hai fatto di bello oggi?*
Olga	I worked all day.
You	*Non hai visto il tuo ragazzo?*
Olga	Yes. At lunchtime.
You	*Avete mangiato insieme?*
Olga	Yes. At a smart trattoria in Via Manzoni.
You	*Perchè non sei contenta allora?*
Olga	Because *I* had to pay for the lunch.

Unit 16

Dialoghi

1 (a) L'immigrato ha lavorato prima a Bedford. (b) È andato ad abitare a Londra. **2** (a) V. (b) Spera di ritornare in Italia. **3** (a) V. (b) È partito col/con il treno delle dieci e quaranta. **4** (a) V. (b) (Non l'accetta) perchè deve scappare.

Attività

1 (a)...lunedì scorso è andato a teatro. (b) ...martedì scorso ha cenato tardi. (c) ...mercoledì scorso non ha studiato affatto. (d) ...giovedì scorso ha lavorato fino alle dieci. (e) ...venerdì scorso ha mangiato fuori. (f) ...sabato scorso ha giocato a scacchi. (g) ...domenica scorsa ha dormito fino a mezzogiorno.

2 Lunedì scorso sono andato a teatro. Giovedì scorso ho lavorato fino alle dieci. Domenica scorsa ho dormito fino a mezzogiorno.

3 (b) Paolo Nuzzo è nato nel '69. È stato in Austria per due anni. È andato a Vienna. Poi è tornato in Italia. (c) Mirella Perrone è nata nel '57. È stata in Francia per un anno. È andata a Parigi. Poi è tornata in Sicilia. (d) I signori Caraffi sono nati nel '58. Sono stati in Spagna per dodici anni. Sono andati a Barcellona. Poi sono tornati in Sardegna. (e) Anna e Silvia sono nate nel '71. Sono state in Grecia per sei anni. Sono andate ad Atene. Poi sono tornate a Roma.

4 (b) Ci sono andata in aprile. (c) Ci sono ritornata nel mese di agosto. (d) Ci sono andata in macchina. (e) No. Ci sono andata con la mia amica Francesca.

5 (a) Non la vede da due anni. (b) La conosce da molti anni. (c) Lo suona da nove anni. (d) Lo studia da sei mesi. (e) Non lo vedono da molto tempo. (f) L'aspettano da poco tempo.

6 (a) Mara è andata a fare la spesa due ore fa. (b) Sergio è venuto a pranzo un'ora fa. (c) Mario è tornato dal lavoro un'ora e mezza fa. (d) Carlo è andato a letto mezz'ora fa. (e) Filippo è uscito cinque minuti fa.

7 Ora tocca a te!

Giornalista	Do you ever go to Italy?
You	*Sì. Ci vado quasi ogni anno.*
Giornalista	Where did you go last year?
You	*Sono andato a Venezia e a Verona.*
Giornalista	Did you stay long in Verona?

You	*Due sere. Per l'opera.*
Giornalista	Did you go with friends?
You	*No. Preferisco viaggiare da solo.*
Giornalista	(But) you speak very well! Are your parents Italian?
You	*Sì. E ... Ho studiato l'italiano all'università.*
Giornalista	Where? In Italy?
You	*Prima in Italia, poi all'università di Londra.*
Giornalista	How long ago?
You	*Due anni fa.*

Informazioni

Si trovano in Sicilia.

Unit 17
Dialoghi

1 (a) Marisa è andata al supermercato con Valeria. (b) (L'ha messo) in frigorifero. **2** (a) Daniele e Sonia hanno comprato una cravatta di seta pura per Sandro. (b) (Non li hanno prenotati) perchè non hanno avuto tempo. **3** (a) V. (b) Ha tolto la spina.

Attività

1 (a) Ne ho mandato uno. (b) Ne ho visti molti. (c) Ne ho spedite sei. (d) Ne ho scritte quattro. (e) Ne ho visitata una. (f) Ne ho spesi molti. (g) Ne ho cambiate poche. (h) Ne ho bevuti tre.

2 (a) Le ho già scritte. (b) Li ho già comprati. (c) Li ho già visti. (d) Le ho già fatte. (e) L'ho già sbrigata. (f) L'ho già finito. (g) Li ho già preparati. (h) L'ho già consultata.

3 (a) No. Non l'ho ancora fatto. (b) No. Non l'ho ancora pulito. (c) No. Non l'ho ancora pagato. (d) No. Non l'ho ancora fatta. (e) No. Non li ho ancora comprati. (f) No. Non l'ho ancora riparata.

4 (a) ... ho scritto ... (b) ... l'ho letto. (c) ... l'ho ascoltata. (d) ...l'ha bevuta. (e) ... l'ha messo. (f) ... hanno perso il treno.

5 Ora tocca a te!

Moglie	Are we leaving then, dear?
You	*Non sono ancora pronto.*
Moglie	What are you looking for?
You	*Il passaporto. Ma dove l'ho messo? L'hai preso tu?*
Moglie	No. Have you looked in the car?
You	*Sì. Ho guardato. Non c'è.*

Moglie Didn't you leave it in the bank this morning when you changed your money?

You *No. Ah ... Un momento ... Forse l'ho messo in camera da letto.*

Moglie No. It's not there. I've cleaned (in) every room and I haven't seen anything.

You *Non l'hai mica messo con gli altri documenti?*

Moglie No, no. I've only got the train tickets in my bag.

You *Che guaio! Come facciamo ora senza passaporto?*

Moglie Have you looked in the study?

You *Sì. Ho guardato dappertutto.*

Moglie My goodness! And the train leaves in half an hour!

Informazioni

They are supposed to be ideal with aubergines and clams.

Unit 18
Dialoghi

1 (a) Renzo non usa mai il profumo./Renzo il profumo non lo usa mai. (b) Perchè è il suo compleanno. **2** (a) Beatrice prende un disco di musica classica per Renzo. (b) Vuol(e) telefonare a Renzo. **3** (a) V. (b) Devono andare a pranzo da Carla.

Attività

1 (a) Anna gli dà una cravatta. (b) Renzo gli dà un libro. (c) Beatrice gli porta un CD. (d) Livio gli manda una cassetta. (e) Matteo gli regala un profumo. (f) Maria gli telefona per fargli gli auguri.

2 (a) Le telefono stasera. (b) Gli telefono più tardi. (c) Gli telefono dopo cena. (d) Le scrivo domani. (e) Le scrivo oggi. (f) Gli parlo dopo la lezione./Parlo loro dopo la lezione.

3 (b) A chi vuole mandare la cartolina di auguri? Voglio mandarla a Beatrice. (c) A chi vuole regalare la borsa di pelle? Voglio regalarla a Maria. (d) A chi vuole portare i cioccolatini? Voglio portarli a Marco. (e) A chi vuole dare il portafoglio? Voglio darlo a Gino.

4 il francobollo – Non ce l'ho. – non lo compri? – la posta è chiusa – il tabaccaio è aperto – non c'è un tabaccaio – vuoi spedirla – devo mandargli – devi mandarli?

5 (a) S'incontrano. (b) Si vedono. (c) Si parlano. (d) Si salutano. (e) Si baciano. (f) Si abbracciano.

6 Ora tocca a te!

Giorgio Where are you going, Carla?
You   Prima vado alla posta, poi vado a comprare il regalo per Antonio.
Giorgio Why? Is it his birthday?
You   No. È il suo onomastico.
Giorgio What are you buying him?
You   Non lo so ancora.
Giorgio Does he like reading?
You   Mi sembra di no.
Giorgio How much do you want to spend?
You   Non troppo.
Giorgio Do you know whether he likes music?
You   So che gli piace ascoltare la musica quando guida.
Giorgio You can buy him a cassette then.
You   Ottima idea!

Informazioni

(a) No. È un fascio di rose. (b) Ce ne sono quindici. (c) They are made in Perugia. (d) Mother's day.

Unit 19

Dialoghi

1 (a) V. (b) No. Non c'è mai stata. **2** (a) V. (b) (C'è andata) per quattro giorni. **3** (a) Marcello lavora in una fabbrica. (b) Si trova bene.

Attività

1 Marco si è iscritto all'università di Roma. Si è laureato in medicina in sei anni. Anna si è iscritta all'università di Bologna. Si è laureata in matematica e fisica in sette anni. Carlo e Fillippo si sono iscritti all'università di Napoli. Si sono laureati in legge in quattro anni.
2 Mi sono vestito… ho fatto colazione … ho comprato … ho telefonato … gli ho chiesto … sono andato … ho detto … ho preso … ho fatto …
3 (b) Ci siamo visti. (c) Ci siamo parlati. (d) Ci siamo salutati. (e) Ci siamo baciati. (f) Ci siamo abbracciati.
4 (a) di cui. (b) con cui. (c) da cui. (d) per cui. (e) a cui.
5 Ora tocca a te!

Giornalista Are you German?
You   No. Siamo inglesi.
Giornalista How long have you been here?

You	*Siamo qui da una quindicina di giorni.*
Giornalista	Did you come by air?
You	*No. Siamo venuti in macchina.*
Giornalista	And why did you come to Perugia?
You	*Perchè ci siamo iscritti all'università per studiare l'italiano.*
Giornalista	How long does the course last?
You	*Dura un mese.*
Giornalista	Have you visited any other places?
You	*Non molti. Ma/però domenica scorsa ci siamo alzati presto e siamo andati ad Assisi.*
Giornalista	Did you enjoy yourselves?
You	*Ci siamo divertiti moltissimo.*

Informazioni

(a) Cenano sulla spiaggia. (b) Il pomeriggio vanno al parco. (c) La fanno sul Mare Adriatico.

Unit 20

Dialoghi

1 (a) La signorina prende le compresse senz'acqua. (b) Ne prende una. **2** (a) V. (b) Deve andare in farmacia. **3** (a) La signora ha mal di denti. (b) Le dà uno spazzolino e un dentifricio speciali. **4** (a) V. (b) Deve riparare gli occhiali dell'avvocato.

Attività

1 Anna: Mi fa male il braccio. Giorgio: Mi fa male il naso. Alessandro: Mi fa male il ginocchio. Livio: Mi fanno male gli occhi. Orazio: Mi fanno male i piedi. Gina: Mi fanno male le gambe.

2 (a) ... le fa male il braccio. (b) ... gli fa male il naso. (c) ... gli fanno male gli occhi. (d) ... gli fanno male i piedi. (e) ...le fanno male le gambe. (f) ... gli fa male il ginocchio.

3 (a) ... ha mal di gola. (b) ... ha mal di testa. (c) ... ha la febbre. (d) ... ha mal di stomaco. (e) ... ha mal di denti. (f) ... ha il raffreddore.

4 (a) ... si riposi! (b) ...si asciughi! (c) ... si lavi i denti! (d) ... si metta il cappotto! (e) ... si diverta!

5 (a) Non le prenda! (b) ... Non li faccia! (c) ... Non gli telefoni! (d) ... Non le scriva! (e) ... Non l'apra! (f) ... Non le chiuda!

6 Ora tocca a te!

You	*Non mi sento bene.*
Mara	What's the matter? Have you got a headache?
You	*No. Mi fanno male gli occhi.*
Mara	Why don't you put your glasses on?
You	*Purtroppo sono dall'ottico.*
Mara	But I can drive if you like.
You	*Va bene. Così mi riposo un po'.*
Mara	How about stopping a moment at the chemist's?
You	*Buon'idea! E poi possiamo andare a prendere qualcosa da bere.*
Mara	So first we'll stop at the chemist's and then we'll go to the Quattro Fontane Bar.
You	*E così posso anche telefonare al medico.*

Unit 21

Dialoghi

1 (a) V. (b) Andranno in Calabria dai loro parenti. **2** (a) Il sole non dà fastidio a Massimo. (b) Perchè dovrà ricominciare a lavorare. **3** (a) V. (b) La rivedrà sabato. **4** (a) La signorina vuole consultare il catalogo dei nuovi dischi. (b) Deve riportarlo/lo deve riportare al commesso. **5** (a) V. (b) Dovrà richiederli/Li dovrà richiedere alla casa discografica.

Attività

1 (b) Berrò ... (c) Andrò ... (d) Farò ... (e) Pulirò ... (f) Preparerò ... (g) Sparecchierò ... (h) Laverò ... (i) Mi riposerò ... (j) Prenderò ... (k) Andrò ... (l) Finirò ... (m) Uscirò ...

2 (a) ... Usciranno ... (b) ... Resteranno ... (c) ... Verranno ... (d) ... Potranno farlo ... (e) Saranno qui ... (f) ... Lo faranno ... (g) ... Arriveranno ... (h) ... La costruiranno ...

3 ... andremo ... ... staremo ... trascorreremo ... torneremo ... daremo ... inviteremo ... guarderemo ... andremo ... ci siederemo ... prenderemo ... ascolteremo ...

4 (a) Me la riparerà il meccanico. (b) Me le cambierà il cassiere. (c) Ce lo prenoterà il nostro amico Sandro. (d) Me lo farà un pittore francese. (e) Ce lo porterà un nostro collega. (f) Me la disegnerà un architetto italiano. (g) Me lo regalerà mia sorella. (h) Ce lo troverà nostro cugino.

5 Ora tocca a te!

You　　*Vorrei un libro sull'Italia.*

Libraio What type of book? Do you want something on politics or economics?

You　　*Veramente cerco un libro per turisti.*

Libraio So it's a guide you are after?

You　　*Sì. Vorrei fare il giro dei laghi.*

Libraio Ah! Then you need a book on Northern Italy.

You　　*Esattamente! Posso vedere ciò che ha?*

Libraio I'm sorry, but at the moment we haven't got anything.

You　　*Come mai?*

Libraio Unfortunately I sold the last one an hour ago.

You　　*Non ne aspetta altri?*

Libraio Of course. But when are you leaving?

You　　*Partirò il primo giugno.*

Libraio Good. If you come here at the end of May I'll have just what you want.

You　　*Posso prenotarne una copia adesso?*

Libraio Of course. Leave me ten per cent deposit and your address. When the book arrives I'll let you know.

Informazioni

(a) Per vedere **la Mostra dei mobili antichi** si deve andare a **Cortona**. (b) Per vedere la **Mostra (internazionale) dei telefilm** si deve andare a **Chianciano Terme**. (c) Per vedere **la Festa del lago** si deve andare a **Castiglione del Lago**.

Unit 22

Dialoghi

1 (a) V. (b) No. La trovava molto monotona. **2** (a) Quando Nino e Dario erano scapoli uscivano ogni sera. (b) Dicevano sempre che non volevano sposarsi. **3** (a) Eugenio Parisi lavorava in un'azienda agricola. (b) Perchè non ha potuto./Perchè suo padre era gravemente ammalato e non poteva più mantenerlo. **4** (a) V. (b) No. Suonava la chitarra.

Attività

1 (b) Faceva così caldo; fa così freddo. (c) C'era tanto sole; c'è tanta pioggia. (d) Uscivo ogni sera; non esco mai. (e) Venivano a trovarmi tante persone; non viene a trovarmi nessuno. (f) Andavo ogni domenica alla spiaggia; vado qualche volta in piscina. (g) Parlavo con

tanta gente; non parlo con nessuno. (h) Bevevo caffè e vino; bevo
tè e birra.

2 (a) Perchè era troppo forte. (b) Perchè mi faceva male un dente.
(c) Perchè costavano poco. (d) Perchè dov'ero prima dovevo lavorare
troppo. (e) Perchè era troppo cara. (f) Perchè non avevamo appetito.
(g) Perchè avevano sete. (h) Perchè eravamo stanchi morti. (i) Perchè
non mi sentivo bene. (j) Perchè aveva bisogno di soldi.

3 (a)…si radeva, ha telefonato … (b) … scriveva, si è rotta …
(c) … riparava, è arrivata … (d) … cucinava, si è scottato …
(e) … leggeva, se n'è andata … (f) … guardava … gli ha chiesto …

4 i (a) No. È laureata da poco tempo. (b) Si offre come baby-sitter di
pomeriggio e di sera. (c) Vive a Bergamo. ii (a) Ha il diploma di
ragioniera. (b) Vuole lavorare per mezza giornata. (c) Bisogna
telefonarle nelle ore dei pasti. iii(a) No. Sono prossimi alle nozze.
(b) No. Vogliono prenderlo in affitto. (c) No. Può essere anche
piccolo. iv(a) No. È laureato in scienze politiche. (b) Ha trent'anni./Ne
ha trenta. (c) No. Lavora da molto tempo. (d) Conosce il francese,
l'inglese e il tedesco.

5 A Ma come! Già te ne vai? **B** Eh, sì. Me ne devo andare. **A** E Bruna,
se ne va anche lei? **B** No. Bruna non se ne va ancora. Però Anna e
Roberto se ne vanno. E voi quando ve ne andate? **A** Noi ce ne andiamo
più tardi.

6 Ora tocca a te!

You	*Dove lavorava, signora, quando era a Napoli?*
Signora	I worked in an agricultural co-operative which exported fruit all over Europe.
You	*Ma lei, che faceva di preciso?*
Signora	I checked the quality of the fruit.
You	*Trovava il lavoro difficile?*
Signora	Yes. Because a minor error was enough to lose very important customers.
You	*Quanto tempo ha lavorato in quell'azienda?*
Signora	Three and a half years. Then we went to Sorrento because my father was tired of living in a big town.
You	*È per questo che vuol cambiare lavoro?*
Signora	Yes. mainly because of that.

Informazioni

2 (a) È il 91%

Unit 23

Dialoghi

1 (a) Quando hanno suonato, Bruna è andata ad aprire la porta. (b) Le ha scritto il suo indirizzo. **2** (a) V. (b) No. (Gianna) ha smesso di fumare./Non fuma più. **3** (a) V. (b) No. Non gli piace,

Attività

1 (b) Torna…! (c) Va'…! (d) Copriti…! (e) Prendi …! (f) Chiama …! (g) Rimani …! (h) Non preoccuparti di…!

2 (a) Non fumare! (b) Prendi l'aereo! (c) Non insistere! (d) Non parcheggiare lì! (e) Va' in macchina! (f) Porta l'ombrello! (g) Metti la data…! (h) Usa la scheda telefonica!

3 (b) Non usarla! (c) Non comprarlo! (d) Non pagarlo! (e) Non berla! (f) Non prenderlo! (g) Non attraversarla! (h) Non perderli!

4 (a) Luigi, sta' zitto! (b) Alfredo, fammi assaggiare il gelato! (c) Elena, va' all'altra tavola! (d) Vittorio, dammi il bicchiere! (e) Maria, passami il sale e il pepe! (f) Nina, dimmi cosa vuoi per secondo piatto!

5 (a) … sta facendo il bagno. (b) … sta cucinando. (c) …sta piovendo. (d) … sta per sposarsi. (e) … sta suonando. (f) … stanno per partire.

6 i (e) Sta mangiando. ii(f) Stiamo comprando … iii (c) Stanno facendo …iv(b) Sta cucinando. v(d) Sta lavorando. vi(a) Stanno chiacchierando.

7 Ora tocca a te!

Mamma	What are you doing up so early? It's not yet five o'clock!
You	*Vorrei studiare un po'.*
Mamma	At this time? How's that?
You	*Ma non sapevi che oggi ho un esame?*
Mamma	Oh! I'd completely forgotten. Shall I make you a cup of coffee?
You	*No grazie. Ritorna a letto.*
Mamma	Have you still got a lot to do?
You	*No. Non molto.*
Mamma	You're studying so much, it's true; but in a couple of years' time you'll be a doctor.
You	*Sì. Ma solo se supero questo esame. È uno dei più difficili.*
Mamma	But why are you so worried?
You	*Perchè questa volta non sono sicuro di me.*
Mamma	Don't worry. Everything will be fine. You'll see.

Unit 24

Dialoghi

1 (a) V. (b) (Se n'è accorta) quando è uscita dal Duomo. **2** (a) V. (b) È nata a Lugano nel '70. **3**(a) V. (b) di usare il suo telefono; di aiutarla a cercare il numero telefonico del suo medico. **4**(a) V. (b) Ha telefonato al pronto soccorso. **5**(a) La macchina è della signora. (b) No. Gli ha chiesto di controllare (solo) l'olio e l'acqua.

Attività

1 (a) Lavatevi le mani! (b) Aspettate qui! (c) Venite a tavola!
(d) Sedetevi! (e) Non gridate! (f) Non fate troppo rumore! (g) Non toccate i fiori sulla tavola! (h) Bevete piano piano! (i) Non parlate con la bocca piena!

2 i(i) ii(f) iii(a) iv(c) v(b) vi(e) vii(d) viii(g) ix(h).

3 (a) … Glieli faccio io. (b) …Glielo compro io. (c) … Glieli cambio io. (d) … Glieli riporto io. (e) …Gliela imbuco io. (f) … Glielo prendo io. (g) … Gliele chiudo io.

4 (a) È sua. (b) È suo. (c) È mio. (d) Sono suoi. (e) Sono miei. (f) Sono sue. (g) Sono miei. (h) Sono suoi. (i) Sono mie.

5 (b) È suo quest'ombrello? (d) Sono suoi questi occhiali? (f) Sono sue quelle chiavi? (h) Sono suoi quei giornali?

6 Ora tocca a te!

You	*Ho perso la patente di guida e non so (che) cosa fare.*
Signorina	Do you know where you lost it?
You	*Non ne sono certo. Forse l'ho lasciata in macchina. Durante la notte qualcuno è entrato nella mia auto e ha preso tutto.*
Signorina	Don't worry. There's a good chance of recovering it, because usually they send it to the 'Questura'.
You	*Che cos'è la Questura?*
Signorina	It's the police headquarters. Go there and report the loss.
You	*E sa dov'è, per cortesia?*
Signorina	Certainly. It's in Via Mazzini.
You	*Grazie.*
Signorina	Don't mention it. But before going there, buy a sheet of stamped paper at the tobacconist's for your statement.
You	*E intanto, come faccio senza patente?*
Signorina	For the moment you can use a copy of the statement as a document.

Informazioni

Il 113.

Unit 25

Dialoghi

1 (a) V. (b) È di Milano ed il giornale che di solito legge è *Il Corriere della Sera*. **2** (a) V. (b) No. Escono ogni settimana. **3** (a) V. (b) Secondo lui ci dovrebbero essere più documentari. **4** (a) Ezio non è d'accordo col suo amico sui programmi televisivi. (b) Vorrebbe abolire le televisioni private.

Attività

1 (a) La berrei … (b) Li mangerei … (c) Lo metterei … (d) Le prenderei … (e) L'ascolterei … (f) Lo guarderei …
2 (a) Ada vivrebbe in città. Comprerebbe un piccolo appartamento. Andrebbe ogni sera a ballare. Imparerebbe a guidare. (b) Vivrei al mare. Comprerei una villa. Andrei spesso a nuotare. Imparerei a suonare la chitarra. (c) I signori Miele vivrebbero in montagna. Comprerebbero una casetta. Andrebbero ogni tanto a sciare. Imparerebbero a dipingere.
3 i(g) ii(h) iii(d) iv(f) v(a) vi(b) vii(e) viii(c).
4(a) Te le porterei io … (b) Te la porterei io … (c) Te la farei io … (d) Te lo pulirei io … (e) Te le cambierei io … (f) Te la farei io … (g) Te la imbucherei io …
5 Ora tocca a te!

You	*Ciao Renata! Puoi venire alla mia festa stasera?*
Renata	I'd love to, but I'm very busy at the moment.
You	*Ma cos'hai di così importante da fare?*
Renata	I've got to tidy up the house, I've got to do some washing, I'm on my own and I have to think of everything.
You	*E non potresti fare tutte queste cose in un altro momento?*
Renata	Yes, I could, only that my parents are coming back from their holiday abroad today.
You	*Ma non dovevano ritornare la settimana prossima?*
Renata	Yes. In fact they would have liked to stay for five or six days longer, but my aunt has had a baby and so they decided to come back early.
You	*A che ora arriveranno?*

Renata They should be at the airport at six. I'll go and collect them myself by car.

You *Comunque, se cambi idea, puoi sempre farmelo sapere. Chiamami quando vuoi.*

Renata Thank you. If I can, I'd love to come, if it's only to greet you and give you my best wishes.

Informazioni

(a) RAI: Radio Televisione Italiana.

(b) *La Stampa*, *La Repubblica* e (il) *Corriere della Sera*.

ITALIAN–ENGLISH VOCABULARY

a *at, to, in, on*
a destra *on the right*
a piedi *on foot*
a presto! *see you soon!*
a sinistra *on the left*
abbastanza *enough*
abbastanza bene *pretty well*
abbigliamento *clothing*
abbonato/a *subscriber*
abbracciare *to embrace, hug*
abbraccio *embrace, hug*
abitante (m *or* f) *inhabitant*
abitare *to live*
abituato/a *used to*
abolire *to abolish*
accanto a *near, next to*
accendere (p.p. acceso) *to light, turn on*
acceso *from* accendere
accettare *to accept*
acciuga *anchovy*
accomodarsi *to sit down, take a seat*
accompagnare *to accompany*
accordo: essere d'accordo *to agree*
accorgersi (p.p accorto) *to notice, realise*
aceto *vinegar*
acqua *water;* – minerale *mineral water*
acquaio *sink*
acquistare *to acquire, purchase*
acustico/a *acoustic*
ad = a *at, to, in, on*
adesso *now*
aereo *aeroplane*
aeroporto *airport*
affare (m): gli affari *business*
affatto (non) *not at all*
affettuoso/a *affectionate*
affittare *to let, rent*

affitto *rent*
agenda *diary*
agente (m) immobiliare *estate agent*
agenzia di viaggi *travel agency*
agenzia immobiliare *estate agents*
agenzia pubblicitaria *advertising agency*
agitarsi *to get upset, excited*
agli = a + gli
aglio *garlic*
agnello *lamb*
agosto *August*
ai = a + i
aiutare *to help*
aiuto *help*
al = a + il
albergo *hotel*
albero *tree*
alcuni/e *a few, some, several*
alfabeto *alphabet*
all' = a + l'
all'aperto *in the open*
all'estero *abroad*
alla = a + la
alle = a + le
allo = a + lo
alloggio *lodging*
allora *so, then*
alto/a *tall*
altrimenti *otherwise, or else*
altro ieri (l') *the day before yesterday*
altro/a *other* senz'altro *certainly* altro?
   anything else?
altrochè! *you bet I do! certainly*
alzare la voce *to raise one's voice*
alzarsi *to get up*
amaro/a *bitter*
ambulanza *ambulance*

americano/a *American*
amica/o *friend (f/m)*
ammalato/a *ill, sick*
ammobiliato/a *furnished*
anch' = anche
anche *also,too*
ancora *still,yet, again, more*
andare (irr.) *to go, to suit, to fit*
andare a + inf. *to go and ...*
andare d'accordo *to get on with*
andare in giro *to travel round*
andarsene (irr.) *to go away, to be off*
anello *ring*
angolo *angle, corner*
animale (m) *animal*
anno *year*
anticipo *deposit;* in – *early*
antico/a *ancient, old*
antipasto *starter(s), hors d'oeuvre*
anzi *as a matter of fact, and even, on the contrary*
aperto/a *open*
appartamento *flat*
appena *as soon as, just, barely*
appetito *appetite*
approvare *to approve of*
appuntamento *appointment, date, rendez-vous*
aprile *April*
aprire (p.p. aperto) *to open*
apriscatole (m) *tin-opener*
aranciata *orangeade*
architetto *architect*
argento *silver*
armadio *wardrobe*
arrivederci, arrivederla *goodbye*
arrivo *arrival*
arrosto *roast*
arte (f) *art*
arte culinaria *cookery*
artista (m or f) *artist*
ascensore (m) *lift*
asciugamano *towel*
asciugarsi *to get dry, wipe oneself*
ascoltare *to listen to*
aspettare *to wait for*
aspettarsi *to expect*
aspirapolvere (m) *vacuum cleaner*

aspirina *aspirin*
assaggiare *to taste, try*
assegno *cheque*
attendere (p.p. atteso) *to wait*
  – in linea *to hold the line*
attenzione! *be careful!*
attento/a *attentive*
attimo *moment*
attività *activity*
attraversare *to cross*
attraverso *across, through, by means of*
attuale *present*
attualmente *at present*
auguri (m pl) *best wishes, greetings*
aumento *rise, increase*
australiano/a *Australian*
auto (f) *car*
autoambulanza = ambulanza
autobus (m) *bus*
autostrada *motorway*
autunno *autumn*
avanti! *forward! come in!*
avere (irr.) *to have*
avvicinare *to draw near, approach*
avvicinarsi *to approach*
avvocato *lawyer*
azienda agricola *agricultural co-operative*
azienda *business, firm*
azzurro/a *blue*

baciare *to kiss*
bacio *kiss*
bacione (m) *big kiss*
bagagli (m pl) *luggage*
bagnato/a *soaked, wet*
bagno *bath, bathroom*
balcone (m) *balcony*
ballare *to dance*
bambina *little girl*
bambino *child, baby, little boy*
banana *banana*
banca *bank*
bancario/a *banking*
bar (m) *bar, café*
basta *enough;* basta così *that's enough*
be', beh *well*
beata lei! *lucky you!*
beato/a *lucky*
bei *from* bello/a

bel *from* bello
bel tempo *fine weather*
bellino/a *pretty*
bello/a *beautiful, nice, handsome*
bene *well*
benissimo! *great! very well*
benzina *petrol*
benzinaio *petrol-pump attendant*
bere (irr; p.p. bevuto) *to drink*
bevuto/a *from* bere
bianco/a *white*
biblioteca *library*
bicchier(e) (m) *glass*
bicchierino *small glass*
bicicletta *bicycle*
bidè (m) *bidet*
biglietteria *ticket office*
biglietto *(bank)note, ticket*
binario *platform*
birra *beer*
biscotto *biscuit*
bisognare *to need, to be necessary*
bisogno di; aver – *to need*
bistecca *steak*
blu *navy blue*
bocca *mouth*
boh! *I don't know*
bollente *boiling*
borsa *bag, handbag*
bosco *wood*
bottiglia *bottle*
box (m) *garage*
bracciale (m) *bracelet*
braccio *arm*
brasato/a *braised*
bravo/a *good, clever*
breve *brief, short*
brutto tempo *bad weather*
buca delle lettere *letter-box*
buon = buono
buonanotte (f) *goodnight*
buonasera *good evening, etc*
buongiorno *good morning, etc*
buono/a *good*
burro *butter*
busta *envelope*

c'è *there is, it's there, he's in, she's in*
cadere *to fall*

caffè (m) *coffee*
calamari (m pl) *squid*
calcio *football*
caldo/a *hot*
calendario *calendar*
calmarsi *to grow calm, calm down*
calzino *sock*
cambiamento *change*
cambiare *to change*
cambiare discorso *to change the subject*
cambiare idea *to change one's mind*
cambiarsi *to get changed*
cambio *exchange (rate)*
camera (da letto) *(bed) room*
cameriera *waitress, maid*
cameriere (m) *waiter*
camicetta *blouse*
camicia *shirt*
camminare *to walk*
campagna *country-(side)*
campanello *(door)bell*
campeggio *camping*
campo da tennis *tennis court*
candelina *little candle*
cane (m) *dog*
canzone (f) *song*
capire *to understand*
capito *from* capire
capolinea (m) *terminus, end of the line*
cappello *hat*
cappotto *coat*
cappuccino *white coffee*
capsula *capsule*
carattere (m) *character*
caratteristico/a *characteristic*
carciofo *artichoke*
cariato/a *decayed*
carino/a *pretty*
carne (f) *meat*
caro/a *expensive, dear, darling*
carriera *career*
carta *paper, card*
carta bollata *stamped paper*
carta di credito *credit card*
carte (f pl) *playing-cards*
cartolina *postcard*
casa *house, home*
casa discografica *record company*

casetta *small house*
caso *chance;* per – by chance
cassetta *cassette*
cassetto *drawer*
cassettone (m) *chest of drawers*
cassiere (m) *cashier*
castello *castle*
catalogo *catalogue*
cattedrale (f) *cathedral*
cattivo tempo *bad weather*
celeste *light blue*
cena *dinner, supper*
cenare *to have dinner, dine*
cento *hundred;* per – *per cent*
centrale *central*
centralinista (m or f) *phone operator*
centralino *phone exchange*
centro *centre*
centro città *city centre*
cercare *to look for*
certamente *certainly*
certo/a *certain, sure*
certo *certainly*
che ora/ore..? *what time..?*
che cos'è? *what is it?*
che *that*
che? che cosa? *what?*
chi *who, whom*
chi si vede! *look who's here!*
chiacchierare *to talk, chat*
chiamare *to call*
chiamarsi *to be called*
chiaro/a *clear, light*
chiave (f) *key*
chiedere (p.p. chiesto) *to ask*
chiesa *church*
chiesto *from* chiedere
chilo *kilo*
chitarra *guitar*
chitarrista (m or f) *guitarist*
chiudere (p.p. chiuso) *to close*
chiuso/a *closed*
ci *here, there; us, ourselves, each other*
ci vediamo! *see you!*
ci vogliono *it takes*
ci vuole *it takes*
ciao! *hello, hi! goodbye*
cin cin! *cheers!*

cinema (m) *cinema*
cinese *Chinese*
cinquanta *fifty*
cinque *five*
ciò che *what*
cioccolatino *small chocolate*
cioccolato *chocolate*
cioè *that is*
cipolla *onion*
circa *about*
citofono *entry-phone*
città *town*
civico *civic*
classe (f) *class*
classico/a *classical, classic*
cliente (m or f) *customer*
cognome (m) *surname*
colazione (f) *breakfast*
collega (m or f) *colleague*
colloquio *interview*
colore (m) *colour*
Colosseo *Coliseum*
coltello *knife*
come *sorry? pardon? how, what, as*
come no! *of course*
come si dice in italiano? *how do you say
    (it) in Italian?*
come sta? *how are you?*
come stai? *how are you?*
cominciare a *to begin to*
commerciale *commercial*
commessa/o (f/m) *shop assistant*
commissariato *police station*
comodino *bedside table*
comodità *comfort, convenience*
comodo/a *comfortable*
compleanno *birthday*
completo/a *full, no vacancies*
complimenti! *congratulations!*
senza –! *no need to be polite*
comprare *to buy*
compreso/a *included*
compressa *tablet*
comunicazione (f) *communication*
comunità *community*
comunque *anyway, however*
con *with*
concerto *concert*

condire *to season*
condominio *block of flats*
conferenza *lecture*
confortevole *comforting, comfortable*
confronto *comparison*
  in confronto a *compared with*
congelatore (m) *freezer*
conoscere *to know*
conseguire *to obtain*
conservare *to keep*
consigliare *to advise*
consolato *consulate*
consonante (f) *consonant*
consultare *to consult*
comsumare *to use*
contabilità *book-keeping*
contattare *to contact*
contatto *contact;* mettersi in – *to contact*
contento/a *pleased, happy*
continuare a *to continue to*
conto, per – mio *personally, on my own,*
  by myself
conto *bill*
contorno *side-dish*
contratto *contract*
controllare *to check*
conveniente *convenient*
convento *convent*
conversazione (f) *conversation*
coperta *blanket*
coperto *cover*
coppa di gamberetti *prawn cocktail*
coprire (p.p. coperto) *to cover*
coprirsi (p.p. coperto) *to cover oneself*
correre (p.p. corso) *to run*
corrispondenza *correspondence*
corsa *run, race*
corso *from* correre
corso *course, avenue*
cortesia, per – *please*
cortile (m) *courtyard*
corto/a *short*
cos'è? *what is (it)?*
cosa da niente *nothing*
cosa sono? *what are (they)?*
cosa *thing*
cosa? che –? *what?*
così *as, so, like this;* basta – *that's enough*

costare *to cost*
costruire *to build*
costruzione (f) *building*
costume (m) (da bagno) *bathing costume,*
  swimsuit
cotoletta *cutlet, escalope*
cotone (m) *cotton*
cotto/a (*from* cuocere) *cooked*
cottura *cooking time*
cravatta *tie*
creare *to create*
credere *to think, believe*
crisantemo *chrysanthemum*
cristallo *crystal*
crudo/a *raw, uncooked*
cucchiaino *tea/coffee spoon*
cucchiaio *spoon*
cucina *kitchen, cooker, cooking*
cucinare *to cook*
cugino/a *cousin*
cui *whom, which* il/la – *whose*
culturale *cultural*
cuocere *to cook*
cuoio *leather*

d'accordo *agreed, alright;* essere – *to agree*
da bere *to drink*
da *from, at, to, by, for, as, like, since*
da questa parte *this way, over here*
da solo/a *on one's own*
dappertutto *everywhere*
dare *to give*
dare fastidio *to bother, annoy, disturb*
dare su *to look out over, to give onto*
dare un'occhiata *to have a look*
data *date*
datore (m) di lavoro *employer*
davanti a *in front of*
decimo/a *tenth*
dei = di + i
delizioso/a *delicious*
della = di + la
dente (m) *tooth;* al – *slightly underdone*
dentifricio *toothpaste*
dentista (m or f) *dentist*
dentro *inside, in*
denuncia *statement*
deposito *deposit*
desidera? *can I help you?*

desiderare *to desire, want, wish*
destra: a destra *on the right*
destro/a *right*
detto *see* dire
devo *see* dovere
di che nazionalità? *what nationality?*
di dov'è? *where are you from?*
di dove sei? *where are you from?*
di fronte *opposite, in front of*
di qua *this way*
di solito *usually*
dialogo *dialogue*
diamoci del tu (from dare) *let's use* tu
diapositiva *slide, colour transparency*
dica! *(from* dire*) go ahead! tell me!*
dicembre (m) *December*
diciannove *nineteen*
diciassette *seventeen*
diciotto *eighteen*
dieci *ten*
dietro *behind*
differenza *difference*
diffuso/a *widely circulated, popular*
dilettante (m or f) *amateur*
dimorante *staying at*
dipendere *to depend*
dipingere (p.p. dipinto) *to paint*
diploma (m) *diploma*
dire irr. (p.p. detto) *to say, tell*
diretto/a *direct, through*
direttore (m) *director*
dirigente (m or f) *manager*
disco *record, cd*
discoteca *discotheque*
discretamente *reasonably well*
disegnare *to draw, design*
distinto/a *distinguished*
distrarsi (p.p. distratto) *to take one's mind off things*
disturbare *to disturb, bother*
disturbo *disturbance, inconvenience*
disturbo allo stomaco *stomach upset*
dito *finger*
ditta *firm, business*
divano *sofa*
diventare *to become*
diversi/e (pl) *several*
diverso/a *different*

divertimento *entertainment*
divertire *to amuse, entertain*
divertirsi *to enjoy oneself, have a good time*
dizionario *dictionary*
do *from* dare
doccia *shower*
documentario *documentary*
documento *document*
dodici *twelve*
dolce (m) *dessert, sweet*
dollaro *dollar*
domani *tomorrow*
domenica *Sunday*
domestico/a *domestic*
donna *woman*
dopo *later, after, then, beyond*
dopodomani *the day after tomorrow*
doppio/a *double*
dormire *to sleep*
dott. = dottore
dottore (m or f) *doctor*
dov'è? *where is (he/she/it)?*
dove *where*
dovere (irr.) *to have to, owe, be supposed to*
due *two*
dunque *well, where was I?*
Duomo *cathedral*
durante *during*
durare *to last*
duro/a *hard, solid*

è *is, it's, you are, is it? etc.*
e, ed *and*
ecc. = *etc.*
eccetto *except*
eccezione (f) *exception*
ecco fatto! *there you are*
ecco! *here is, here are; look!*
economia *economy*
economico/a *economic, economical*
ed = e
edicola *news-stand*
edificio *building*
effettivamente *actually, really*
elegante *smart, elegant*
elettricista (m or f) *electrician*
elettrodomestici (m.pl.) *household appliances*

entrare *to enter*
entrata *entrance*
entro *within, on or before*
ero *from* essere
esame (m) *examination*
esaminare *to examine, consider*
esatto/a *exact(ly)*
esco *from* uscire
esempio *example*
esistere (p.p. esistito) *to exist*
esperienza *experience*
esportare *to export*
esposizione (f) *exhibition*
espressione (f) *expression*
espresso *express/fast train*
espresso *expresso (coffee)*
essere (irr.) *to be*
estate (f) *summer*
esterno/a *outer, external*
estero *foreign;* all'- *abroad*
età *age*
etto *100 grams*
europeo/a *European*
evidente *evident*

fabbrica *factory*
facile *easy*
fagiolino *green bean*
fai *you do*
falso/a *false*
fame (f) *hunger*
fame, aver – *to be hungry*
famiglia *family*
far(e) complimenti *to pay compliments*
– così *to do like this*
– male *to hurt*
– sapere *to inform*
– tardi *to be late*
fare (irr; p.p.fatto) *to do, make*
fare i bagagli *to pack*
fare il bagno *to have a bath, to swim*
fare il biglietto *to buy a ticket*
fare il conto *to make out the bill*
fare il pieno *to fill up*
fare una domanda *to ask a question*
farmacia *chemist's shop*
farmacista (m or f) *chemist*
fascio *bunch*
fastidio *trouble, bother*

fatto *from* fare
favore (m) *favour*
fazzoletto *handkerchief*
febbraio *February*
febbre (f) *temperature, fever*
felicità *happiness, joy*
ferie (f pl) *holidays, leave*
fermarsi *to stop (oneself), stay*
fermata *(bus) stop*
ferragosto *August bank holiday*
ferri: ai ferri *grilled*
ferrovia *railway*
Ferrovie dello Stato *State Railways*
festa *fete, party, public holiday, fair*
fetta *slice*
fiammifero *match*
fidanzato/a *engaged, boyfriend, girlfriend*
figli *children*
figlia *daughter*
figlio *son*
figurarsi *to imagine, fancy*
figuri *see* si figuri
fila *queue*
film (m) *film*
finanziario/a *financial*
finchè *(non)* till, until
fine (f) *end*
finestra *window*
finire *to finish*
finito/a *finished*
fino a *until, up to*
fioraio/a *florist;* fiore (m) *flower*
Firenze (f) *Florence*
firma *signature*
firmare *to sign*
fisica *physics*
fisso/a *fixed*
fiume (m) *river*
foglio *sheet*
fondo *see* là in fondo
fontana *fountain*
forchetta *fork*
formaggio *cheese*
forno *oven*
forte *strong, loud*
fotografia *photograph*
fra *in. among, between*
fra poco *soon*

fra un'ora *in an hour's time*
fragola *stawberry*
francese *French*
Francia *France*
franco *franc*
francobollo *stamp*
fratello *brother*
freddo/a *cold*
frequentare *to attend, go to*
frequente *frequent, often*
fresco/a *fresh, cool*
frigorifero *fridge*
fritto/a *fried*
frontemare (m) *seafront*
frutta *fruit*
fruttivendolo *fruiterer, greengrocer*
fungo *mushroom*
fuori *out, outside*

gabinetti *toilets*
gamba *leg*
gamma *range*
garage (m) *garage*
garantire *to guarantee*
garanzia *guarantee*
gas (m) *gas;* con – *sparkling;* senza gas *still (water)*
gatto *cat*
gazzetta *gazette*
gelateria *ice-cream parlour*
gelato *ice cream*
generale *general*
generalità (f pl) *particulars*
generi (m pl) alimentari *groceries*
generoso/a *generous*
genitore (m) *parent*
gennaio *January*
Genova *Genoa*
gente (f) *people*
gentile *kind*
Germania *Germany*
ghiaccio *ice*
già *already*
giacca *jacket*
giallo/a *yellow*
giapponese *Japanese*
giardino *garden;*– pubblico *park*
ginocchio *knee*
giocare a *to play (game)*
gioco *game, amusement*

giornale (m) *newspaper*
gionalista (m or f) *journalist*
giornata *day;* che bella – *what a nice day!*
giorno *day*
giorno, un – qualunque *just an ordinary day*
giovedì (m) *Thursday*
gioventù (f) *youth*
girare *to turn*
giugno *June*
gli *the, (to) him*
glielo = gli + lo
gola *throat*
gomma *tyre, rubber*
gonna *skirt*
gorgonzola (m) *a type of cheese*
grammo *gram*
gran *big large;* in – parte *to a great extent*
Gran Bretagna *Great Britain*
grande *big, large, grown up*
granita di caffè *crushed ice with coffee*
granita di limone *crushed ice with lemon*
gratuito/a *free of charge*
grave *serious, seriously ill*
grazie (mille) *(many) thanks*
greco/a *Greek*
gridare *to shout*
grigio/a *grey*
griglia alla griglia *grilled*
gruppo *group*
guadagnare *to earn*
guaio *trouble, problem;* il – è *the trouble is* che – *what a nuisance!*
guanto *glove*
guardare *to look at, watch*
guasto/a *out of order, broken down*
guida (f) *guide*
guidare *to drive*

ha (*from* avere) *you have, he/she has*
hai (*from* avere) *you have*
hanno (*from* avere) *they have*
ho (*from* avere) *I have*
ho capito (*from* capire) *I understand, understood*

i (m pl) *the*
idea *idea*

ideale *ideal*
ieri *yesterday*
il (m s) *the*
imbucare *to post*
immaginare *to imagine*
immediato/a *immediate*
immigrato/a *immigrant*
imparare *to learn*
impegnato/a *busy, engaged*
impermeabile (m) *raincoat*
impiegarsi *to get a job*
impiego *employment, job*
importa *it matters;* non – *it doesn't matter*
importante *important*
impossibile *impossible*
in fondo *see* là in fondo
in giro *out and about*
in *in, inside, to, at, into*
in piedi *standing*
incidente (m) *accident;* – stradale *road accident*
incominciare a = cominciare a
incontrare *to meet*
incontrarsi *to meet each other*
incrocio *crossroads*
indirizzo *address*
infatti *indeed, in fact*
infine *finally*
influenza *influence, influenza*
informare *to inform*
informatica *computer science*
informazione (f) *(piece of) information*
ingegnere (m or f) *engineer*
ingegneria *engineering*
Inghilterra *England*
inglese *English*
ingrediente (m) *ingredient*
ingresso *entrance hall, entrance*
insalata *salad*
insegnante (m or f) *teacher*
insegnare *to teach*
inserzione (f) *advertisement*
insieme *together*
insolazione (f) *sunstroke*
intanto *meanwhile, to begin with*
intelligente *intelligent*
interessante *interesting*
interessare *to interest*
interno *flat number ...*

intervista *interview*
intervistare *to interview*
invece *on the other hand, instead, but, on the contrary*
inverno *winter*
invitare *to invite*
io *I, me*
Irlanda *Ireland*
iscriversi (p.p. iscritto) *to enrol, register*
istituto *institute*
Italia *Italy*
italiano/a *Italian*

jeans (m pl) *jeans*
jogging (m) *jogging*

lagnarsi *to complain*
lago *lake*
lana *wool*
lasagne al forno *baked lasagne*
lasciare *to leave, let*
latte (m) *milk*
laurea *degree*
laurearsi *to graduate*
laureato/a *graduate*
lavanderia *laundry;* – a secco *dry cleaning*
lavandino *washbasin*
lavare *to wash, clean*
lavarsi *to get washed, clean*
lavastoviglie (f) *dishwasher*
lavatrice (f) *washing machine*
lavorare *to work*
lavorativo/a *working, of work*
lavoro *work, job*
le (m or f) *to you*
le (f pl) *the*
legge (f) *law*
leggere (p.p. letto) *to read*
lei parla –? *do you speak –?*
lei *she, her, you*
lenzuolo (pl lenzuola) *sheet*
lettera *letter*
letto *bed*
letto *(from* leggere)
lezione (f) *lesson*
lì (over) *there*
libero/a *free*
libreria *bookshop, bookcase*
libro *book*
licenziare *to dismiss, sack*

liceo *secondary school*
lieto/a *happy, glad, delighted*
limonata *lemonade*
limone (m) *lemon*
linea *line, figure*
lingua *language*
liquore (m) *liqueur*
lira *lira*
litro *litre*
Livorno (f) *Leghorn*
lo *the, it*
locale (m) *room*
locale *local*
Londra *London*
lontano *far* – da *far from*
loro (to) *them, they, their, theirs*
luce (f) *light*
luglio *July*
lui *he, him*
lunedì (m) *Monday*
lungo/a *long*

ma *but*
macchè! *not at all*
macchina *car*
macedonia (di frutta) *fruit salad*
macellaio *butcher*
macelleria *butcher's shop*
madre (f) *mother*
magari *maybe, I wish I could, I'd love to*
magazzino *store*
maggio *May*
maglietta *T shirt, vest*
mai *never, ever*
maiale (m) *pork, pig*
mal (m) di gola *sore throat*
mal (m) di testa *headache*
mal di denti (m) *toothache*
male *badly, bad;* non c'e male *not bad*
mamma *mother, mummy*
mancia *tip*
mandare *to send*
mangiare *to eat*
mano (f) *hand*
mantenere (irr.) *to retain, maintain, keep*
manzo *beef*
marche da bollo *revenue stamps*
mare (m) *sea*
marinaro/a *sea-* (adj)

marmellata *jam*
marrone *brown*
martedì (m) *Tuesday*
marzo *March*
matematica *mathematics*
matita *pencil*
matrimoniale: camera – *room with a double bed*
mattina *morning*
maturità classica *school leaving cert. in classics*
me (*to/for*) *me*
meccanico *mechanic*
medicazione (f) *dressing, treatment*
medicina *medicine*
medico *doctor*
meglio *better*
mela *apple*
melanzana *aubergine*
melone (m) *melon*
meno *less*
meno male *thank goodness, a good job that*
mentre *while*
menù (m) *menu*
mercato *market*
mercoledì (m) *Wednesday*
merluzzo *cod*
mese (m) *month*
messaggio *message*
messicano/a *Mexican*
metro *metre, underground (abbrev.)*
metropolitana *underground*
mettere (p.p. messo) *to put*
mettere da parte *to put aside*
mettere in ordine *to tidy up*
mettersi *to put on, wear*
mettersi in contatto *to contact*
mezza pensione *half-board*
mezzanotte (f) *midnight*
mezzi (m pl) *means*
mezzi di comunicazione (di massa) *mass media*
mezzo/a *half*
mezzogiorno *midday*
mi (*to/for*) *me, myself*
mi dispiace *I'm sorry*
mica: non ... mica *not really, by any chance*
migliore *better, best*

mila *thousands*
milione (m) *million*
mille *a thousand*
minerale *mineral*
minestra *soup*
minestrone (m) *vegetable soup*
minicrociera *mini-cruise*
minuto *minute*
mio/a *my, mine*
misto/a *mixed*
mittente (m) *sender*
mobili (m pl) *furniture*
moderno/a *modern*
modo *manner*
modulo *form*
moglie (f) *wife*
molti/e *many*
molto *very, very much*
molto/a *much*
momento *moment*
mondo *world*
monotono/a *monotonous*
montagna *mountain*
monumento *monument*
morire irr.(p.p. morto) *to die*
mortadella *Bologna sausage*
morto/a *dead*
mostra *exhibition*
mostrare *to show*
municipio *town hall*
museo *museum*
musica *music*
musicassetta *music cassette*

Napoli (f) *Naples*
naso *nose*
Natale (m) *Christmas*
nativo/a *native*
nato/a *born*
natura *nature*
naturalmente *naturally*
nazionale *national*
nazionalità *nationality*
nè ... nè *neither ... nor*
neanche *not even, neither*
necessario/a *necessary*
necessità *necessity*
negli = in + gli
negozio *shop*
nei = in + i

nel = in + il
nell' = in + l'
nella = in + la
nelle = in + le
nello = in + lo
nero/a *black*
nessuno/a *no, not any, no-one*
neve (f) *snow*
nevicare *to snow*
niente *nothing*
nipote (m or f) *nephew, niece*
Nizza *Nice*
no *no*
no, grazie *no thank you*
noi *we*
nome (m) *forename, name*
non *not*
non ... ancora *not yet*
non ... affatto *not at all*
non c'è male *not too bad*
non fa niente *it doesn't matter*
non importa *it doesn't matter*
non lo so *I don't know*
non ... proprio *not at all*
nonna *grandmother*
nonno *grandfather*
nono/a *ninth*
normale *normal;* benzina – *two star petrol*
nostalgia *nostalgia;* sentire la – *to feel homesick, to miss*
nostro/a *our, ours*
notizia *(piece of) news*
notte (f) *night*
novanta *ninety*
nove *nine*
novembre (m) *November*
nulla *anything, nothing*
numero *number, size*
nuotare *to swim*
nuoto *swimming*
nuovo/a *new*

o *or*
obbligatorio/a *compulsory*
occhiali (m pl) *glasses*
occhiata *glance, look*
occhio *eye*
occorrere (p.p. occorso) *to be necessary, to need*
occuparsi di *to deal with, look after*

occupato/a *engaged, busy, taken*
oddio! *my goodness!*
odore (m) *smell*
offrire *to offer*
oggetto *object*
oggi (m) *today*
ogni *every, all, any*
ogni tanto *now and then*
olimpico/a *Olympic*
olio *oil*
oliva *olive*
oltre a *besides, apart from*
ombrello *umbrella*
ombrellone (m) *beach umbrella*
onomastico *name-day*
opera *opera*
operaio *worker, employee*
opinione (f) *opinion*
opinioni a confronto *opinions compared*
oppure *or, or else*
ora *hour, o'clock*
ora *now*
orario *timetable,* in – *on time*
ordinare *to order*
ordine (m) *order*
orecchio *ear*
organizzare *to organise*
origine (f) *origin*
oro *gold*
orologio *watch, clock*
ospedale (m) *hospital*
ospitalità *hospitality*
ospite (m or f) *guest*
ostello *hostel*
ottanta *eighty*
ottavo/a *eighth*
ottico *optician*
ottimo/a *excellent*
otto *eight*
ottobre (m) *October*

pacco *parcel*
padre (m) *father*
padrona di casa *landlady*
padrone (m) *owner, landlord*
Paese (m) *country*
paese (m) *village, small town*
pagare *to pay*
paio *couple, pair*
palazzo *palace, building*

pallone (m) *ball*
pane (m) *bread*
panetteria *baker's*
panettiere (m) *baker*
panino *roll*
pantaloni (m pl) *trousers*
pappagallo *parrot*
parcheggiare *to park*
parcheggio *car-park*
parco *park*
parecchio tempo *quite a time*
parecchio/a *quite a lot, several*
parente (m or f) *relative, relation*
parere *to appear, seem*
Parigi (f) *Paris*
parla? *do you speak?*
parlare *to speak*
parlarsi *to speak to each other*
parlo *I speak*
parola *word*
parrucchiere (m) *hairdresser*
parte (f) *side, part;* a– *apart*
partenza *departure*
parti, da queste – *in/to these parts*
partire *to leave*
passaggio, di – *passing through*
passante (m or f) *passer-by*
passaporto *passport*
passare *to pass, spend*
passato *past*
passeggiata *walk*
passeggiero *passenger*
passo *step*
passo, a due passi da ... *very near ...*
pasta *pasta, cake*
pasticceria *patisserie*
pasticciere (m) *pastrycook, confectioner*
pasto *meal*
patata *potato*
patatina *chip*
patente (f) di guida *driving licence*
paura: aver – *to be afraid*
pazienza! *never mind*
peccato! che – *what a pity!*
pelle (f) *leather*
pendente *leaning*
penna *pen*
pennette rigate (f pl) *pasta quills*
pensare *to think, believe*

pensiero *thought*
pensione (f) *guest house, pension*
pensione completa *full board*
pepe (m) *pepper*
peperone (m) *pepper (veg)*
per *in order to, for, through, by*
per *for, around, about, through, to*
per carità! *not at all*
per favore *please*
per forza *at all costs, necessarily*
per piacere *please*
per strada *in the street*
per terra *on the floor*
pera avocado *avocado pear*
pera *pear*
percentuale (f) *percentage*
perchè *why, because*
perdere (p.p. perso) *to loose, miss*
pericoloso/a *dangerous*
periferia *outskirts, suburbs*
periodo *period*
permesso! *excuse me! may I come in?*
però *however, but*
perso *from* perdere
persona *person*
personale (m) *personnel, personal*
personalmente *personally*
pesca *peach*
pesce (m) *fish*
pescheria *fishmonger's*
pescivendolo *fishmonger*
piacciono *from* piacere
piace di più *from* piacere *to prefer*
piace: mi piace *I like*
piacere *to please, to like*
piacere (m) *pleasure, favour*
piacere! *pleased to meet you, how do you do?*
pianista (m or f) *pianist*
piano *quietly, slowly*
piano *floor*
pianoforte (m) *piano*
pianta *plan, plant, map*
pianterreno *ground floor*
piatto *plate, dish*
piazza *square*
piccolo/a *small, little*
piede (m) *foot;* a piedi *on foot;* in piedi
  standing
pieno/a *full*

pigiama (m) *pyjamas*
pillola *pill*
pioggia *rain*
piombare *to fill (of teeth)*
piovere *to rain*
piscina *swimming pool*
pittore (m) *painter*
più *more, most*
più avanti *further on*
più presto (al) *as soon as possible*
più tardi *later*
piuttosto *rather*
pizza *pizza*
plastica *plastic*
po': un po' di *a bit of, a little*
poco a poco *little by little*
poco/a *a few, little*
poi *then, after*
politica *politics*
politico/a *political*
polizia *police*
pollo *chicken*
poltrona *armchair*
pomeriggio *afternoon*
pomodoro *tomato*
ponte (m) *bridge*
porta *door, gate*
portafoglio *wallet*
portare *to take, bring, wear, carry*
portiere (m) *porter*
portoghese *Portuguese*
possibile *possible*
possibilità *possibility, chance*
posso *from* potere
posta *post office*
posto *place, seat, job*
posto di lavoro *place of work*
potabile *drinkable*
potere (irr) *to be able*
povero/a *poor*
pranzare *to lunch*
pranzo *lunch*
pratico/a *practical*
preferenza *preference*
preferenza: di – *mostly, preferably*
preferibilmente *preferably*
preferire *to prefer*
preferito/a *favourite*
prego *don't mention it, can I help you, etc.*

prende *has, have, take(s)*
prendere (p.p.preso) *to have, take, get, buy*
prendo *I take, have*
prenotare *to book*
prenotazione (f) *booking*
preoccuparsi *to worry*
preparare *to prepare*
presa *socket*
preso *from* prendere
presso *care of*
prestare *to lend, borrow*
presto *early, soon;* far – *to be quick, hurry up*
prezzo *price*
prima *at first*
prima di *before*
prima di tutto *first of all*
primavera *spring*
primi (i) di agosto *early August*
primo = primo piatto
primo/a *first*
principale *main, principal*
privato/a *private*
problema (m) *problem*
processione (f) *procession*
produrre irr. (p.p. prodotto) *to produce*
produzione (f) *production*
prof. = professore
professionista (m or f) *professional, expert*
professor = professore
professore (m) *teacher, professor*
profondo/a *deep, thorough*
profumo *perfume*
progetto *project, plan*
programma (m) *programme*
proibire *to forbid*
promettere (p.p. promesso) *to promise*
pronto soccorso *casualty (department), first aid*
pronto/a *ready:* pronto? *hello! (telephone)*
pronuncia *pronunciation*
proposta *proposal, proposition*
proprio *just, really*
proprio/a *one's own, real, really, just*
prosciutto *ham;* – crudo *Parma ham*
prossimo/a *near, next*
provare *to try (on), taste*
pubblico/a *public*

pulire *to clean*
pullman (m) *coach*
punto: in – *punctually*
puntuale *punctual*
può *from* potere
pure *too, also, by all means*
puro/a *pure*
purtroppo *unfortunately*

qua *see* di qua
quadro *picture*
qual = quale
qualche *some, one or two*
qualcosa *something*
qualcuno *someone, anyone, one or two*
quale *which, what*
qualunque *any, whatever*
quando *when*
quanti/quante? *how many?*
quanto fa? *how much does it come to?*
quaranta *forty*
quarto/a *fourth, quarter*
quasi *almost, nearly*
quattordici *fourteen*
quattro chiacchiere *chat*
quattro *four*
quegli *those; from* quel
quel/quello/a *that (one)*
questo/a *this (one)*
questura *police station (HQ)*
qui *here*
qui vicino *near here*
quindi *so, well, therefore*
quindici *fifteen*
quindicina: una – *about fifteen*
quinto/a *fifth*
quotidiano/a *daily*

racchetta *tennis racket*
raccolta *collection*
raccomandata *registered letter*
radersi *to shave*
radio (f) *radio*
raffreddore (m) *cold*
ragazza *girl, girlfriend*
ragazzo *boy, boyfriend*
ragione (aver) *to be right*
ragione (f) *reason*
ragioneria *book-keeping, accountancy*
ragioniera/e (f or m) *accountant*

rallegramenti! *congratulations!*
rapido *express, fast train*
rapporto *report, link, relationship*
rasoio *razor*
ravioli (m pl) *ravioli (pasta)*
recente *recent*
regalare *to give as a present*
regalo *present*
regolare *regular*
religioso/a *religious*
reparto *department*
repubblica *republic*
residente *resident*
residenziale *residential*
respirare *to breathe*
restare *to remain, stay*
resto *change, balance*
ricetta *prescription*
ricevere *to receive*
ricevuta *receipt*
richiamare *to call back*
richiedere *to ask for, order*
ricordarsi *to remember*
rientrare *to come back, re-enter*
rilassarsi *to relax*
rilevante *important, relevant*
rimanere irr. (p.p. rimasto) *to remain, stay*
rimasto *from* rimanere
ringraziare *to thank*
riordinare *to tidy up*
riparare *to repair*
ripetere *to repeat*
riportare *bring back*
riposarsi *to (have a) rest*
riposo *rest*
risolto *from* risolvere
risolvere (p.p. risolto) *to solve*
risotto *risotto (rice)*
rispondere (p.p. risposto) *to answer, reply*
risposta *answer*
ristorante (m) *restaurant*
ritardo *lateness, delay;* essere in *– to be late*
ritirare *to collect, get back*
ritornare *to return*
ritorno *return, way back*
ritrovare *recover, find*
riunione (f) *meeting*
riuscire irr. (p.p. riuscito) *to manage,
  succeed*

rivestirsi *to get dressed again*
rivista *magazine*
rivolgersi *ask, apply*
roba *thing, stuff*
Roma *Rome*
romanzo *novel*
rompere (p.p. rotto) *to break*
rosa *rose, pink*
rosso/a *red*
rosticceria *take-away*
rotto *from* rompere
ruba: andare a *– to sell like hot cakes*
rumore (m) *noise*
ruolo *role*
Russia *Russia*
russo/a *Russian*

sa *from* sapere
sa: non sa di niente *it has no taste*
sabato *Saturday*
sacco *sack;* un *– di soldi pots of money*
sala da pranzo *dining room*
salame (m) *salame sausage*
salato/a *salted*
saldi (m pl) *sale(s)*
sale (m) *salt*
salire *to go up, get on*
salmone (m) *salmon*
salone (m) *large sitting room*
salotto *sitting room*
salsa *sauce*
salumeria *grocery*
salumiere (m) *grocer*
salutare *to greet*
salutarsi *to greet each other*
salute (f) *health;* alla–! *cheers!*
saluto *greeting*
San Marco *St Mark*
San Pietro *St Peter*
sandalo *sandal*
sanitario/a *of health, sanitary*
sanno *see* sapere
santo/a *saint*
sapere *to know*
sarete *you will be, from* essere
sbagliato/a *wrong*
sbaglio *mistake*
sbrigare *to deal with*
sbrigarsi *to hurry up*
scacchi (m pl) *chess*

scaffale (m) *bookshelf*
scambio di ospitalità *exchange*
scambio *exchange (money)*
scapolo *bachelor*
scarpa *shoe*
scatola *tin, box*
scelta *choice*
scendere giù *to go/come down(stairs), to get off*
scheda telefonica *phonecard*
schiena *back*
sci (m) *skiing*
sciare *to ski*
scientifico/a *scientific*
scienza *science*
scienze economiche *economics*
sciopero *strike*
sconto *discount*
scontrino *ticket, receipt*
scorso/a *last*
scottarsi *to get burnt*
scritto *from* scrivere
scrivania *desk*
scrivere (p.p. scritto) *to write*
scuola *school*
scuro/a *dark*
scusare *to excuse*
scusi! *excuse me*
se *if*
secco/a *dry*
secolo *century*
secondo *according to*
secondo/a *second*
sede (f) centrale *head office*
sedere (irr.) *to sit (down)*
sedersi (irr.) *to sit (down)*
sedia (a sdraio) *(deck) chair*
sedici *sixteen*
seduto/a *seated*
segnale (m) acustico *(sound) signal, beep*
segretaria *secretary*
segreteria telefonica *answer-phone*
sei *six*
sei *you are (from* essere)
semaforo *traffic light*
sembrare *to seem, appear*
semola di grano duro *durum wheat*
semplice *simple*

sempre *always*
sempre dritto *straight ahead*
sentire *to hear, feel*
sentir dire *to hear of;* senti! *listen!*
sentirsi *to feel*
sentirsi male/bene *to feel ill/well*
senz' = senza
senz'altro! *of course, definitely*
senza *without*
separato/a *separated*
sera *evening*
servire *to serve; need*
servirsi da soli *to help oneself*
servizio *service*
sessanta *sixty*
sesto/a *sixth*
seta *silk*
sete (f) *thirst;* aver – *to be thirsty*
settanta *seventy*
sette *seven*
settentrionale *northern, north*
settimana *week*
settimanale *weekly*
settimo/a *seventh*
si dice *one says (it)*
si figuri! *not at all, it's no trouble*
si *one, oneself, you (impersonal)*
si prega di *please*
sì *yes (I do)*
sì, grazie *yes please*
siciliano/a *Sicilian*
sicuro/a *sure, safe*
sig. = signore
sig.na = signorina
sig.ra = signora
sigaretta *cigarette*
signor = signore
signora *lady, woman, Madam, Mrs*
signore (m) *(gentle)man, Mr, Sir*
signorile: appartamento – *luxury flat*
signorina *young lady, woman, Miss*
simpatico/a *nice, pleasant*
singolo/a *single*
sinistro/a *left;* a- *on the left*
sistema (m) *system*
sistemare *to fix, arrange*
sistemarsi *to get settled*
smarrimento *loss*

smarrire *to lose, mislay*
smettere (p.p. smesso) *to stop*
so *from* sapere; non lo so *I don't know*
soccorso *assistance, help*
sociale *social*
società *company, society*
soddisfatto/a *satisfied, happy*
soggiorno *living room*
sogliola *sole*
sognare *to dream*
solamente *only*
soldi (m pl) *money*
sole (m) *sun*
solito *see* di solito
solo *only*
solo/a *alone*
soltanto *only*
sono *I am; they are: from* essere
sono io *it's me*
sopportare *to bear*
sopra *up(stairs)*
soprattutto *above all*
sorella *sister*
sorpreso/a *surprised*
sotto *under, underneath*
sottopassaggio *underpass*
spaghetti (m pl) *spaghetti*
Spagna *Spain*
spagnolo/a *Spanish*
sparecchiare *to clear the table*
spazzolino *toothbrush*
specchio *mirror*
speciale *special*
specialità *speciality*
spedire *to post, despatch, send*
spegnere (irr.) *to turn off, switch off*
spendere (p.p. speso) *to spend*
spensierato/a *carefree*
spento *from* spegnere
sperare di *to hope to*
spesa *shopping*
speso *from* spendere
spesso *often*
spettacolo *show*
spiacere = dispiacere
spiaggia *beach*
spiccioli (m pl) *small change*
spiegazione (f) *explanation*
spina *plug*

sport (m) *sport*
sportello *counter, window counter*
sposarsi *to get married*
sposato/a *married*
sposo/sposa *bridegroom/bride*
sta: come –? *How are you?*
stadio *stadium*
stagione (f) *season*
stamattina *this morning*
stampa *press*
stanco/a *tired*
stanotte *tonight, last night*
stanza *room*
stare *to be, stay*
stare + gerund *to be doing*
stare attento *to be careful*
stare male *to be/feel unwell*
stare meglio *to be/feel better*
stare peggio *to be/feel worse*
stare per *to be about to*
stasera *this evening*
Stato *State*; gli Stati Uniti *USA*
stato *from* essere *or* stare
statua *statue*
stazione (f) di servizio *service station*
stazione (f) *station*
stereo *stereo*
sterlina *£ sterling*
stesso (lo) *all the same*
stesso/a *same*; io – *I myself*
stia tranquillo/a! *don't worry!*
stipendio *salary, wages*
stomaco *stomach*
strada *street, road*
straniero/a *foreign*
strano/a *strange, odd, funny*
studente (m) *student*
studentessa (female) *student*
studiare *to study*
studio *office*; – legale *lawyer's office*
stufo/a (di) *fed up (with)*
su *on*
subito *straight away, immediately*
succedere (p.p. successo) *to happen*
successo *from* succedere
sud (m) *south*
sugo *sauce*
suo/a *his, your(s), her(s)*
suonare *to play (an instrument), ring*

super: benzina – *four-star petrol*
superare *to pass (an exam)*
supplemento *supplement*
svegliare *to wake someone up*
svegliarsi *to wake up*
Svizzera *Switzerland*
svizzero/a *Swiss*

tabaccaio *tobacconist*
tabaccheria *tobacconist's*
tabacco *tobacco*
taglia *size*
tagliatelle *pasta strips*
taglio *cut*
tanti/e *so many*
tanto da vedere *so much to see*
tanto/a *so much*
tappeto *carpet*
tardi *late*
tasca *pocket*
tassì (m) *taxi*
tavola *table*
tavolino *small table*
tavolo *table*
tazza *cup*
tazzina *coffee/espresso cup*
tè (m) *tea*
teatro *theatre*
tecnico/a *technical, technician*
tedesco/a *German*
telefonare *to phone*
telefonata *phone call*
telefonino *mobile phone*
telefono *telephone*
telegramma (m) *telegram*
televisione (f) *television*
televisivo/a *television (adj)*
tema (m) *theme*
tempio *temple*
tempo *time, weather*
tenda *curtain*
tenere (irr.) *to keep, hold*
terrazza/o *terrace, balcony*
terzo/a *third*
testa *head*
testo *text, words*
ti *(to/for) you, (to/for) yourself*
tipo *type, kind*
tirare *to pull; –* vento *to be windy*

titolo di studio *qualification(s)*
tocca a te! *it's your turn*
toccare *to touch*
togliere *to take off, pull out*
tolto *from* togliere
Torino (f) *Turin*
tornare = ritornare
torre (f) *tower*
torto (aver) *to be wrong*
tosse (f) *cough*
tovagliolo *serviette, table napkin*
tra = fra
traduzione (f) *translation*
tramezzino *sandwich*
tranquillo/a *quiet*
trascorrere (p.p. trascorso) *to spend*
trasferirsi *to move*
trasporto *transport*
trattare *to treat, deal with*
trattoria *modest restaurant*
traversa *turning*
tre *three*
tredici *thirteen*
treno *train*
trenta *thirty*
trentenne *thirty-year-old*
trentina, una – *about thirty*
Trento *Trent*
trimestre (m) *term*
troppo *too, too much*
troppo/a *too*
trota *trout*
trovare *to find, see, visit*
trovarsi *to be; –* bene *to be happy*
tu *you (informal)*
tuo/a *your(s)*
turismo *tourism*
turista (m or f) *tourist*
tutti e due / tutte e due *both (of them)*
tutto a posto *everything in order*
tutto *all, everything*
tutto/a *all, whole, every*
tv privata *independent tv*

ubriacarsi *to get drunk*
uccello *bird*
ufficio *office*
uliva = oliva
ultimo/a *last*

un *a, an*
un po' di *a bit of*
un' (f) *a, one*
una *a, an, one*
università *university*
universitario/a *(of the) university*
uno/a *one*
uomo (pl uomini) *man*
uovo (pl uova) *egg*
urgente *urgent*
usare *to use*
uscire (irr.) *to go out*
uscita *exit, way out*
utile *useful*
uva (s) *grapes*

va bene *alright, fits*
va *from* andare
vacanza *holiday*
vado *from* andare
vaglia (m) *postal order*
vasca da bagno *bathtub*
vasto/a *huge*
vecchio/a *old*
vedere (p.p. visto) *to see*
vediamo un po' *let's have a look*
vegetariano/a *vegetarian*
veloce *fast*
vendere *to sell*
vendita *sale*
vernerdì (m) *Friday*
Venezia *Venice*
venire (irr. p.p. venuto) *to come*
venti *twenty*
ventina, una – *about twenty*
ventisei *twenty-six*
vento *wind*
ventotto *twenty-eight*
ventuno *twenty-one*
venuto *see* venire
verde *green*
verde: al – *broke*
verità *truth*
vero/a *true;* vero? *isn't it? don't you? etc.*
versare *to pour*
verso *at, about*
vestirsi *to get dressed*
vestito *suit, dress*
vestito da sera *evening dress*

Vesuvio *Vesuvius*
vetrina *shop window*
ve *(to/for) you, yourselves*
via *street, road, away*
viaggiare *to travel;* il- *travelling*
viaggiatore (m) *traveller*
viaggio *journey*
vicino *near;–* a *next to, near*
vicino/a di casa *neighbour*
video *video*
videoregistratore (m) *video recorder*
vietato/a *forbidden, prohibited*
villa *villa*
villaggio *village*
villeggiatura *holiday*
villetta *small villa*
vino *wine*
violinista (m or f) *violinist*
violino *violin*
visione (f) *vision*
visitare *to visit, examine*
vissuto *from* vivere
visto *from* vedere
vita *life*
vitello *calf, veal*
vittoria *victory*
vivere (p.p. vissuto) *to live*
vocale (f) *vowel*
voce (f) *voice*
vogliamo *see* volere
voi *you(pl)*
volentieri *willingly*
volere *to wish, want*
voltare *to turn*
vongola *clam*
vorrei *I would like*
vostro/a *your, yours*
vuole *from* volere
vuoto/a *empty*
water (m) *w.c.*

zero *nought, zero*
zia *aunt*
zio *uncle*
zitto/a *quiet*
zona *zone*
zucchero *sugar*
zucchino *courgette*

GLOSSARY OF GRAMMATICAL TERMS

Active and passive voice

Most actions can be viewed in two different ways:

    1. The dog bit the postman   2. The postman was bitten by the dog

Because in the first example the dog is clearly the doer of the action (or the *agent*) and the postman receives or suffers the action, this type of sentence is referred to as being in the *active voice*.

In the second example, the postman occupies first position in the sentence even though he is not the doer of the action, but the recipient or sufferer of it. The agent, the dog, is now in third position (after the verb) and could even be omitted. This type of sentence is referred to as being in the *passive voice*.

Adjectives

Adjectives are used to provide more information about nouns. In English they can appear in front of a noun or they can stand on their own after a verb such as *to be* or *to seem*:

    (a)   The *new* school opens today.
    (b)   That school is very *good*.
    (c)   That *new* school seems *excellent*.

In many languages certain adjectives come after the noun, rather than in front of it.

Possessive adjectives

Words such as *my*, *your*, *her* are given the term *possessive adjective*.

Adverbs

Just as adjectives provide more information about nouns, so *adverbs* tend to provide more information about verbs:

    (a)   Wayne ran *quickly* down the stairs.

    (b)   Tracy fell *heavily* to the ground.

But adverbs can also provide more information on adjectives:

    (a)   I was *completely* exhausted.

    (b)   The town centre was *totally* empty.

In English adverbs often (but not always) end in *-ly*.

Articles

definite article This is the term given to the word *the*.
indefinite article This is the term given to the words *a* and *an*.

Auxiliary verbs

Auxiliary verbs are used as a support to the main verb, for example, I *am* working, you *are* working … Here *am* and *are* support the verb *work*. By its very nature an auxiliary verb does not normally stand on its own, because it is the main verb that carries the meaning. *Working* gives us the information as to what activity is going on; *am/are* tell us that is in the present continuous.

The most important auxiliary verbs in English are *to be*, *to have* and *to do*. We use *do*, for example, to ask questions and to negate statements:

    Do you work on Saturdays?   Yes, but I *do* not work on Sundays.

We also use auxiliary verbs to form compound tenses, for instance:

    I *have* just seen a very good film.

Conjunctions

Conjunctions are words such as *and* and *although*. They link words, or clauses or sentences together:

    (a)   bread *and* butter

    (b)   We went to London *but* we didn't see Trafalgar Square.

    (c)   We went for a walk *although* it was raining.

Other conjunctions are *but, when, if, unless, while*.

Imperative

The *imperative* is the form of the verb used to give orders or commands:

    (a)   Give me a hand.

    (b)   Help Sharon with her homework.

Infinitive

The *infinitive* is the basic form of the verb. This is the form that you will find entered in the dictionary. In English the infinitive is usually accompanied by the word *to*, e.g. *to go*, *to play*.

Masculine/feminine

In English, gender is usually linked to male and female persons or animals, so for example, we refer to a man as *he* and to a woman as *she*. Objects and beings of an indeterminate sex are referred to as having *neuter* gender. So for instance, we refer to a table as *it*.

In many languages nouns have a gender irrespective of sex. So although the gender of the words for female persons and jobs tend to be feminine and the gender of the words for male people and jobs tends to be masculine, this cannot be taken for granted. While there *are* some rules to help you, you have to accept that the gender of every noun has to be learned.

Nouns

Nouns are words like *house*, *bread* and *beauty*. They are often called 'naming words'. A useful test of a noun is whether you can put *the* in front of it: e.g. *the house*, *the bread*. Adjectives are often used in front of nouns:

The big house, a wild cat.

Number

The term *number* is used to indicate whether something is singular or plural; see **singular**

Object

The term *object* expresses the 'receiving end' relationship between a noun and a verb. So, for instance,the postman is said to be at the receiving end of the biting in the sentence:

The dog bit the postman.

He is therefore said to be the *object* of the sentence.

Not all verbs need an object:

The dog barked.

See also **subject**

In sentences such as

My mother gave my wife an expensive ring.

The phrase 'an expensive ring' is said to be the *direct object*, because the ring is actually what the mother gave. The phrase 'my wife' is said to be the *indirect object* because the wife was the recipient of the giving (and **not** the person who was giving to someone else).

Plural *see* **singular**

Pronouns

Pronouns fulfil a similar function to nouns and often stand in the place of nouns which have already been mentioned:

The *house* is over 200 years old. *It* is very beautiful.
noun   pronoun

Personal pronouns

As their name suggests, *personal pronouns* refer to persons:

	Singular	Plural
First person	I	we
Second person	you	you
Third person	he, she, it	they

Relative pronouns see **relative clauses**
Reflexive pronouns words such as *myself, yourself, himself* are called *reflexive pronouns*.
See also **reflexive verbs**
Possessive pronouns Words like *mine, yours, his* are called *possessive pronouns*.
Demonstrative pronouns Words like *this, that, these, those*, when they stand on their own, are called *demonstrative pronouns*:

I like *these* better than *those*.

Prepositions

Words like *in*, *on*, *between*, *for* are called *prepositions*. Prepositions often tell us about the position of something. They are normally followed by a noun or pronoun:

(a)   Your book is in my drawer.
(b)   The bank is between the bank and the church.
(c)   This present is for you.

Reflexive verbs

When the *subject* and the *object* of a verb are one and the same, the verb is said to be reflexive.

(a)   Gary hit himself on the head with a book.
(b)   I washed myself thoroughly.

Relative clauses

A *relative pronoun* such as *which, who* or *that* can be used to provide more information on a noun which had just been mentioned. The resulting clause is called a *relative clause*:

(a)   I know the man <u>*who* lives next door to you</u>.
(b)   He has a problem <u>*that* is impossible to solve</u>.

Relative pronouns can often be omitted in English:

(a)   The man *(who)* I go to work with has three children.

More formal and now antiquated version: The man with *whom* I go to work...

(b)   The car *(which)* I drive is nearly 6 years old.

NB: Most other European languages do not allow you to omit the relative pronoun.

Singular

The terms *singular* and *plural* are use to make the contrast between 'one' and 'more than one':

dog/dogs, book/books, hat/hats

Most plural forms in English are formed by adding an -s, but not all:

child/children, woman/woman, mouse/mice

Pronouns too can be singular or plural:

    (a)   I have a new book. It is very good.

    (b)   I have some new books. They are very good.

Some nouns do not normally have plurals and are said to be *uncountables:*

    the milk, the air, flour

Subject

The term *subject* expresses a relationship between a noun and a verb. So, for instance, in the sentence:

    The dog bit the postman.

because it is the dog that does the biting, the dog is said to be the subject of the verb *to bite*.

Superlative

The *superlative* is used for the most extreme version of a comparison:

    (a)   This shirt is the cheap*est* of all.

    (b)   This blouse is the *most* expensive of all.

See also **Comparative**.

Tense

Most languages use changes in the verb to indicate an aspect of time. These changes in the verb are traditionally referred to as tense, and the tenses may be *present*, *past* or *future*. Tenses are often reinforced with expressions of time:

    Past: Yesterday I went to London.

    Present: Today I am staying at home.

    Future: Tomorrow I'll be flying to Berlin.

Verbs

Verbs often communicate actions, states and sensations. So for instance, the verb *to play* expresses an action, the verb *to exist* expresses a state and the verb *to see* expresses a sensation. A verb may also be defined by its role in the sentence or clause and usually has a *subject*:

    My head aches.

    Subject   verb

A verb often has an object as well:

> My daughter plays tennis.
> *Subject   verb object*

Irregular verbs

Life would be considerably easier if all verbs behaved in a regular fashion. Unfortunately, all European languages have verbs which do not behave according to a set pattern and which are therefore commonly referred to as *irregular* verbs.

Transitive/intransitive verbs

Verbs that need an object to complete the sentence are usually known as *transitive* verbs:

(a) The doctor is visting a patient.
(b) I need a glass of water.

Verbs that do not need an object to complete the sentence are usually known as *intransitive* verbs:

(a) My friends are waiting.
(b) The value of the pound is rising.

Some normally transitive verbs can be used intransitively:

> Today the doctor is *visiting* (i.e. making visits to patients).

GRAMMAR INDEX